THE INFLUENCE OF BEAUMONT AND FLETCHER ON SHAKSPERE

THE INFLUENCE OF BEAUMONT
AND FLETCHER ON SHAKSPERE

ASHLEY H. THORNDIKE, Ph. D.

NEW YORK / RUSSELL & RUSSELL

1965

FIRST PUBLISHED IN 1901
REISSUED, 1965, BY RUSSELL & RUSSELL
L.C. CATALOG CARD NO: 65—17924
PRINTED IN THE UNITED STATES OF AMERICA

PREFACE.

This volume is based on a portion of a dissertation on "Some Contemporary Influences on Shakspere," which was presented to the Faculty of Arts and Sciences of Harvard University to fulfill a requirement for the degree of Doctor of Philosophy. That dissertation dealt with the relations of *As You Like It* to pastoral and Robin Hood plays, and of *Hamlet* to tragedies of revenge, as well as with the influence of Beaumont and Fletcher on Shakspere's romances. This last division has been rewritten and considerably enlarged and forms this volume. My conclusions in regard to the indebtedness of the romances to the contemporary drama are thus offered without the support which might perhaps have been afforded by the co-ordinate investigations.

A study, however, of Shakspere as an adapter requires less apology now than it would have four years ago when I first began this work. Shaksperean criticism has made a decided advance since then toward the adoption of the point of view and methods of historical criticism. Mr. Sidney Lee's discussion of the sonnets as a representative of a current literary form has opened the field and pointed the way for future students of the plays. My incentive to a historical study came entirely from the lectures of Professor Barrett Wendell at Harvard University and from his suggestive study, *William Shakspere*. While the hypothesis in regard to the influence of Beaumont and Fletcher with which I began my work was the immediate result of my reading and, so far as I know, has never been advanced before, whatever merit there may be in the general method and point of view of this essay is due to the instruction and example of Mr. Wendell. I venture to hope that, however my conclusions may be estimated, the investigation on which they are based will be of some interest in illustrating the application of the historical method to the study of Shakspere.

In condensing the results of my work for publication, it has been necessary to omit some investigations not closely connected with the main thesis and merely to note the results of others. Among these are a discussion of the Revels companies, 1601-1611, additional notes on the plays of Beaumont and Fletcher after 1611, an alphabetical list of plays acted 1601-1611, some tables illustrating the use of colloquialisms, of 'em and them, and various verse tests.

Like every other student in the history of the drama, I owe much to the books of Mr. Fleay. I have found many occasions to differ with him and to criticise his methods, but I have also had abundant opportunity to admire his extensive knowledge and brilliant inductions. My indebtedness to Mr. Wendell's book on Shakspere is apparent; in expressing my thanks I wish I could also indicate the extent of my obligations to his friendly and stimulating criticisms and suggestions made while my investigation was in progress. I am also greatly indebted for helpful criticism to Professor George L. Kittredge, to whom I have frequently turned for suggestion and guidance, and to Mr. Jefferson B. Fletcher, and Professor George P. Baker.

ASHLEY H. THORNDIKE.

WESTERN RESERVE UNIVERSITY,
CLEVELAND, OHIO.

CONTENTS.

BIBLIOGRAPHICAL NOTE.

Texts.

Shakspere's plays. "Globe Edition." W. G. Clark and W. A. Wright. All line references are to this edition.

"The Two Noble Kinsmen." Ed. by Harold Littledale. New Shakspere Society. Series II. 7, 8. 15. London, 1885.

Plays of Beaumont and Fletcher. "Works." Ed. by Rev. Alexander Dyce. 11 vols. London, 1843. Page references are to this edition.

"Works." Ed. by George Darley. Routledge's "Series of the Old Dramatists." 2 vols. This edition is used when there is no reference to Dyce.

Critical Works, Etc.

The following list includes only those books or articles which are repeatedly referred to and often in abbreviated form. Where the abbreviations are not evident they are given in this list. Other books referred to are named in full in the foot notes.

A Biographical Chronicle of the English Drama, 1559-1642. F. G. Fleay. 2 vols. London, 1891. Referred to as *Chr.* When no page number is given, the reference is invariably to the play under discussion and can be found without difficulty.

A Chronicle History of the London Stage, 1559-1642. F. G. Fleay. London, 1890. *H. of S.*

A Chronicle History of the Life and Work of William Shakespeare. F. G. Fleay. London, 1886.

Outlines of the Life of Shakespeare. J. O. Halliwell Phillipps. Sixth Edition. London, 1886. *H. P. Outlines.*

A Life of William Shakespeare. Sidney Lee. London and New York, 1899.

A History of English Dramatic Literature. A. W. Ward. 3 vols. New and revised edition. London, 1899.

History of English Dramatic Poetry to the time of Shakespeare, and Annals of the Stage. J. Payne Collier. 3 vols. London, 1874. Abbreviated, *Collier.*

A New Variorum Edition of Shakespeare. H. H. Furness. Philadelphia. *The Tempest.*

The Diary of Philip Henslowe from 1597 to 1609. J. Payne Collier. London. For the Shakespeare Society, 1845. *H. D.*

Annales or a Generall Chronicle of England. Begun by John Stow. Continued to 1631 by Edmund Howes. London, 1631. *Stow.*

The Progresses and Public Processions of Queen Elizabeth. New edition in 3 vols. John Nichols. London, 1823.

The Progresses, Processions . . . . . . of King James the First, etc. John Nichols. 4 vols. London, 1828.

Extracts from the Accounts of the Revels at Court. P. Cunningham. For the Shakespeare Society. London, 1842.

William Shakspere. A Study in Elizabethan Literature. Barrett Wendell. New York, 1894.

Quellen Studien zu den drama Ben Jonson's, John Marston's und Beaumont und Fletcher's. Münchener Beiträge VI. E. Koeppel. Erlangen und Leipzig. 1895.

Die Englischen Maskenspiele. Alfred Soergel. Halle, 1882.

Francis Beaumont. A Critical Study. G. C. Macaulay. London, 1883.

ERRATA.

Page 37, line 11 ; for period after "side," substitute a comma.

Page 41, line 6 of the foot-note ; the reference should be to page 31.

Page 43, line 15 ; insert a reference to the foot-note after "doors."

Page 58, line 5 ; "the two allusions"—omit "the."

Page 74 ; Fleay's identification of the "miraculous maid" is correct. *The Fasting of a Maiden of Confolens* was published in 1604, with introductory verses by Dekker.

Pages 91 and 93 ; for *Lover's Progress*, read *Lovers' Progress*.

Page 107, foot-note ; the *Wit of a Woman*, probably acted 1600–1604 is another play which I have not seen.

Page 112, line 4 ; read " as that of Leontes."

Page 125, line 23 ; for " thown," read " thrown."

CHAPTER I.

INTRODUCTION.

In considering the question of Shakspere's indebtedness to two of his contemporaries, we can have no better starting point than the earliest known reference to Shakspere as a dramatist, a passage written by a contemporary play-wright, Robert Greene.

"For there is an upstart Crow, beautified with our feathers, that with his *Tyger's heart wrapt in a Player's hide*, supposes that he is as well able to bumbast out a blanke verse as is the best of you: and being an absolute *Johannes fac totum*, is in his owne conceit the onely Shake-scene in a countrie."[1]

Although no one believes that in our sense of the word Shakspere was a plagiarist, Greene's accusation contains an element of truth worth keeping in mind.

There is no doubt that Shakspere began play-writing by imitating or re-vamping the work of others. *Titus Andronicus* and *Henry VI*, so far as they are his, are certainly imitative of other plays of the time, while *Richard II* and *Richard III* show the influence of Marlowe's tragedies, and *Love's Labour's Lost*, the influence of Lyly's comedies. During the period that he was learning his art and experimenting with various kinds of plays, it is generally recognized that he was indebted to the dramatists and the dramatic conventions of his time.

After this early experimental period, however, his indebtedness to his contemporaries has received little notice. In fact, the idea that Shakspere in his maturity imitated, adapted, or to any considerable extent made use of the work of his fellow dramatists, has to most students seemed absurd. His plays are so immensely superior to those of his contemporaries that, when resemblances have been noticed, critics have been wont to say: 'Shakspere must have originated this and the other man copied it.' There is a fallacy here which we must avoid; for the mere fact that Shakspere's work is the better by no means proves that it is the original, and in general we may well question if his superiority so much disproves as conceals his indebtedness to his contemporaries.

Whatever he touched, he transformed into a permanent work of art; but it is no less true that in his work of transformation

---

[1] Greene's Groatsworth of Wit. 1592.

I

or creation he was working under the same conditions as his fellow play-wrights. He was an actor, and a theater-owner, conversant with all the conventions of an Elizabethan theater and practically interested in the stage fashions and stage rivalries of his time. He made plays that paid, situations that held the interest of the audiences, characters that were effective in London theaters. He must have understood and been influenced by the stage demand whose varying wants he and his fellow dramatists were engaged in supplying. As in the case of any other Elizabethan dramatist, we may be reasonably sure that the final character of his work must have been partly determined by definite objective causes. Moreover, since he sometimes wrote in co-operation with and, doubtless still oftener, in competition with other dramatists, and since many of these were writers of great originality, it is almost inconceivable that his work was not directly influenced by theirs.

Still further, there is much clear evidence of his use of contemporary conventions and dramatic forms. It will be remembered, for example, that he continued to write chronicle-histories even after that form had been ridiculed as antiquated and that *Hamlet* and *Lear* contain traces of the "tragedy of blood" type. A closer adherence to current forms can be seen in the relation between the *Merchant of Venice* and the *Jew of Malta* or in the many points of similarity between *Hamlet* and the other Elizabethan tragedies dealing with the theme of blood-revenge. Characters, too, are often clearly developments of types familiar on the stage; as, for example, Iago is a development of the conventional stage villian. Such facts as these have been frequently noticed and commented upon, but even they have not led to any careful investigation of Shakspere's indebtedness to his contemporaries.

Such investigation finds encouragement not only in Shakspere's relation as a play-wright to his fellow play-wrights, but also in the almost invariable law of art forms that the developer excels the innovator. We know that no one wrote any English dramas until a long period of miracle and morality plays had prepared the way. We know that we can trace the rise and development of a number of dramatic forms in the thirty years preceding Shakspere's first masterly work. We know that the Elizabethan literature in general and the history of its drama in particular were characterized by experiment, invention, and discovery. In the history of dramatic art, then, in a period characterized by an abundance of new forms, it is only natural to expect that the genius who brought many of these to their highest perfection should not have been so much an innovator as an adapter. We may naturally expect that Shakspere's transcendent plays owe a considerable debt to the less perfect but not less original efforts of his contemporaries.

In this investigation I have undertaken to study some of Shakspere's plays in connection with the conventions and fashions of the Elizabethan theater. I have also undertaken the study of these plays in connection with similar plays by his contemporaries. I have by no means exhausted the field of possible contemporary influences. Any one play, I believe, shows almost countless effects of preceding plays; and only the most exhaustive study of Shakspere's work could treat adequately of his total indebtedness. Aiming at definiteness rather than completeness, I have merely considered the influence on Shakspere of one current and popular dramatic form. I have taken as a point of departure some of the plays of Beaumont and Fletcher and studied their possible influence on *Cymbeline, the Tempest,* and *the Winter's Tale.*

Beaumont and Fletcher began to write plays toward the end of Shakspere's dramatic career; and by the time of his withdrawal from the stage, they were probably the most popular play-wrights of the day. The popularity of their plays seems, indeed, to have been established almost at the start and to have continued well into the eighteenth century. Nor was their literary pre-eminence less readily recognized; their work was thought worthy of being classed with Shakspere's by poets and critics from Webster to Dryden. Even in the opinion of critics to-day, two or three of their masterpieces, the *Maid's Tragedy* in particular, can well contest with any other Elizabethan tragedies for the rank next to Shakspere's. Moreover, even from our modern point of view, it is easy to find qualities in many of their plays, such as their variety of situations and their surprising climaxes, which made them better acting plays, greater stage successes even than Shakspere's.

Our main interest in Beaumont and Fletcher's work to-day is, however, probably an historical one. Their work marks a new development in the Elizabethan drama, and their influence is seen in nearly all the dramatists from 1610 to 1640, to say nothing of those of the Restoration. A few of the well known facts of their lives will at once suggest some of the marked distinctions which separated them from the earlier dramatists.

In the first place, Beaumont and Fletcher were gentlemen of birth and breeding; they numbered, as we learn from dedications and commendatory verses, many friends among the gentlemen and noblemen of the day; they had little in common with the Bohemian actor-play-wrights of Elizabeth's reign. They have, indeed, been accused by Coleridge of being "servile *jure divino* royalists." Their political opinions are not so much in evidence as this accusation would indicate, but the tone of their work is decidedly the tone of the fashionable world.

In the second place, as became friends of Jonson, they began writing with considerable notion of the rules and requirements

3

of dramatic art. This is, perhaps, best illustrated by a few lines from Beaumont's verses on Jonson's *Volpone*.[1]

> "I would have shown
> "To all the world, the art, which thou alone,
> "Hast taught our tongue, the rules of time, of place,
> "And other rites, delivered with the grace
> "Of comic style, which only, is far more
> "Than any English stage hath known before."

Fletcher, too, in the address to the reader prefixed to the *Faithful Shepherdess*, shows a similar critical knowledge of the rules of his art. Many of their plays, also, satirize the faults of the contemporary drama, and the *Knight of the Burning Pestle* abounds in ridicule of the absurdities of the popular plays of the day. They placed themselves, then, in opposition to the vulgar taste of the time, and were conscious of the demands of a refined taste and a requiring art.

Nevertheless, there is by no means an absolute disconnection between their plays and the plays of the preceding half-century. Although we shall have occasion to dwell on the novelty of their plays, they are, of course, far from being new. Possibly, there is scarcely a situation or a character which might not be traced back to an early original; certainly, there is no play which separates itself entirely from relationship with its Elizabethan predecessors. Indeed one needs to make but a cursory study of the Elizabethan drama to convince oneself that this is true of all plays as late as 1600. The continuity of theatrical tradition is rarely broken. The girl in doublet and hose, the deep-dyed villain, the braggart coward, the faithful friend, can all be traced at least as far back as the earliest days of the drama. A situation or a plot once successful was sure to be copied and varied and developed. However much the Elizabethan dramatists studied and pictured human life, they also kept closely in touch with theatrical conventions.

A single example may be permitted to illustrate these observations. In 1566, a play, *Palamon and Arcyte*, was performed before Queen Elizabeth at Oxford; and among other things concerning it, we learn from Wood's Ms.[2] "There was a good part performed by the the Lady Amelia, who for gathering her flowers prettily in a garden there represented and singing sweetly in the time of March, received eight angels for her gracious reward by her Majesty's command." There, perhaps, was the germ of a situation used over and over again in later plays and adapted by Shakspere into the scene in which Perdita distributes her flowers in the *Winter's Tale*.

Beaumont and Fletcher, like Shakspere and all other Eliza-

---

[1] 4to, 1607, acted 1605.
[2] Nichols' Progresses of Queen Elizabeth, I.

4

bethan dramatists, took their material where they could find it, and availed themselves of whatever had found favor on the stage. There can be no doubt, however, that their plays seemed very different to the spectators of their day from any which preceded. This is true of their comedies, with which as a class we shall have little to do, and it is still more true of their tragi-comedies and tragedies which I shall include by the term romances.[1] In the period 1600–1615 there are certainly few plays by other authors that resemble these romances. They are nothing like the revenge plays which were prevalent at the beginning of the period, nor the "tragedies of blood" of Webster and Tourneur, nor Chapman's *Bussy d'Ambois* and *Byron*, nor the classical tragedies of Jonson and Shakspere. Neither are they like *Macbeth*, *Othello*, or *Lear*, tragedies which deal with one main emotion and center about one character. If they differ from the plays which immediately preceded or were contemporary with them, they differ still more from the earlier chronicle-histories or tragedies. Beaumont and Fletcher, in fact, created a new dramatic form, the heroic romance. I shall later endeavor to establish this assertion by showing how their romances differ from all other plays of the time and how closely they themselves adhere to a definite type. For the present, we may well enough rest on a statement which no one will deny, that their romances were distinguished by much that was new in situations, plots, characters, and poetic style.

The production of such a series of plays within a few years of each other must certainly have influenced contemporary play-writing. And our knowledge of Shakspere surely justifies us in suspecting that no dramatist was more ready than he to make use of whatever was popular and suited to his purpose on the stage.

It becomes a significant fact, then, that at just about the time Beaumont and Fletcher's romances appeared, Shakspere, who had for a number of years been chiefly engaged on his tragedies, began writing a series of plays differing from any he had previously written and perhaps, also, best designated as romances. The common name 'romance' indicates a real resemblance. We saw a moment ago that Beaumont and Fletcher's romances differed markedly from almost all the notable tragic plays of their period; they have, however, at least a class resemblance to *Cymbeline*, the *Winter's Tale*, and the *Tempest*. Especial prominence given to a sentimental love-story, a rapid succession of tragic situations, a happy ending, are examples of resemblances which must occur to everyone.

[1] Typical examples are: *Philaster, Four Plays in One, Thierry and Theodoret, Cupid's Revenge, A King and No King, The Maid's Tragedy.*

5

Critics have, in fact, specifically noted the similarities between *Philaster* and *Cymbeline*[1].

Moreover, there is an abrupt change from Shakspere's previous work to his romances. Sometime between 1601 and 1608 he wrote the series of tragedies from *Hamlet* to *Antony and Cleopatra;* sometime between 1608 and 1612, he wrote *Cymbeline*, the *Winter's Tale*, and the *Tempest*. There were other plays probably during these two periods — *Troilus and Cressida, Measure for Measure, Pericles, Timon* — but some of these are not wholly Shakspere's, and all are of more doubtful date. They perhaps indicate periods of weakness in creative power, of searching after new forms,[2] but they cannot be classified under either of the groups above — the great tragedies or the romances. These two groups are absolutely distinct; they differ enormously in general effect. Still further, this transition from the tragedies to the romances was accomplished in one or two years at most; for the student of Shakspere's art, therefore, the hiatus has not been an easy one to bridge.

The only explanation that I know to have been offered, is that of a subjective change in Shakspere. It is stated that he passed out of a period of life, gloomy, passionate, full of suffering, into one of philosophic calm, renewed optimism, and final reconciliation: or as Mr. Dowden puts it, he passed "out of the depths" and rested "on the heights." It would be stupid to deny the possibility of such a change. No one imagines that Shakspere's mind was the same when he was writing *Hamlet* as when he was writing the *Tempest;* and what actual personal circumstances may have accompanied these varying creative moods is certainly open to conjecture without any possibility of disproof. Such subjective explanations, however, are at best only attempts to interpret the author's moods in terms of the æsthetic effect his work exerts upon us: and they give us few clues as to the actual methods of his creative art. We are on far safer grounds when we study objective influences; and a mere re-insistance on our point of view — the study of Shakspere as an Elizabethan dramatist — must lead to the conclusion that no decided change in the character of his plays would have been likely to take place without some objective cause.

Such a cause for his change from the tragedies to the romances I find in the production at about the same time of a series of romances by Beaumont and Fletcher. I think, also, that Shakspere's romances show definite evidences of the influence of Beaumont and Fletcher. In order to establish any probability for these opinions, there is necessary (1) an examination of the dates of Shakspere's and of Beaumont and Fletcher's

---

[1] See B. Leonhardt. *Anglia* 8.
[2] See *William Shakspere* by Barrett Wendell. p. 334.

6

romances in order to determine if the latter preceded, and (2) an examination of such of Beaumont and Fletcher's romances as date early enough in order to discover their distinguishing characteristics, and a like examination of Shakspere's three romances in search of indications of Beaumont and Fletcher's influence.

In addition to these two principal investigations there are some minor ones involved by them. The rather general opinion that both Shakspere and Fletcher are concerned in the authorship of *Henry VIII* and the *Two Noble Kinsmen*, is important in its bearing on the investigation of Fletcher's influence on Shakspere. We shall consider, therefore, the dates, the authorship and the possible collaboration in these plays. Their discussion, together with that of the lost *Cardenio*, also attributed to Fletcher and Shakspere, will be included for convenience in the first main division of the investigation, that of the chronology of the plays. *Pericles* is often spoken of as a precursor of Shakspere's romances and must therefore receive at least brief consideration. This will be postponed to the appendix.

Inasmuch as in investigating the chronology of the Beaumont-Fletcher plays I shall take Mr. Fleay's conclusions as a basis, some of his theories must first be considered, and with them some matters of the stage history of the period and some general methods used in the subsequent investigation. As this introduction to the Beaumont-Fletcher chronology also, in some details, affects the Shakspere chronology, it will precede the latter as well as the former.

An examination of the plays acted in the eight or ten years preceding the romances will also be necessary in order to determine to what extent they were innovations on contemporary practice.

In discussing the characteristics of the romances of Beaumont and Fletcher and their influence on Shakspere's we should naturally expect to find in *Cymbeline*, probably the earliest of the latter, more distinct traces of the influence of Beaumont and Fletcher than in the *Winter's Tale* and the *Tempest*; for in these later plays Shakspere, once accustomed to the new style of drama, would more completely transform it. I shall, therefore, consider separately the influence of *Philaster* on *Cymbeline*, and in still another chapter discuss the *Winter's Tale* and the *Tempest*.

My investigation, therefore, will be presented in the following somewhat arbitrary order.

(I.)

1. Introduction to the chronology of the plays of Beaumont and Fletcher and the stage history of 1605–1615.

7

2. Chronology of Shakspere's three romances.
3. Chronology and discussion of *Henry VIII*, the *Two Noble Kinsmen*, and *Cardenio*.
4. Chronology of the plays of Beaumont and Fletcher.

(II.)

5. The drama 1601–1610.
6. General characteristics of the romances of Beaumont and Fletcher.
7. General characteristics of Shakspere's romances.
8. *Cymbeline* and *Philaster*.
9. A *Winter's Tale* and the *Tempest*.
10. (Appendix). *Pericles*.

In spite of the somewhat wide latitude of the investigation, its two main objects must not be lost sight of: (1) to show that so far as dates and facts of stage history are concerned, it is entirely possible that the Beaumont-Fletcher romances may have influenced Shakspere, and (2) to show a probability that they did definitely influence his romances.

CHAPTER II.

INTRODUCTION TO CHRONOLOGY AND STAGE HISTORY.

Before attempting to fix the dates of the plays of Beaumont and Fletcher, it is necessary to understand the few facts known of their lives and reputations as dramatists and to discuss a few important features of the stage history of the time. In discussing the separate plays, I shall take as a basis the conclusions of Mr. Fleay in his *Chronicle of the English Drama*; and these conclusions rest so often on his special theories in regard to the general stage history that, in order even to understand his dates for the plays, those theories must be carefully examined.

A. Biographies.

Francis Beaumont, third son of Judge Beaumont of Grace Dieu in Leicestershire, was born about 1585 and died March 6, 1616. He was admitted gentleman commoner at Broadgates Hall, Oxford, in 1597, and was entered at the Inner Temple, London, Nov. 3, 1600. *Salamis* and *Hermaphrodite*, 1602, may possibly have been written by him. He was married, possibly about 1613,[1] and left two daughters (one, a posthumous child). He was buried in Westminster Abbey.

John Fletcher, son of Richard Fletcher, Bishop of Bristol, was baptized at Rye in Sussex, where his father was then minister, Dec. 20, 1579, and died of the plague Aug. 25, 1625. He was entered as a pensioner at Bene't College, Cambridge, 1591.

It is not known just when Fletcher came to London or when he began writing plays or when he first became acquainted with Beaumont. Davenant in a prologue to the *Woman Hater* at a revival, evidently alluding to Fletcher, declares that "full twenty years he wore the bays:" this would place the beginning of his play-writing 1604–5. In 1607, both he and Beaumont prefixed verses to *Volpone* (acted 1605.) Beaumont addresses Jonson as "my dear friend," praises him for teaching "our tongue the rules of time, of place," and shows a characteristic scorn of the audiences of the day. Fletcher also classes himself among Jonson's friends and speaks of the latter's foes. In 1607, then, they were well acquainted with Jonson and

---

[1] Fleay: Chr. I, p. 170.

probably with each other. Beaumont wrote commendatory verse for *Epicœne* (1609) and both Beaumont and Fletcher for *Catiline* (1611). Beaumont also wrote commendatory verses, together with Jonson, Chapman, and Field for Fletcher's *Faithful Shepherdess* (4to 1609?) *The Woman Hater*, probably by Beaumont alone, was published anonymously, 1607. Beaumont's oft-quoted epistle to Jonson, is entitled in the 1679 folio, " written before he and Master Fletcher came to London with two of the precedent comedies, then not finished, which deferred their merry meetings at the Mermaid." [1] The reference in the letter to Sutcliffe's wit seems to refer to the pamphlets produced by him in 1606. [2] In 1610, Davies' *Scourge of Folly* was published, containing an epigram on *Philaster*. In 1612, in the address to the reader, prefixed to the *White Devil*, [3] Webster praises " the no less worthy composures of the both worthily excellent Master Beaumont and Master Fletcher," ranking them on equal terms with such scholars and experienced dramatists as Chapman and Jonson, and apparently above Shakspere, Dekker, and Heywood. Before 1612, then, the reputation of Beaumont and Fletcher as dramatists must have been well established.

Beaumont, in addition to his plays, wrote elegies on the Lady Markham who died in 1609, the Countess of Rutland who died in 1612, and Lady Penelope Clifton who died in 1613. He also addressed some verses to the Countess of Rutland, and in 1613 wrote a masque for Lady Elizabeth's marriage, which was performed with great splendor by the gentlemen of the Inner Temple and Gray's Inn. We shall find no direct evidence that he wrote anything for the stage during the last four years of his life. At the same time there is no positive reason to believe that he stopped play-writing so long before his death.

Beaumont was buried in Westminster Abbey close by Chaucer and Spenser; and the verses on Shakspere, usually attributed to William Basse, bid

> " Renowned Spencer lye a thought more nye
> To learned Chaucer, and rare Beaumont lye
> A little nearer Spenser, to make roome
> For Shakespeare in your threefold, fowerfold Tombe.
> To lodge all fowre in one bed make a shift
> Until Doomesdaye, for hardly will a fift
> Betwixt *this* day and *that* by Fate be slayne,
> For whom your curtaines may be drawn againe."

There is no doubt, indeed, that Beaumont's reputation as a poet was very high even before his death. The commendatory

---

[1] Whether there is any evidence for the connection between the epistle and " two of the precedent comedies " is a matter of conjecture.
[2] *Cf.*, Chr. I p. 170.
[3] Acted before 1612, perhaps 1607-8 (Fleay).

verses prefixed to the Beaumont and Fletcher folio of 1647 show that then they were probably the most popular of the Elizabethan dramatists. How high their literary reputation was, can be seen from the fact that either during their lives or after their deaths, their praises were heralded by Jonson, Chapman, Webster, Waller, Denham, Lovelace, Cartwright, Herrick, Brome, and Shirley. Perhaps no other poet of the Elizabethan period—certainly not Shakspere—received such a volume of praise.

B. Connections with Theatrical Companies.

We have next to examine some of Mr. Fleay's theories, and from the examination arrive at some important facts of the stage history. We may first consider Beaumont and Fletcher's connections with the theatrical companies.

Some of the Elizabethan playwrights were actors and wrote for the companies in which they acted; some were hackwriters whose services were engaged for certain periods by certain companies. Some, like Shakspere, wrote for one company throughout their career; some changed back and forth at fairly traceable intervals from one company to another. Beaumont and Fletcher were neither actors, nor managers, nor hackwriters; they were gentlemen and poets. They were probably no more closely attached at any one time to any one company than a dramatist of to-day would be bound to one manager, or a novelist to one publisher. Not only is there no evidence that their services were subsidized for definite periods by particular companies; on the contrary there is clear evidence that they belonged to the class of writers who were independent of all such theatrical engagements.

That there was such a class of dramatists may be clearly seen from a cursory examination of Ben Jonson's dramatic career. The following list shows his career up to 1616,[1] giving date, play, company, and theater.

1597, Dec. 3.	Henslow, "a book."		
1598, Aug. 19.	Hot Anger soon Cold.*	Henslow, Admirals.	Rose.
1598, (before 1599.)	The Case is Altered.	Chapel Children.	
1598.	Every Man in his Humour.	Lord Chamberlain's.†	Curtain.
1599.	Every Man out of his Humour.	Lord Chamberlain's.	Globe.
1599, Aug. 10, Sep. 2.	Page of Plymouth.	Henslow, Admiral's.	Rose.
1599, Sep.	Robert II, King of Scots.*	Henslow, Admiral's.	Rose.
1600.	Cynthia's Revels.	Chapel Children.	Blackfriars
1601.	The Poetaster.	Chapel Children.	Blackfriars
1601. (?) Fleay.	Tale of a Tub.	Chapel Children. (?)	
1601-2, Sep. 25, June 24.	The Spanish Tragedy, Additions.	Henslow, Admiral's.	Fortune.
1602, June 24.	Richard Crookback.	Henslow, Admiral's.	Fortune.

* With collaborators.
† Also acted by another company; Fleay thinks before 1603 by Chapel Children.

[1] The dates can be verified by Henslow's diary and Jonson's 1616 folio.

II

1603.	Sejanus.	King's.	Globe.
1604–5.	Eastward Ho.*	Queen's Revels.	Blackfriars
1605.	Volpone.	King's.	Globe,
1609.	Epicoene.	Queen's Revels.	?
1610.	Alchemist.	King's.	Blackfriars
1611.	Catiline.	King's.	Blackfriars
1614.	Bartholemew Fair.	Lady Elizabeth's.	Hope.
1616.	The Devil is an Ass.	King's.	Blackfriars

* With collaborators.

It is absurd to say, as Mr. Fleay does, that Jonson left this company and went to that; one has to trace twelve such changes for twenty plays. "This continual change of company,"[1] which Mr. Fleay says is peculiar to Jonson, simply indicates that he never had any definite connection with any company.

During their joint career as dramatists, Beaumont and Fletcher are as 'peculiar' as Jonson in the continual changing of company. The following are the only certain dates of plays before 1616, (Beaumont's death) and they show how impossible it is to arrange the plays by periods in which the authors were writing for different companies.

1607.	Woman Hater, printed.	Paul's Boys.
Before Oct., 1610.	Philaster, acted.	King's Men.
1612.	Coxcomb, acted at court.	Rossiter's Queen's Revels
1612–3.	Captain. acted at court.	King's Men.
1612.	Cupid's Revenge, acted at court.	Queen's Revels.
In or before 1611.	Maid's Tragedy, acted.	King's Men.
1611.	A King and No King, acted.	King's Men.
1613.	Honest Man's Fortune, acted.	Lady Elizabeth's Men.

This list at least shows the difficulty of dividing the plays chronologically into groups written for different companies; yet this is just what Mr. Fleay tries to do, and he also tries to trace the changes of Beaumont and Fletcher in conjunction with Jonson's. This method has vitiated his entire chronology. To what extent it rests on ill-founded conjectures and neglect and misstatement of facts, we shall have occasion to notice in other places. Here, we can only point out the absurdity of the whole proceeding.

Up to about September, 1610,[2] he thinks Beaumont and Fletcher were writing for the Revels children, (Blackfriars Company and its successor at Whitefriars); and so all the plays acted by the Revels Company are crowded into the years before that date. Then in company with Jonson,[3] he thinks they left the Revels boys for the King's men, where they took the place of Shakspere.[4] But Shakspere's *Tempest*, according to Mr. Fleay's own statement[5] was not yet produced, and Beaumont and Fletcher's *Philaster* was produced some time before Oct. 8, 1610. Moreover, Jonson's leaving the Revels for the

[1] Chr. I, p. 346.
[2] Except the *Woman Hater* for Pauls Boys. For date see Chr. I, p. 188.
[3] Chr. I, p. 188, Chr. I, p. 349.
[4] Chr. I, p. 370.
[5] Life of Shakspere, p. 248.

King's men amounts to just this; from 1605 to the end of 1610, he wrote one play, *Epicoene*, (1609) which was acted by the Revels boys, and in 1610, his *Alchemist* was acted by the King's men. Jonson did not change in September, 1610, neither did Beaumont and Fletcher.

From 1610 to 1613, Mr. Fleay keeps them busy writing plays for the King's men; but in 1613, he thinks "Fletcher, still following Johnson, now left the King's men"[1] and wrote 1613–16 for the Lady Elizabeth's men. In 1613, as a matter of fact, Jonson was in France with Sir Walter Raleigh's son, so it is hard to see in what way Fletcher followed him. The facts are simply these: Jonson's *Catiline* was acted in 1611 by the King's men, and his next play was acted three years later by the Lady Elizabeth's men. Beaumont and Fletcher's *A King and No King* was acted by the King's men in 1611, and *The Honest Man's Fortune*, in which Fletcher, at least, had a share, was acted by Lady Elizabeth's men in 1613. There are no other plays by Fletcher which were certainly acted 1613-16 by Lady Elizabeth's men.

Mr. Fleay's method of arranging the plays certainly tends to distort the facts and may well be dispensed with. The relations between the dramatists and the companies do, however, afford some assistance in determining the dates of plays. From 1619 and perhaps from as early a date as 1616, Fletcher seems to have been writing only for the King's men; at least, so many of his plays were produced by that company, there is small likelihood that he wrote for any other. Before 1616, there is no definite evidence connecting either Beaumont or Fletcher for fixed periods with any company.[2] The fact, however, that one of their plays was produced by a given company at a certain date, makes it somewhat likely that other plays were produced by the same company at about that time. If they wrote some plays for the Revels boys before 1611, there is a consequent likelihood that they wrote others. If none of their plays, so far as is known, were presented by the Queen's men, there is a strong presumption against any particular play of theirs being acted by the Queen's men. There is, however, no reason to suppose that different plays of theirs may not have been given first presentations by different companies in the same year. There is no reason why they may not have been writing in the same year one play particularly suited to one of the companies of children and another play for the King's men.

I shall therefore attempt to determine the date of each play

---

[1] Chr. I, p. 195.
[2] They wrote for Paul's boys, Queen's Revels, Rossiter's (Second Queen's) Revels, King's men, and Lady Elizabeth's men.

13

without any assistance from a conjectural division of Beaumont and Fletcher's dramatic career into periods marking their connection with different companies.

C. The Plague and the Closing of the Theaters.

"In the reigns of James and Charles," writes Mr. Fleay, "the plagues were so frequent that the theaters were often closed in consequence. This took place whenever the deaths from plague amounted to forty per week."[1] He then goes on to show that this regulation was rigidly enforced because from an examination of Henslow's diary for 1593, it appears that the theater was closed from May 3 to Dec. 27, while the deaths exceeded forty a week from April 28 to Dec. 15. He, therefore, concludes that the theaters were closed during all periods when the plague deaths per week were above forty; and hence in the later half of each of the five years 1606–10 inclusive, from about July 1 to the last of November, and particularly, from July 28 to Dec. 22, 1608, and from Dec. 26, 1608, to Nov. 30, 1609.

This theory, especially in respect to the closing of the theaters for sixteen months in 1608–9, is of great importance in Mr. Fleay's chronology of plays. It is, in fact, constantly leading him into trouble. He is obliged to assign the *Scornful Lady*, *Monsieur Thomas*, and any other plays which he thinks date 1609, to the small part of December which would remain after the announcement had been made that the deaths were less than forty. He is also obliged to explain the acting of *Epicoene* in 1609[2] by the old style calender. One suspects, indeed, that his theory that the theaters closed entirely was an offspring of his theories about the Blackfriars House, for in his *Life of Shakspere*[3] he assigns *Cymbeline* to the autumn of 1609 and merely remarks, "this being a plague year, there was little dramatic activity."

At all events, considered point by point, his theory proves untenable. In the first place, it is not clear just what the regulation was for closing the theaters. Mr. Fleay insists that forty is the correct number of deaths,[4] but in Middleton's *Your Five Gallants*,[5] the following passage indicates that the number was thirty,—"'tis e'en as uncertain as playing, now up and now down; for if *the bill down rise to above thirty, here's no place for players.*" Again in the rough draft of a patent for

---

[1] H. of S. p. 162.
[2] So stated in quarto and folio of 1616.
[3] p. 162.
[4] H. of S. p. 191. So stated in Privy Seal to King's Men, 1619–20.
[5] Licensed March 22, 1608.

14

the Earl of Worcester's men, published by Collier,[1] it is especially provided that they shall play "when the infection of the plague shall decrease to the number of thirty within our city of London." Again in a letter printed in Winwood's *Memorials*,[2] thirty a week is referred to as if it were the limiting number of deaths. Finally, in none of the eight patents granted to companies from 1603–1615, except in the one just noted is there any reference to a limiting number. In six[3] there is no allusion whatever to the plague; and in the remaining one to the King's men,[4] they are to act "when the infection of the plague shall decrease." There is no reference to the forty limit until the Privy Seal to the King's men in 1620.[5]

In the second place there is no certainty that any regulation prohibiting theatrical performances during the plague was rigidly enforced. Mr. Fleay's conclusion rests on the closing of Henslow's theater for seven months during a year when the deaths numbered 11,503; but because a theater was closed when the plague was so prevalent, it clearly does not follow that any regulation was strictly enforced fifteen years later when the deaths were averaging about twenty-five hundred yearly. A passage in Middleton's *A Mad World my Masters*[6] makes it certain that theaters were sometimes closed because of the plague, but also makes it evident that the players decidedly objected to such regulations. When fear of the plague was not excessive, it seems reasonable to suppose that the regulations were unenforced or evaded.

---

[1]Vol. I, p. 336. Fleay suspects, to be sure, that this draft of a patent may be a forgery, but one of the chief reasons for his suspicion is that the number of deaths is stated at thirty instead of forty. H of S. p. 140.

[2]Vol. II, p. 140. "The sudden riseing of the sickness to thirty a "week and the infesting of nineteen parishes, made us think the Term, "or Parliament, or both, might be prolonged and put off, but the "abating of some few this week makes us all hold on."
Also printed Nichols I, 562. Dated Oct. 12, 1605.

[3]Privy Seal, Jan. 30. 1604. Her Majesty's Revels. Collier I, 340. Privy Seal, March 30, 1610. Duke of York's. Shak. Soc. Papers, IV. 47. Privy Seal, April 15, 1609. Queen's Men. Shak. Soc. Papers, IV. 44. Privy Seal, April 30, 1607. Prince's Men. Shak. Soc. Papers, IV, 42. Privy Seal, Jan. 4, 1613. Palsgrave's Men. Collier I, 365. Privy Seal, May 30, 1615. Philip Rossiter et al. *English Drama and Stage*, p. 46. Roxburgh Library (1869).

[4]Patent, May 17, 1603, King's Men. Collier I, 334. This patent was granted in the great plague year of 1603, when the deaths were over 30,000.

[5]Patent, March 27, 1620. *English Drama and Stage.* Roxburgh Library, 1869, p. 50.

[6]Quarto 1608; acted (Fleay) 1606; "But for certain players, there "thou liest, boy, they were never more uncertain in their lives; "now up, and now down; they know not where to play, or what to "play, nor when to play for fearful fools." Act V, sc. 1.

In the third place, Mr. Fleay's table of the periods 1606–1610 when the deaths exceeded forty per week, is open to suspicion. I have not been able to examine the mortality tables, but it seems curious that the deaths were less than forty *per week* for a period *Dec. 22 to 26*, 1608. At any rate, for five years the deaths averaged about 2,500 a year, and in 1609, the year in which the plague was severest, they were only a little over 4,000. This plague had been prevalent since the great outbreak of 1603; and one would hardly suppose it sufficient to close the theaters entirely during sixteen months in 1608–9.

There is, in fact, very definite evidence that it did not. On the 5th of April, 1609, J. Hemings was paid for twelve plays performed at court by the King's men the Christmas before; and on the same date there was a payment for three plays by the Prince's men, presumably also given in the Christmas season 1608–9. At that time, according to Mr. Fleay, the theaters had been closed five months, and we have to suppose that the travelling companies[1] were summoned back to London to play at court during the plague. A more likely inference is that the companies were playing in London both at the time of the court performance and the later payment. There is, in fact, no evidence that theaters, pageants, or business in general were to any extent interrupted by the plague in 1608–9. The *Masque* of *Queens* was performed Feb. 2, 1609 before the royal family at Whitehall; the king and royal family visited the Tower June 23, 1609, and the Bourse (new Exchange) was dedicated April 10, 1609. Moreover, in April, 1609, we find a patent granted to the Queen's players "to shewe and exercise publickly as well within their nowe usual houses called the Redd Bull, etc."[2] Apparently the theaters and companies were then in full swing.

Jonson's *Epicœne*, too, was certainly acted in 1609, as stated in the first quarto and the carefully edited folio of 1616. Mr. Fleay assumes that Jonson is using the old calendar and that 1609 may include Jan.–March 1610, hence he dates the play 1610,[3] because he thinks the theaters were closed during 1609, and because he sees in the prologue a reference to the Whitefriars theater which he thinks was occupied by a company of Revels boys in 1610. The last reason is one of Mr. Fleay's wildest, and may be at once dismissed; "the daughters of Whitefriars"

---

[1] They were presumably away from London, unless they returned for the period Dec. 22–Dec. 26, when Fleay thinks the plague deaths were less than forty a week.

[2] Fleay (Chr. I, 31) says "they did not play until December on account of the plague."

[3] Chr. I, p. 374.

has no reference to the theater.[1] The assumption that Jonson used the old style calendar, beginning the year March 26, is equally contrary to fact but has some value as a typical example of Mr. Fleay's methods.

In fixing the date of *Epicœne* in 1610, he remarks, " this play like *the Fox* and other plays, has hitherto been dated a year too early, in consequence of the use of the old style dates."[2] Nevertheless, earlier in the same volume, he expressly states: "Jonson and Chapman begin their year Jan. 1; most other writers March 26."[3] Fortunately we have the means for determining which of these two contradictory statements is true by comparing the dates given in the quartos and folio for several of the masques with the known dates of their presentation. The following table will make it perfectly plain that in dating his productions Jonson began the year with January first.

Date given in Quarto.	Date given in 1616 Folio.	New style date of Court Perf'r'nce.	Masque.
1605 and 1608.	1605 and 1608.	Jan. 1, 1605, and Jan., 1608.	*Blackness.*
Jan. 6, 1606.	not dated.	Jan. 6, 1606.	*Hymen.*
1608.	1608.	Jan. 14, 1608.	*Beauty.*
Quarto, entered S. R., Feb. 22, 1609.	Feb. 2, 1609.	Feb. 2, 1609.	*Queens.*
	1608.	Feb., 1608.	*Hue and Cry. after Cupid.*

The evidence[4] (note particularly the date given for the *Masque of Queens*) seems to be conclusive that the 1609 date given in the Folio for *Epicoene* means from Jan. 1 to Dec. 31, 1609.

Finally, then, Mr. Fleay's deductions from his theory of the closing of the theaters add nothing to its plausibility. In addition to placing *Epicoene* in 1610, he places the *Scornful Lady, Ram Alley*,[5] *Monsieur Thomas*, and quite possibly other plays I have not noticed, in December, 1609. In the week ending Nov. 30, the plague deaths exceeded forty; another

---

[1] *Epicœne.* Prologue. . . " Some for lords, knights, 'squires;
" Some for your waiting wench, and city wives,
" Some for your men and daughters of Whitefriars."
See, also, *Volpone*, IV. 1., "Ay, your Whitefriars nation." Gifford explains the passage: "Whitefriars was at this time a privileged spot in which fraudulent debtors, gamblers, prostitutes, and other outcasts of society usually resided." See, also, *The Blacke Booke* 4to 1604. B. 8, p. 30, "drabs in Whitefriars" and *Father Hubbard's Tales*, Bk 8, p. 78, "Whitefriar's nunnery," Bk 8, p. 84, "Whitefriars, Pict.-hatch, and Tumball Sheet."
[2] Chr. I, p. 374.
[3] Chr. I, p. 65, foot-note.
[4] The only case I have noted in which the folio does not date by the new style is in that portion which Mr. Fleay himself says was not supervised by Jonson, *i. e.*, which is without marginal notes and whose statements are less correct. Theré, the *Golden Age Restored*, acted Jan. 1 and 6, 1616, is dated 1615.
[5] He is in doubt between Dec., 1609 and 1610.

week must have elapsed in which they were less than forty, and at least a few days more according to his theory before the companies could have acted.[1] He supposes, then, that after sixteen months of idleness or absence from London, the companies at once began playing and that one of them, the Queen's Revels, brought out two new plays in the last two weeks of December, 1609. This supposition alone is enough to throw suspicion on his theory.

On the whole, the most that can be safely asserted is that the theaters were very possibly closed during the summer and autumn months of 1609-10, when the plague was more fatal than common. During these months the companies probably spent some of the time in travelling. There is positive evidence that the theaters were not closed during sixteen or seventeen months 1608-1609, and the only safe assumption is Mr. Fleay's earlier one that theatrical activity may have been considerably lessened because of the plague in 1609.

D. *The Occupancy of Blackfriars by the King's Men.*

Mr. Fleay dates all the plays of Beaumont and Fletcher acted by the King's men later than the fall of 1610. He does this because he thinks Beaumont and Fletcher then left the Revels children and joined the King's men, and because he thinks the King's men had then just begun playing in Blackfriars, where he seems to imagine all Beaumont and Fletcher's plays were first acted. The first reason we have already found to be groundless; the second is of enough importance in Mr. Fleay's chronology to require special attention.

The date of the occupancy of Blackfriars by the King's men, he reaches by a curious process. The Blackfriar Share Papers, first published by Mr. Halliwell-Phillipps in his *Outlines of the Life of Shakespeare*, proved that Burbadge took back the lease of Blackfriars from Evans (given in 1600) and established a men's company there instead of the boys, taking Underwood and Ostler[2] from the boys' company into the King's men. Mr. Halliwell-Phillipps stated the date of the change to be December, 1609.[3] Thereupon, Mr. Fleay in his *Life of Shakespeare*[4] took Mr. Halliwell-Phillipps to task for merely guessing. Mr. Fleay declared that Burbadge bought the remainder of the lease probably on Lady's Day, 1610 and then took possession of the building. Then Mr. Green-

---

[1] Mr. Fleay seems to think the theaters were opened before any announcement was made or the deaths were less than forty a week, for he speaks of the re-opening of the theaters Dec. 1. *Chr. 1, 31.*

[2] Field's name is also mentioned, but this seems surely a misstatement. He does not appear with the King's men until about 1616.

[3] *Outlines*, p. 150.

[4] p. 164.

street's discovery of the papers of the Kirkham-Burbadge case, proved that Burbadge actually bought back the lease in August, 1608. Mr. Fleay, however, clung to as much of his former theory as he possibly could. The King's men did not take possession, he affirmed in his *History of the Stage*,[1] until December 24, 1609. He seems to have finally arrived at Mr. Halliwell-Phillips' earlier guess.

Now, this date, December 24, 1609, involves the following improbable theory : Although Burbadge bought back the lease in August, 1608, the theater was closed by the plague until Nov. 30, 1609; just as soon as possible after the deaths were less than forty a week (Dec. 1 to 7), the company which had occupied the theater before 1608, the Queen's Revels children, began playing again in Blackfriars; on December 24, they gave it up to Burbadge and the King's men. Mr. Fleay's support for this theory is three-fold : (1) the *Scornful Lady* was acted at Blackfriars in 1609, by the Queen's Revels; (2) a new company of boys, a successor of the old Queen's Revels, was formed by Rossiter in January, 1610, and the first Revels did not leave Blackfriars until then; (3) the plague closed all the theaters from July 28, 1608, to Nov. 30, 1609.

These supports are all conjectural and groundless. The first we have already seen to be improbable, as will appear more conclusively in our discussion of the *Scornful Lady*. The second has no ground, for the Revels company was certainly on the verge of dissolution in 1608, and there is no reason to be sure that it kept together until Rossiter's company was formed. Further, the Revels children might conceivably have left Blackfriars some time before they joined Rossiter's company, or they might have shared the Blackfriars for a while with the King's men, as Collier suggested.[2] At any rate, the Revels company in a disbanded state wouldn't have been very likely to occupy Burbadge's theater to the exclusion of the King's men. The third conjecture, in regard to the plague, has already been shown to be without foundation.

So much for Mr. Fleay's theory. The facts are clear enough. Just what became of the remnant of Queen's Revels from 1608-1610 is, indeed. open to conjecture, but there can be no doubt about the King's men. Evans sold back his lease to Burbadge in August, 1608. The reasons for the transfer are stated to have been legal inhibitions and financial difficulties. Burbadge placed men players in Blackfriars ; but before doing so, according to the testimony of his children,[3] he took Ostler and Under-

---

[1] p. 200. *et passim.*
[2] Vol. I, p. 360. Mr. Fleay also states that two companies may have sometimes shared the same theatre. *Life Shaks.*, p. 164.
[3] Blackfriars Share Papers. H. P. *Outlines*, V. I, p. 286-293.

wood into the King's men. The King's men probably occupied Blackfriars from 1608 on, as is indicated by the statement of John Hemings in a legal paper, dated Nov. 5, 1612, who declares that for four years past he had received (as a partner of Burbadge) a share in the profits of the Blackfriars house, *i. e.*, since the surrender of the lease by Evans.[1] There is nothing, moreover, to oppose the natural conclusion that the King's men took possession of Blackfriars very soon after August, 1608.

E.   The Revels Companies.

We have already examined Mr. Fleay's theory of the career of the Queen's Revels in so far as it was affected by the plague years and the closing of Blackfriars. His further discussion of this and the other Revels companies seems to me inadequate ; but since it does not affect the dates of any of the Beaumont and Fletcher plays, I shall merely note the conclusions reached in my investigations without discussing the changes of the companies in detail.

On the whole the most reasonable chronology is that in 1605, after their difficulty over *Eastward Ho*, the Queen's Revels boys ceased for a time to use that name but continued in Blackfriars until August, 1608, when the company was broken up and the lease resold to Burbadge. The King's Revels appear as early as 1607 (when the Paul's boys disbanded), and not later than 1610 ; they employed some of the poets and possibly some of the actors of the Queen's Revels. Possibly the Queen's Revels kept up some sort of an organization from 1608 to 1610, but, surely, in 1610 the name was associated with a new company of children, including some from both the King's and the Queen's Revels, which was managed by Rossiter and acted at Whitefriars. This chronology is not without difficulties, and cannot be relied upon with certainty in establishing dates of plays. We have not enough evidence to trace out in detail the history of the Revels Companies from 1604-1613, but the important facts are certain. In 1608 the first Queen's Revels disbanded, and in 1610 a new company of Queen's Revels was established.

F.   Shakspere with Beaumont and Fletcher, writing for the King's Men.

Still another theory of Mr. Fleay's requires especial examination. He asserts that Shakspere gave up writing for the King's men in the autumn of 1610,[2] and that Jonson, Beau-

---

[1] Greenstreet Papers. H. of S., p. 238. The joint and several answers of John Hemings and Richard Burbadge, etc.
[2] Chr. I, p. 170.

mont, and Fletcher succeeded him about September. Mr. Fleay thinks that before this date Beaumont and Fletcher wrote for the Queen's Revels at Blackfriars, until December, 1609, and for Rossiter's new company at Whitefriars in 1610. We have seen how little basis there is for any theory that traces the careers of these dramatists by their connections with companies. In regard to Shakspere there is no evidence, whatever, that he left writing in the fall of 1610. There is, on the contrary, important evidence, as we shall see later, that he wrote for the King's men even until 1613.[1]

Mr. Fleay's theory, however, can be disproved without going outside of his own discussions. He fixes the date of the *Tempest*,[2] as do most critics, after Jourdain's narrative, published October 13, 1610 ; so Shakspere was, according to Mr. Fleay's own account, writing for the King's men after that date. In Davies' *Scourge of Folly* (entered S. R., October 8, 1610) there is an epigram on *Philaster*.[3] This play, in the first quarto, is stated to have been " acted at the Globe by his Majesty's Servants ;" therefore Beaumont and Fletcher were certainly writing for the King's men before Shakspere stopped writing for that company.

In addition to the evidence of the date of the *Tempest*, we may note that the evidence of the date of the *Winter's Tale*, and the opinion of his most competent biographers agree in placing Shakspere's withdrawal from dramatic writing later than the latest possible date for *Philaster*.

To show how these theories of Mr. Fleay's have vitiated his results, it will be enough to state that, owing to his conjectures that the King's men did not occupy the Blackfriars house until December, 1609, and that the plague closed all the theaters for seventeen months, and that Beaumont and Fletcher did not join the King's men until the autumn of 1610, he has placed the first productions of six of their best plays in the ten months from December, 1609, to September, 1610. He places the *Scornful Lady* and *Monsieur Thomas* at the Blackfriars in 1609, the *Knight of the Burning Pestle*, the *Coxcomb*, and *Cupid's Revenge* at the Whitefriars in 1610 ; and *Philaster* at the Blackfriars by the King's men before Oct. 8, 1610. Without considering the evidence for the date of each play, the production of these six plays in ten months is improbable. According to Mr. Fleay, Beaumont wrote almost the whole of two of these and a large share in three others, which is a very large proportion of his life's work to assign to so short a period ; besides,

---

[1] See discussion of *Henry VIII* and *Two Noble Kinsmen*, Chapter IV.
[2] Life of Sh., pp. 248-9.
[3] Correctly stated by Fleay. Chr. II, 189.

the six plays show wide differences in style and dramatic methods.

Leaving Mr. Fleay's theories, we may again repeat the important facts. In August, 1608, Burbadge took back his lease of Blackfriars. During 1609 the plague was more severe than usual. Beaumont and Fletcher were certainly writing for the King's men before Shakspere left the company.

G. *Evidence of Folios, Quartos, and Verse-tests.*

In addition to the foregoing remarks on stage-history, there are some general considerations in respect to the evidence of folios and quartos and of verse-tests which may best be stated now. Beaumont and Fletcher, like Shakspere, took no care about publishing their plays. Only four were printed before Beaumont's death in 1616, and his name appears on none of these. Fletcher's name appears on only the *Faithful Shepherdess* and *Cupid's Revenge*. In general, their plays seem to have held the stage and to have been kept from the printers; at any rate, only fourteen plays were published in quartos before the folio of 1647, which contained thirty-six plays never before published. These were all assigned to Beaumont and Fletcher; but Beaumont certainly had no share in many of them, Fletcher probably had no share in a few, while Massinger certainly had a large share in many, and other dramatists in a few. The evidence of both quartos and folio on the question of authorship is nearly valueless.

In the second folio of 1679, the plays previously published in quarto were added to those of the first folio; and to these latter, lists of the chief actors were in many cases supplied. These lists were added to all the plays of the first folio certainly acted by the King's men and to three others, and are an important aid in determining the dates of those plays. Seven lists have Burbadge at the head, so the plays must have been acted before his death in 1619; and the remaining plays by the King's men without Burbadge's name date pretty certainly after 1618. The presence or absence of other actors on these lists helps to fix their dates more exactly.

From 1622 on, we also have the dates of licensing given in Herbert's office book. A number of plays, however, have neither actors' lists nor are on Herbert's books. The presumption, therefore, is that they were not acted by the King's men and that they date before 1622; or—since the time 1618–1622 is well filled with plays by the King's men—probably before 1618.

A further means of fixing the dates of these plays is that of verse-tests, used primarily to determine the authorship of the plays. These have been applied to Beaumont and Fletcher's

22

plays by[1] Fleay, Macaulay, Boyle, and Oliphant, to whose work I shall have frequent occasion to refer. Beaumont seems to have stopped writing for the stage 1611–12, at least, no plays in which he certainly had a share date later than that; so if the critics agree in giving Beaumont a share in a play, the date is presumably before 1612, and certainly before 1616. The trouble is they don't agree; still, including disputed cases, there are only some fifteen plays which Mr. Fleay, or Mr. Macaulay, or Mr. Boyle assigns to Beaumont. Mr. Oliphant, however, thinks that a great number of the plays of uncertain date were first written by Beaumont and Fletcher, or by one of them alone, and later revised by other authors.

The reasons which lead him to such a conclusion may be briefly summarized. (1) If a play is not on Herbert's licensing books, it was originally produced before 1622, and probably, as noted above, before 1618. (2) Many of these plays according to all investigators, show signs of revision by other authors than Beaumont or Fletcher. (3) If written within a few years before 1622, it is odd that they should be revised shortly after Fletcher's death in 1625. There is a probability, therefore, that they were early plays; and in addition to these general considerations, (4) he finds in some specific indications of Beaumont's authorship. In this way he places before 1612 some twelve plays in addition to those so dated by Mr. Fleay. This obliges him to date the beginning of Beaumont and Fletcher's writing for the stage as early as 1604; a reference to the known facts of their lives will show that this date is probable enough.

Mr. Oliphant's general reasoning is plausible, but his attempts to separate the work of two original authors and two revisers with their various permutations, are, from their nature, not of a sort to excite unlimited faith. Unless there is direct corroborating evidence of an early date, his conclusions in respect to a play must clearly be viewed with the utmost caution. At the same time, there is no doubt that a number of these plays were revised; and, *a priori*, there is almost a probability that some in their present form may be revisions of early plays.

In general, I shall avoid questions of authorship except

---

[1] F. G. Fleay: *Transactions New Shakespeare Society*, 1874. *Chronicle of the English Drama*, 1891.
G. C. Macaulay: *Francis Beaumont, a critical study*, 1883, London.
R. Boyle: *Englische Studien*, V, VII, VIII, IX, X—1881-2—1886.
Transactions New Shakespeare Society, 1886.
E. F. Oliphant: *Englische Studien*, XIV, XV, XVI, 1890-92.
In referring to these I shall use simply the author's name unless special reference is necessary.
A. H. Bullen in the article on Fletcher in the Dict. of Nat. Biog. has also discussed the authorship of the plays.

when they directly affect the date; but as a number of such cases occur, a word may be added here on the subject. Fletcher's style is so clearly distinguishable that any one who has read him carefully may recognize it with some degree of certainty. Nevertheless, his *Faithful Shepherdess*[1] is written in a very different style and suggests that Fletcher may have varied his versification in other plays. Of Fletcher's work, however, we may generally be sure; Massinger's style, though by no means as distinctive as Fletcher's, is somewhat readily distinguished by verse-tests from either Fletcher's or Beaumont's. Beaumont's versification rests on a somewhat doubtful canon; when a play is known to be by Beaumont and Fletcher, the part not in Fletcher's recognized manner is accredited to Beaumont. This separation was accomplished, however, with great skill by Mr. Macaulay[2] and has been substantiated in the main by other critics. When a play is probably too late for Beaumont, the part neither in Massinger's nor in Fletcher's style goes begging. Field seems to be the favorite, but the verse-tests show little difference between his work and Beaumont's. Mr. Fleay seems confident that he can tell the difference, but he observes : " Mr. Boyle is, as I have frequently pointed out, incapable of distinguishing Field's work from Beaumont's."[3] Mr. Oliphant frankly confesses that the distinction between Field and Beaumont is one of the critic's most difficult tasks. He excepts the determination of the authorship of prose passages, and here the basis of analysis seems to be individual opinion rather than scientific demonstration.

H. The " 'em-them " test.

I venture to offer a new test which I think may be of service in testing the analysis already made by critics. Slight though it may seem, it certainly has the merit of definiteness. It is simply an author's use of ' them ' and ' 'em.' Every one who has read many of Fletcher's plays must have noticed the great frequency with which he uses ' 'em ' instead of ' them '— ' kill 'em,' ' with 'em,' etc. This fact led me to count the ' thems ' and ' 'ems ' in *Henry VIII* and the *Two Noble Kinsmen* with a view of testing the generally accredited divisions of those plays between Fletcher and Shakspere. The results given

---

[1] Mr. Fleay has no doubt that Beaumont had a share in this, Chr. I, p. 178, but the external evidence is strong to the contrary.

[2] Of the other critics, it may be noted that Mr. Fleay, after his usual fashion, gives his conclusions and ingeniously conceals his reasons. Mr. Boyle and Mr. Oliphant are scientific in their methods, but Mr. Boyle is a bit over-fond of discovering Massinger, and Mr. Oliphant often carries his analysis of revised plays beyond the limits of plausibility.

[3] Chr. I, 206.

in another place are rather surprising.   A little more counting
showed that the preference for either ' them ' or ' 'em ' is, so far
as it goes, a fair indication of authorship.

Thus Fletcher, in the *Woman's Prize*[1] uses sixty 'ems to four
thems ; in *Bonduca*,[2] eighty-three 'ems to six thems ; in the two
last plays of *Four Plays in One*,[3] fifteen 'ems to one them.

These plays, as all others mentioned here, were selected
purely at random, and probably indicate fairly Fletcher's decided preference for ' 'em.'[4]   Moreover, he seems to have a
special fondness for bunching several 'ems in a few lines, as :

> " Bring 'em in,
> Tie 'em and then unarm 'em."[5]

> " Now look upon 'em, son of Earth, and shame 'em ;
> Now see the faces of thy evil angels ;
> Lead 'em to Time, and let 'em fill his triumph !"[6]

> " Cæsar's soft soul dwells in 'em,
> Their mother got 'em sleeping. Pleasure nursed 'em !"[7]

Shakspere differs very noticeably from Fletcher, and uses 'em
only sparingly.   In *Cymbeline*[8] there are sixty-four ' thems ' and

---

[1] Woman's Prize, I, 1, o them, 2 'ems ; I, 2, 1 them, 3 'ems ; I, 3, 2
thems, 10 'ems ; I, 4, o them, 1 'em ; II, 1, o them, 3 'ems ; II, 2, o them,
1 'em ; II, 3, o them, o 'em ; II, 4, o them, 1 'em ; II, 5, o them, 7 'ems ;
II, 6, o them, 9 'ems ; III, 1, o them, 3 'ems ; III, 2, o them, 3 'ems ; III,
3, o them, o 'em ; III, 4, o them, 4 'ems ; IV, 1, 1 them, 3 'ems ; IV, 2,
o them, o 'em ; IV, 3, o them, 1 'em ; IV, 4, o them, 1 'em ; IV, 5, o
them, o 'em ; V, 1, o them, 5 'ems ; V, 2, o them, 2 'ems ; V, 3, o them,
o 'em ; V, 4, o them, 1 'em. Total, 4 thems, 60 'ems.

[2] Bonduca, I, 1, 10 'ems, o them ; I, 2, 8 'ems, 1 them ; II, 1, 4 'ems,
o them ; II, 2, 1 'em, o them ; II, 3, 17 'ems, o them ; II, 4, 5 'ems, 1
them ; III, 1, 4 'ems, 1 them ; III, 2, 1 'em, o them ; III, 3, 5 'ems, o
them ; III, 4, o 'em, o them ; III, 5, 13 'ems, 1 them ; IV, 1, o 'em, 1
them ; IV, 2, 1 'em, 1 them ; IV, 3, 4 'ems, o them ; IV, 4, 1 'em, o
them ; V, 1, 2 'ems, o them ; V, 2, 2 'ems, o them ; V, 3, 5 'ems, o them.
Total, 83 'ems, 6 thems.

[3] Triumph of Death, 10 'ems, o them.
Triumph of Time, 5 'ems, 1 them.
Fletcher's Share in Four Plays, 15 'ems, 1 them.

[4] ' Them,' however, is used in the *Faithful Shepherdess;* but that play,
if Fletcher's, seems to be an exception to every rule that can be determined for him.

[5] *Bonduca*, III, 5.
[6] *Triumph of Time*, Scene IV, near end.
[7] *Bonduca*, I, 1.
[8] Cymbeline, I, 1, 3 thems, o 'em ' I, 4, o them, 1 'em [prose] ; I, 5, 3
thems, o 'em ; I, 6, 5 thems, o 'em ; II, 1, 2 thems, o 'em ; II, 3, 1 them,
o 'em ; II, 4, 4 thems, o 'em ; II, 5, 4 thems, o 'em ; III, 1, 3 thems, o
'em ; III, 2, 2 thems, o 'em ; III, 3, 2 thems, 1 'em ; III, 4, 1 them, o
'em ; IV, 1, 6, 3 thems, o 'em ; IV, 1, 1 them, o 'em ; IV, 2, 12 thems,
o 'em ; IV, 3, 2 thems, o 'em ; IV, 4, 1 them, o 'em ; V, 1, 2 thems, o
'em ; V, 3, 2 thems, 1 'em ; V, 4, 5 thems, o 'em ; V, 5, 6 thems, o 'em.
Total, 64 thems, 3 'ems.

three ''ems'; in the *Winter's Tale*,[1] thirty-seven 'thems' and eight ''ems;' and in the *Tempest*,[2] thirty-eight 'thems' and thirteen ''ems.'

So far as my observation goes ''em' occurs with the same comparative infrequency in the earlier plays as in the romances. Massinger invariably uses 'them.' At least, I have gone through seven of his plays without finding a single ''em,' while each play contains from twenty to fifty 'thems.' [3] These seven plays, the *Maid of Honour*, the *Duke of Milan*, *A New Way to Pay Old Debts*, the *Great Duke of Florence*, the *Guardian*, the *Roman Actor*, the *City Madam*, differ widely in character and date and must fairly represent his practice.

Beaumont's practice is less certain. In the first two plays of *Four Plays in One*,[4] which are generally assigned to him, there are four 'thems' and eight ' 'ems.' In the *Woman Hater*, also generally assigned to him, there are twenty-eight 'thems' and seven ''ems.'[5] In *A King and No King*, in the portion assigned to Beaumont by Mr. Boyle,[6] there are

---

[1] Winter's Tale, I, 1, 1 them, 0 'em; I, 2, 2 thems, 0 'em; II, 1, 2 thems, 1 em; II, 2, 1 them, 0 'em; II, 3, 2 thems, 0 'em; III, 1, 1 them, 0 'em; III, 2, 2 thems, 0 'em; III, 3, 1 them, 2 'ems [prose]; IV, 3, 0 them, 2 'ems; IV, 4, 18 thems, 3 'ems [7 thems, 2 'ems, in prose]; V, 1, 3 thems, 0 'em; V, 2, 3 thems, 0 'em [prose]; V, 3, 1 them, 0 'em. Total, 37 thems, 8 'ems.

[2] The Tempest contains in addition four 'ems in one line of a snatch, III, 1, 130.

" Flout 'em and scout 'em,
And scout 'em and flout em."

And one additional them in a song, I, 2, 404. Counting these the total is 39 thems, 17 'ems.

The Tempest, I, 1, 1 them, 0 'em; I, 2, 5 thems, 4 'ems; II, 1, 4 thems, 0 'em; II, 2, 0 them, 1 'em; III, 1, 1 them, 1 'em; III, 2, 3 thems, 1 'em; III, 3, 5 thems, 2 'ems; IV, 1, 7 thems, 0 'em; V, 1, 12 thems, 4 'ems. Total, 38 thems, 13 'ems.

I suspect that this proportion of ''ems' is about Shakspere's maximum.

[3] For table of these plays, see next page.

[4] *Triumph of Honour*, 3 thems 1 'em. *Triumph of Love*, 1 them, 6 'ems. Total, 4 thems, 8 'ems.

[5] The Woman Hater, Prologue, 3 thems, 0 'ems; I, 1, 1 them, 0 'ems; I, 2, 0 thems, 0 'ems, I, 3, 1 them, 1 'em; II, 1, 5 thems, 1 'em; II, 2, 0 thems; III, 1, 1 them, 0 'ems; III, 2, 0 thems, 0 'ems; III, 3, 1 them, 1 em; IV, 1, 8 thems, 0 'ems; IV, 2, 2 thems, 1 'em; V, 1, 1 them, 1 'em; V, 2, 1 them, 0 'ems; V, 3, 0 thems, 0 'ems; V. 4, 2 thems, 0 'ems; V, 5, 2 thems, 0 'ems. Total, 28 thems, 7 'ems.

[6] A King and No King, I, 1, 0 thems, 10 'ems; I, 2, 0 thems, 0 'ems; II, 1, 1 them, 4 'ems; II, 2, 2 thems, 4 'ems; III, 1, 0 thems, 3 'ems; III, 2, 1 them, 3 'ems; III, 3, 0 thems, 3 'ems; IV, 1, 0 thems, 2 'ems; IV, 2, 0 thems, 4 'ems; IV, 3, 0 thems, 0 'ems; IV, 4, 1 them, 9 'ems; V, 1, 0 thems, 3 'ems; V, 2, 0 thems, 1 'em; V, 3, 2 thems, 0 'ems; V, 4, 2 thems, 5 'ems. Total, 9 thems, 51 'ems.*

---

*In a King and No King, Mr. Boyle assigns IV, 1; IV, 2; IV, 3; V, 2 to Fletcher, leaving Beaumont the rest with 7 thems and 42 'ems; but whatever division is made the proportion of thems and 'ems in Beaumont's share will not be greatly changed.

seven 'thems' and forty-two ''ems.' So far as appears on
the face, these results indicate that Beaumont used ''em' and
'them' indiscriminately. Field certainly did; for in his *A
Woman is a Weathercock*, there are, so far as I have counted,
eighteen ''ems' and twelve 'thems.'

The definite results obtained in the cases of Fletcher, Massinger and Shakspere furnish safe standards. Modern texts
follow the first quartos or folios carefully ; and the uniformity
of the results, compared with the diversity of editions, shows
that printers' errors may be disregarded. I cannot find,
either, that any one of these authors is distinctly influenced
in his use of ''em' by the character of the speaker. Thus,
Prospero says ''em' as well as Ariel, Caliban, and Antonio.
Neither does the nature of the subject matter nor the use of
prose make any appreciable difference. The preference for
either ''em' or 'them' seems to have been merely an individual mannerism; and in the case of these three authors, a very
distinct one. Fletcher uses 'them' very rarely, once where he
uses ''em' fourteen or fifteen times ; Shakspere uses ''em'
rarely, and 'them' frequently; Massinger always writes 'them.'

The serviceableness of this test used as a supplement of the
usual verse-tests in determining authorship, must be apparent.
Henry VIII furnishes an example of its use in separating the
work of Shakspere and Fletcher; and a single random example
will show how it may be used in cases of Fletcher-Massinger
authorship. In the *Queen of Corinth* [1] in the part assigned to
Massinger by Mr. Fleay, there are twenty-one 'thems' and one

[1] *Queen of Corinth.* Massinger's Part (Fleay) ; I, 1, 5 thems, o 'ems ;
I, 2, 9 thems, 1 'em; I, 3, b, o thems, o 'ems ; V, 1, 4 thems, o 'ems ;
V, 2, o thems, o 'ems ; V, 3, 3 thems, o 'ems. Total, 21 thems, 1 'em.

Massinger's Plays. Table of 'thems.' No ''ems' occur.

Act	Duke of Milan	Maid of Honour	Great Duke of Florence	Roman Actor	Guardian	New Way to Pay Old Debts	City Madam	
1	5	4	4	6	5	7	7	
2	7	6	4	1	12	4	3	
3	5	5	4	13	3	14	6	
4	4	8	6	7	9	3	6	
5	3	1	3	1	18	3	10	
Total	24	24	21	28	50†	31	32‡	210

† 3 'thems' in prologue. Total without these, 47.
‡ Two of the dramatis personæ are called 'Ding 'em' and 'Have 'em.'

"'em;' in the Fletcher part, one 'them' and six "'ems.' In general, the existence of even a single 'em in a Massinger part is very suspicious, and the existence of a large number of 'ems is a pretty safe indication of Fletcher. The test will also in some cases, I think, serve to call attention to interpolations or additions by a second author, which verse-tests alone would not indicate. Thus, even the single 'em in Massinger's part of the *Queen of Corinth* is enough to warrant special examination of the passage in search of a second hand. Of course, the serviceableness of the test is limited; and it is of little value except as a supplement of the usual verse-tests. Since we are concerned with dates rather than with authorship, there will be little occasion to use it; there will be sufficient occasion, however, to demonstrate its value.

I.   *Court Masques and the Chronology.*

A word or two must be added in regard to the influence of the court-masques on the public drama.

During the reign of James I., court-masques attained a great importance both as splendid spectacles and in the literature of the time. They were very numerous, were produced at great expense, and engaged the services of the best poets of the day. Usually performed at a marriage, or on some festival like those of the Christmas season, they consisted primarily of two parts, (1) the dramatic dialogue usually setting forth some allegorical or mythological device which formed the basis of an impressive spectacle, and (2) the dances interspersed with songs and accompanied by music. These dances were performed by ladies and gallants of the highest court circles, the queen often participating. In addition to these elements, about the year 1608 a third appeared, the anti-masque, consisting of grotesque dances by 'antick' personages. These comic anti-masques at once became exceedingly popular and played no small part in the entertainments. The antic dancers were almost always actors from the public theaters.[1]

Fletcher's Part; I, 3, a, o thems, o 'ems; I, 4, o thems, o 'ems; II, 1, o thems, o 'ems; II, 2, o thems, 1 'em; II, 3, o thems, 1 'em: II, 4, 1 them, 4 'ems.   Total, 1 them, 6 'ems.

[1] For a full account of the English masques, see *Die Englischen Maskenpiele*, Alfred Soergel, Halls, 1882. In addition to the evidence which Dr. Soergel gives for the presence of actors from the theaters, see Middleton's *the Inner Temple Masque;* or *Masque of Heroes*, quarto 1619, where a list of actors from a public company is given. For further illustration of the part which actors played in entertainments and pageants, see the *Athenæum*, May 19, 1888, where Mr. Halliwell-Phillipps shows that Burbadge and Rice were "the players that rodd upon the twoe fishes and made the speeches at the meeting of the highe and mighty prince of Walles upon the river Thames"—June 5, 1610. Burbadge, "Amphion seated on a dolphin," Rice, "a nymph, riding on a whale." See also the *"Entertainment to King James,"* Th.

This last fact points to an interesting connection between the masques and the drama, for it establishes an *a priori* probability that the antic dances used in the masques would be performed again in the theaters. As Mr. Harold Littledale has shown,[1] such a repetition of an anti-masque does undoubtedly occur in the *Two Noble Kinsmen*, borrowed from Beaumont's *Masque of the Inner Temple and Gray's Inn*, 1613, and consequently the play may be dated shortly after 1613. I shall suggest that the date of the *Winter's Tale* is in a similar way determined by the repetition of a dance of satyrs from Jonson's *Masque of Oberon*. The influence of the masques in a more general way on the public drama has been emphasized by Mr. Fleay[2] and treated at length by Dr. Soergel. I shall have occasion to note this influence in the plays of Beaumont and Fletcher and Shakspere. Here I merely wish to call attention to the possible service of a study of this influence in determining the dates of plays. There were forty-nine masques performed at court 1603–1642; and it is very probable that public plays borrowed many details in addition to anti-masques.[3]

Dekker, quarto, 1604. 'Zeal' "whose personage was put on by W. Bourne, one of the servants to the young Prince."

[1] See *The Two Noble Kinsmen*, ed. Harold Littledale, New Shakspere Society. Series II, 7, 8, 15, 1876–85. Mr. Littledale was unacquainted with Dr. Soergel's investigation and gave this borrowing less prominence than it deserves in fixing the date. See the discussion of the play in chapter 4.

[2] Fleay: Chr. I. 12. Soergel, p. 87, seq. Fleay seems to think that masques occur in plays only when they were added for some court performance. So he conjectures that the masques in the *Tempest* and the *Maid's Tragedy* were additions. Dr. Soergel has shown that similar masques occur in other plays; and many features of the court-masque were certainly introduced on the public stage.

[3] Much of the material in this section and in the discussion of the masques in the *Two Noble Kinsmen* and the *Tempest*, has been already published in *Publications of the Mod. Lang. Ass'n of America*. Vol. XV; No. 1. "Influence of the Court-Masques on the drama."

CHAPTER III.

CHRONOLOGY OF SHAKSPERE'S ROMANCES.

These three plays were first entered S. R. and published in folio in 1623. From the agreement of different verse-tests and from the general opinion of critics, they are thought to have been written at the close of Shakspere's career and after all his plays except *Henry VIII* and the *Two Noble Kinsmen*. There is almost no evidence, however, even from verse-tests, to determine the relative order of the three; although the general character of style seems to indicate that *Cymbeline* was the earliest.

The Tragedy of Cymbeline. There is no record of any court performance, and the only evidence for the date [1] is the entry in the note book of Dr. Simon Forman. This entry is not dated; but as the accompanying note on *Macbeth* is dated April 20, 1610, and that of the *Winter's Tale*, May 15, 1611, the Cymbeline entry must belong to those years. Forman died in September 1611, so that is the outside date for the entry. Mr. Fleay, who thinks Shakspere retired from play-writing in 1610, fixes the date of *Cymbeline* in 1609; [2] and since that year was a plague year, thinks the play was perhaps not finished for the stage until after Shakspere's retirement. Yet he thinks *Philaster* (certainly before Oct., 1610) contains passages suggested by *Cymbeline*. [3] He also thinks that the historical parts of *Cymbeline* were written about 1606, when Shakspere may have been using Holinshed for material for *Lear* and *Macbeth*. [4] These are pure conjectures. So far as the plague of 1608–9 may be taken to have diminished theatrical activity, [5] the fact makes 1610 rather than 1609 a probable date. Forman's elaborate description indicates that the play was new to him. The date is probably within a year of 1610.

The Tempest. It was one of the fourteen court plays paid for on May 20, 1613 (Vertue Ms.), [6] and consequently was

---

[1] It is a curious fact that the 1600 quarto of *Much Ado* contains the following opening stage direction: "Enter Leonate (and) Imogen his wife." Imogen does not appear elsewhere in the play.

[2] *Life of Shaks.*, p. 246.

[3] Chr. II, p. 193.

[4] *Life of Shaks.*, p. 246, Chr. II, 193.

[5] See pp. 14–17.

[6] *Sh. Soc. Papers.* II, p. 124.

acted at court in the fall or winter 1612–13. According to the forged revels' accounts of Cunningham, it was also acted at court 1611, Nov. 1; and there is evidence that these forgeries were based in part on fact.[1] It is probably referred to, together with the *Winter's Tale* in the induction to Ben Jonson's *Bartholemew Fair*.[2] The name, Tempest, has been thought by some to have been suggested by the great storms of the fall of 1612; and by others by the tempest encountered by Sir George Somers on his voyage to the Bermudas, 1609.

Malone[3] has shown certain resemblances between passages in the play and passages in Jourdan's *A Discovery of the Bermudas, otherwise called the Isle of Devils, by Sir Thomas Gates, Sir George Somers, and Captain Newport, with divers others*, which was published Oct. 13, 1610. Malone also thought that particulars in the play were derived from *A True Declaration* of the Estate of the Colony of Virginia, published Nov. 8, 1610. Mr. Fleay, on the contrary, thinks the word tragicomedy in this last pamphlet refers to the play, and, hence, he concludes that the *Tempest* was acted between the dates of the publication of Jourdan's narrative and *A True Declaration*. A glance at the passage[4] in question will show how groundless is this conjecture.

Dr. Furness, in his variorum edition of the *Tempest*, is inclined to belittle the importance of both of Malone's suggestions, and thinks that similar resemblances can be shown between particular passages in the play and Wm. Strachey's *A True reporatory of the wracke and redemption of Sir Thomas Gates, Knight upon and from the Islands of Bermudas*, etc., which was published in 1612. This argument is by no means a *reductio ad absurdam*, for Strachey's narrative may possibly have preceded the play. Such evidence as Malone's is not absolutely conclusive, and, in the case of the *True Declaration*, not quite convincing; but the references in the play to the "stillvext Bermoothes[5]" and the detailed points of resemblance

---

[1] See Furness' *Variorum* Edition of *Othello*, pp. 351–360. Also Sidney Lee's *Life*, p. 254, note.

[2] "If there be never a servant-monster in the fair, who can help it, he says, nor a nest of antiques? he is loth to make nature afraid in his play, like those that beget tales, tempests, and such like drolleries, to mix his head with other men's heels; let the concupiscence of jigs and dances reign as strong as it will amongst you, etc."

[3] *Variorum Shakespeare*, 1821.

[4] "What is there in all this tragicall-comædie that should encourage us with the impossibility of the enterprise? When, of all the fleete, one onely ship by a secret leake was indangered, and yet in the gulfe of despaire was so graciously preserved." See Fleay, *Shaks.*, pp. 248, 249.

[5] I, 2, 229.

make it fairly certain that the play was not acted until after Jourdan's narrative was published.[1]

The news of Somer's voyage created great interest in London in September, 1610, and there were four other narratives besides Jourdan's, which was the earliest.[2] The date of the play, then, cannot be earlier than Oct. 13, 1610, and not later than the court presentation, 1613. It was probably written and acted late in 1610 or early in 1611.

A Winter's Tale. Like the *Tempest*, it was one of the fourteen plays acted at court 1613, and was referred to by Jonson in *Bartholomew Fair*.[3] It was described in Dr. Forman's notebook under the date May 15, 1611. This is the final limit for the date.[4] I think the early limit is determined by the date of Ben Jonson's *Masque of Oberon*, Jan. 1, 1611.

This contains an anti-masque of satyrs, and I conjecture that the dance of satyrs in the *Winter's Tale* was directly suggested by the anti-masque. Anti-masques, as we have seen,[5] were first introduced about 1608, and at once became very popular. In *Oberon* there is one of these antic dances, doubtless performed by actors from the public theaters. This was a dance of ten (or twelve)[6] satyrs, "with bells on their shaggy thighs," and is thus described.

"Here they fell suddenly into an antic dance full of gesture and swift motion and continued it till the crowing of the cock."

Again, after the entrance of Oberon, there was a little more dancing by the satyrs.

"And the satyrs beginning to leap, and express their joy for the unused state and solemnity."

In the *Winter's Tale* there is a similar antic dance of twelve

---

[1] There is no other evidence as to date. Gonzalo's description (II, 1, 147) is from Florio's *Montaigue* (1st edition, 1603). The "dead Indian" (II, 2, 36) exhibited for a show, offers no aid in regard to the date. It may refer to one of Frobisher's Indians (1577). There were, also, some Indians brought from New England in 1611. For notice of Fleay's theory that the masque was added by another writer for the court presentation. See p. 29.

[2] See Sidney Lee's *Life*, pp. 252, 253.

[3] It may, also, have been acted at court in Nov., 1611. It is one of the plays assigned to that date in the forged revels' accounts. See p. 30.

[4] No other date can be assigned as a final limit with any probability. Mr. Fleay thinks there are several references to the play in Jonson's address to the reader in the 1612 quarto of the *Alchemist*. The phrase "concupiscence of dances and jigs" reminds one of the wording of the reference in the induction to *Bartholomew Fair;* but the other references which Mr. Fleay sees are less convincing. See *Chr.* I, 275. The passages in the *Alchemist* and *Bartholomew Fair* show that Jonson was decidedly opposed to the introduction of masques and antimasques into plays.

[5] See p. 28.

[6] "Two sylvans" possibly join in the dance.

satyrs which is clearly an addition to please the audiences of the day.

"Servant. Master, there is three carters, three shepherds, three neat-herds, three swine-herds, that have made themselves all men of hair, they call themselves Saltiers, and they have a dance which the wenches say is a gallimanfry of gambols, because they are not in't; but they themselves are o' the mind, if it be not too rough for some that know little but bowling, it will please plentifully.

Shepherd. Away! we'll none on't; here has been too much homely foolery already. I know, sir, we weary you.

Polixenes. You weary those that refresh us: pray, let's see these four threes of herdsmen.

Servant. One three of them, by their own report, sir, hath danced before the king; and not the worst of the three but jumps twelve foot and a half by the squier.

Sheperd. Leave your prating; since these good men are pleased, let them come in; but quickly now.

Servant. Why, they stay at door, sir. [*Exit.*]

Here a dance of twelve satyrs.[1] "

Like the dancers in the masque, these are great leapers and like those they are men of hair. Moreover, three of them by their own report had danced before the king as did the satyrs in the masque.

Now, while satyrs were not altogether uncommon on the Elizabethan stage, a dance of satyrs "full of gesture and swift motion" was certainly an inovation in 1611. Such anti-masques were only introduced about 1608, and such a dance of satyrs is not found in any court masque before, or for that matter after, 1611.[2] The *Winter's Tale* is generally dated about the first of 1611;[3] therefore, either Jonson must have borrowed from the public stage the idea of an antic dance of satyrs for his court masque, or Shakspere must have borrowed

---

[1] IV, 4, ll. 331-353.

[2] There is a dance of "six Sylvans" in act III, scene 2, of Chapman's *the Widow's Tears*, 4to, 1612, acted according to Fleay in 1605. This dance is the main feature of a brief wedding masque. The sylvans bear torches, are "fair" and "fresh and flowery." They lead out the bride and five other ladies, who

"all turn nymphs to-night
To side these sprightly wood-gods in their dances."

Altho the sylvans are elsewhere alluded to as "curveting and tripping on the toe," and their dances are called "active and antic," they evidently were not as active as Jonson's satyrs nor at all grotesque, and their dance was not an anti-masque. It was, in fact, the masque proper, danced with the ladies and closing the entertainment.

[3] Jonson and Shakspere were friends, and at this time both were writing plays for the King's men. Jonson: *Alchemist*, 1610; *Catiline*, 1611.

33

from the court masque this new and popular stage device for his *Winter's Tale*. The second alternative is far more probable because of the great importance of the court masques and the desire for novelty in them, and because the public may naturally be supposed to have been anxious to see a reproduction of a popular anti-masque. It gains additional probability from the fact that actors from the theaters performed in these anti-masques and from the reference to the three who had already danced before the king. It is still more probable because an anti-masque in Beaumont's *Masque of the Inner Temple* is obviously made use of in a similar way in the *Two Noble Kinsmen*.[1] Finally, we may note that the dance is an integral part of the *Masque of Oberon*, while it is a pure addition to the play.[2]

The probability is, then, strong that Jonson devised this dance of satyrs for his *Masque of Oberon*, where it was performed, at least in part, by actors from the King's men, and that Shakspere introduced the dance, doubtless with some variations but with some of the same actors, in the *Winter's Tale*. This fixes the date of the play between Jan. 1, and May 15, 1611. This harmonizes with the generally assigned date 1610–11.

---

[1] See p. 44.
[2] It is worth noting that in the masque the chariot of Oberon was drawn by two white bears. Perhaps here as in the dance, costume and actor reappeared in the play in the bear who chases Antigonous. (III. 3.)

CHAPTER IV.

CHRONOLOGY AND DISCUSSION OF HENRY VIII, THE TWO
NOBLE KINSMEN, AND CARDENIO.

What external evidence there is assigns *Henry VIII* to
Shakspere (the folio of 1623) and the *Two Noble Kinsmen*
to Shakspere and Fletcher (quarto, 1634). Since Mr.
Spedding's essay in 1850,[1] there has been a growing belief
that Fletcher also had a part in *Henry VIII;* and since Mr.
Spaulding's essay in 1833,[2] perhaps a majority of critics have
been inclined to recognize Shakspere's work in the *Two
Noble Kinsmen.* Great diversity of opinion, however, still
exists. While no one doubts Fletcher's share in the *Two
Noble Kinsmen*, there are all sorts of opinions in regard to the
non-Fletcherian part; and in the case of *Henry VIII* some
critics still think it is wholly by Shakspere[3] while others
doubt if he had anything to do with it.[4] A large majority of
competent judges at present recognize Shakspere as author
of a part of *Henry VIII* and Fletcher as author of part of
Two Noble Kinsmen; but we have at most only the support of
a doubtful majority in assigning each play to both Shakspere and Fletcher.

The reasons and authorities for this opinion will be given
in the discussion of each play, but at the start we may note
two general objections which have had great weight with
critics of judgment. In the first place, they have found it
difficult to think of Shakspere condescending to write a play
in company with another dramatist, especially when, as in
Henry VIII, his part is somewhat the less important. Yet
Shakspere apparently had co-adjutors in both *Timon* and
Pericles, and co-adjutors certainly inferior to Fletcher in both
ability and reputation. In 1613, Fletcher was one of the most
prominent dramatists, and it is very doubtful if Shakspere
would have seen any condescension in taking Beaumont's
place. This objection is simply another exhibition of the

---

[1] *Gentleman's Magazine*, 1850, reprinted New Shakespeare Society's
Transactions, 1874.
[2] Reprinted by New Shakespeare Society, 1876. See, also, N. S. S.
Transactions, 1874.
[3] Mr. Halliwell-Phillipps. *Outlines*, II, 292-4.
[4] Mr. Boyle. N. S. S. *Transactions*, 1884.

common fallacy of always regarding Shakspere as a world genius and never as an Elizabethan dramatist. Shakspere's own practices and the general practice of Elizabethan dramatists, show that his collaboration with Fletcher would be no cause for wonder.

In the second place, the inferiority of the supposed Shaksperean parts in comparison with the best of his mature work has led some to question his authorship. In the *Two Noble Kinsmen*, particularly, the non-Fletcherian parts, good as they are, have not seemed quite worthy of Shakspere. The trouble with this objection is that it rather assumes that Shakspere was always at his best and entirely overlooks the fact that his worst was decidedly bad. We must remember that probably at about the same time that he was writing *Antony* and *Cleopatra* he was also writing *Coriolanus*, *Timon* and *Pericles*. When we discern weakness of characterization in *Henry VIII* or the *Two Noble Kinsmen*, we must remember that after creating the Falstaff of *Henry IV* he could produce the Falstaff of *Merry Wives*. There were, of course, no other dramatists who wrote anywhere nearly as well as he did at his best, and to my mind, there were no other dramatists who wrote very much like his style at his best or worst. Anyhow, the question in regard to the supposed Shaksperean parts of these plays is not, are they as good as he could do? but are they like what he did?

So much for these two general objections; the elaborate theories that have been built up in respect to the plays, we can by no means consider in detail. Almost every critic who has dealt with the plays has his own theory of dates and authorship; and many a critic has seen fit to reject his first theory for a second. To discuss all these adequately would require a volume; there are, however, two main positions often taken which seem to me untenable and which will be noted in our discussion of the plays. These two positions may be stated here.

First, apart from the general objection to Shakspere's authorship just noticed, efforts have been made to determine the author of the non-Fletcherian parts of the plays. These parts are thought by some not only unequal to Shakspere but also unlike Shakspere, or at least more like another. Mr. Boyle's papers assigning these parts to Massinger [1] are the most systematic exposition of this opinion, but other students give Massinger a different share and still others think Beaumont, Chapman, or some one else was the author. These theories can only be briefly touched upon in our discussion,

---

[1] N. S. S. *Transactions*, 1880-86; p. 371 seq; p. 443 seq. See, also, *Eng. Studien*, Vol. IV.

but the evidence for Shakspere's authorship will be noted in the case of each play.

Second, many who think Shakspere had a share in one or both of these plays, do not think that he wrote in direct collaboration with Fletcher, but that he left the plays unfinished and they were completed by Fletcher,[1] or as is held by others, by Fletcher and Massinger.[2] We shall later consider some definite evidence against this opinion.

In the main, however, our discussion of the two plays will have little to do with theories. Leaving objections and counter-theories to one side. I shall try to show definite evidence (1) that both plays were first acted in 1613 and (2) that both plays were written by Shakspere and Fletcher in direct collaboration.

HENRY VIII.

Date. First printed in folio of 1623.

On June 29, 1613, while the King's men were acting a play of *Henry VIII* the Globe Theater was burned. The event is described in several letters of the time,[3] but whether the play then being acted was the *Henry VIII* of the folio of 1623, is not absolutely certain. The fact, however, that a *Henry VIII* was played by Shakspere's company at a time when Shakspere[4] was connected with that company and was very possibly in London,[5] makes it practically certain that this was the *Henry VIII* published by two of the company in the folio of 1623.

Moreover, the account given by sir Henry Wotton of the 1613 play, applies in several important particulars to the folio

---

[1] So Mr. Spedding on Henry VIII. N. S. S. *Transactions*, 1874.

[2] Mr. Oliphant and Mr. Fleay think Massinger 'revised Fletcher's work.

[3] *Harleian Ms.* 7002. A letter from Thomas Lorkin to Sir Thomas Pickering, dated "this last of June, 1613." *Court and Times of James I*, 1848, Vol. 1, p. 253.
Winwood's *Memorials*, III, 469. A letter of July 12, 1613, refers to the burning of the theater and the play *Henry VIII*.
Howe's continuation of Stowe's *Chronicles*, p. 1003, also refers to the fire and the play *Henry VIII*.
Reliquiæ Wottonianæ, 1675, pp. 425-6. A letter by Sir Henry Wotton to his nephew dated July 6, 1613, contains an account of the play. "The King's players had a new play, called *All is True*, representing "some principal pieces of the reign of Henry the Eighth, which was "set forth with many extraordinary circumstances of pomp and majesty, "even to the matting of the stage; the Knights of the Order, with "their Georges and Garter, the guards with their embroidered coats, "and the like; sufficient in truth, within a while, to make great-"ness very familiar, if not ridiculous. Now, King Henry making a "mask at the Cardinal Wolsey's house, and certain cannons being shot "off at his entry, some of the paper or other stuff wherewith one of "them was stopped, did light on the thatch "—etc.

[4] Fletcher, too, if one of the authors, had written many plays for the King's men before 1613, and wrote many after that.

[5] Shakspere bought a house in Blackfriars, March, 1613. See H. P. *Outlines* I, 220.

play. Wotton calls it a new play. The title, *All is One*, is alluded to three times in the prologue.[1] The play also contains "some principal pieces of the reign of Henry the Eighth," and these may fairly be said to be "set forth with extraordinary circumstance of pomp and majesty."[2] It also contains Knights of the Order and guards[3] and a masque of King Henry's at Cardinal Wolsey's, in which chambers are discharged.[4] These resemblances increase the probability that the play in the folio was the play of 1613.

Nevertheless, Mr. Halliwell-Phillips[5] and Mr. Fleay in his *Life of Shakspere*[6] have insisted that the plays were not the same. The main reason for their opinion, which is shared by others, is found in an interpretation of a poem which describes the burning of the theater. They think the allusion in this poem to the fool indicates that there was a fool in the 1613 play, and as there is no fool in the folio play, the two must be different plays. The allusion seems to me likely to refer to some member of the company who usually played the fool, or it may be a general allusion with no specific reference. Even if it refers to a fool in the entertainment of June 29, 1613, we need not conclude that the fool was a regular member of the dramatis personæ of the play. Fools who performed between the acts or after the play were common. The reference, then, is at best doubtful and by no means sufficient to contradict the evidence already noted, which favors the identity of the folio and 1613 plays.[7]

Moreover, those who think Shakspere wrote a part of the play now universally consider it one of his later productions, and this is in harmony with the 1613 date. Furthermore, the play can hardly be earlier than 1611 because of the reference to the strange Indian,[8] and surely not earlier than 1607 because

---

[1] Lines 9, 18, and 21.

[2] *e. g.*, note the stage directions, II, 4; IV, 1.

[3] See dramatis personæ.

[4] I, 4. Stage direction after l 48: "Drum and Trumpet, chambers discharged."

[5] *Outlines*, I, 310–311. II, 290-292.

[6] pp. 250, 251. Mr. Fleay, however, seems to have changed this opinion, for in his *Chronicle of the Drama*, II, 193, he dates Shakspere's part of *Henry VIII* about 1611, and says: "Probably completed by Fletcher, and produced as a new play 1613 at the Globe." So I judge he now thinks the folio play the same as the 1613 play.

[7] The fact that the "matting of the stage" mentioned in Wotton's account is not mentioned in the folio play,—and the discrepancy between the shilling alluded to in the prologue and the usual price at the Globe (2d) hardly seem important considerations.

[8] See H. P. *Outlines*, II, 294. Five Indians were brought to England in 1611, and one of great stature was exhibited. This "strange Indian" of the play (V. 4, 34) has suggested many conjectures. To identify him with the "dead Indian" of the *Tempest* is funny enough, but Mr. Boyle's interpretation is surely the most astonishing of all. He mis-

of the reference to Virginia.[1] In short everything points to the identity of the play in the folio with the play at the burning of the Globe. It is possible that the two may be different just as it is perfectly possible to question almost every accepted fact of Elizabethan stage history; but there is no definite evidence to controvert the considerable definite evidence that the *Henry VIII* of the folio was first acted in 1613.

Authorship. The only external evidence that the play is Shakspere's is its place in the folio of 1623. The folio editors are not to be trusted on questions of authorship, for they certainly included some plays not wholly Shakspere's and omitted others in which he had a part; but it is not certain that they included any play in which he did not have a share. In 1623,[2] if no part of the play was by Shakspere his fellow actors must have known it, and there is no reason to imagine that they would have placed it in the folio.

Mr. Spedding's Essay in 1850 conclusively proved that there were two authors of the play and that the second was Fletcher. His essay has been substantiated by many later investigators and has been somewhat generally accepted. The various verse-tests all show two distinct styles, one very like Fletcher's and one very like Shakspere's later style.

Fletcher's share is doubted by no one who has systematically studied his versification, and Mr. Boyle's theory[3] that Massinger wrote the Shaksperean part is certainly not well proved. While we shall keep this and other theories in mind, we shall start with Mr. Spedding's division of the play between Shakspere and Fletcher,[4] which seems to me reasonably conclusive.

Let us see, then, what warrant there is from this division for supposing the play to have been written in direct collabora-

---

understands an obscene allusion, and thinks "the word (tool) was evidently meant for a proper name," and identifies it with the Irishman O'Toole in Middleton's *Fair Quarrel*, IV, 4. Thus, he fixes the date of the play as late as 1617. N. S. S. *Transactions*, 1880-86, p. 464. Series I, 8-10.

[1] V. 5, 51-53.

[2] Those who think the play was not by Shakspere date it later than 1613.

[3] N. S. S. *Transactions* 1880–86, p. 493, seq. Boyle also gives Massinger some scenes generally assigned to Fletcher. The difficulty with any such theory is in proving that any other dramatist wrote in Shakspere's characteristic manner. Mr. Boyle assumes this off hand in the case of Massinger. "From the characteristics of meter alone it would be difficult to decide whether a particular passage, or even play, was written by Shakspere or Massinger, so similar is the latter's style to that of Shakspere's later dramas." This assumption seems to me contrary to fact; and any theory based on it is *a priori*, of doubtful value.

[4] Shakspere: Act I, sc. 1, 2; Act II, sc. 3, 4; Act III, sc. 2 (to exit of King); Act V, sc. 1. The rest by Fletcher.

39

tion. Shakspere was probably in London in 1613, and was still connected with the King's men.[1] Fletcher was a prominent and popular dramatist who had collaborated with Beaumont in writing some very notable plays for the King's men.[2] Beaumont had probably stopped writing for the King's men by 1612[3] and Shakspere's attention seems to have been considerably occupied with other affairs:[4] it seems perfectly possible and natural that Shakspere and Fletcher should have worked together.

Moreover there is no tangible evidence either of interpolation of each other's work or of revision. The play in the folio is divided into acts and scenes; five scenes and the first half of a sixth are by Shakspere, the rest by Fletcher. On the face of things it looks as if, after the usual fashion of Elizabethan collaboration, Shakspere wrote certain scenes and at the same time Fletcher wrote certain others. The various verse-tests, as has been noted, show that this division is almost surely accurate.

The ''em-them' test also presents further evidence on this point. Taking Mr. Spedding's division (the usually accepted one), I have counted the ''ems' and 'thems' in the play. In the *Winter's Tale*, Shakspere uses 37 'thems' and 8 ''ems;' in *Bonduca*, Fletcher uses 83 ''ems' and 6 'thems,' and in the *Woman's Prize*, 60 ''ems' and 4 'thems'[5] The following table will show the results in the Shakspereau and Fletcherian portions of *Henry VIII*.

The ''em-them' test used entirely as a supplement to the other tests very strongly confirms the accepted division of the play between the two authors. It also strongly confirms the

Shakspere's Part.

ACT. SC.	THEM.	LINES.	'EM.	LINES.	TOTAL LINES IN SCENE.
I. 1.	4	8, 9, 25, 30	2	34, 84	226
I. 2.	5	32, 37, 46, 62, 94	2	21, 49	214
II. 3.	0		0		108
II. 4.	2	51, 195	0		241
III. 2a.	3	2, 3, 79	1	195	203
V. 1.	3	145, 151, 152.	0		176
Total.	17		5		1168

[1] H. P. *Outlines* I, 220.
[2] *Philaster, The Maid's Tragedy, A King and No King*, before the end of 1611.
[3] No plays certainly by him after 1611. See p. 10.
[4] H. P. *Outlines* I, 219–220. Sidney Lee's *Life of Shakspere*, Chap. XVI.
[5] See ante Chap. II The figures given here represent the approximate averages.

ACT. SC.	THEM.	LINES.	'EM.	LINES.	TOTAL LINES IN SCENE.
I. 3.	o		7	4,8,12,13,36,42,43	68
I. 4.	1	60	10	4,8,13,23,44,57,58, 58,72,77,78,107	108
II. 1.	o		4	65, 66, 68, 106	169
II. 2.	1	11	2	7, 39	141
III. 1.	o		5	2, 35, 36, 105, 158	184
III. 2b.	1	334	3	234, 244, 399	256 ll 203-459
IV. 1.	1	29	3	9, 79, 80	118
IV. 2.	o		3	147, 149, 150	172
V. 2.	o		3	27, 28, 34	35
V. 3.	o		3	22, 22, 23	182
V. 4.	o		13	7,13,14,14,16,23,32, 58,59,61,62,67,81	94 1-70 prose
V. 5.	o		1	15	77
Total.	4		57		1604

Prologue, 1 them. Epilogue, 2 'ems. These should perhaps be added to Fletcher's share, making the total 5 thems and 59 'ems.

assignment of these parts to Shakspere and Fletcher, since the ratio and the total of 'ems and thems in the former's part corresponds closely with his practice in the *Winter's Tale* (1611), and the ratio and total of 'ems and thems in the latter's part corresponds closely with his practice in *Bonduca* (before 1616). Incidentally, too, it demonstrates the worthlessness of Mr. Boyle's division of the play between Massinger and Fletcher.[1]

---

[1] Mr. Boyle assigns all the Shakspere portion, as given in our table, to Massinger and in addition I, 4, 1–24, 2 'ems; I, 4, 64–108, 4 'ems; II, 1, 1–53, o 'ems; II, 1, 137–169, o 'ems; IV, 1, 3 'ems and 1 them; V, 3, 1–113, 3 'ems. This gives in the total share assigned to Massinger, 18 thems and 17 'ems. Now Massinger as we have seen, uses 210 thems and not a single 'em in the seven plays counted. [See p.   ] An examination of Mr. Boyle's results also shows that he thinks that Massinger not only wrote like Shakspere, but also very like Fletcher, for he assigns to Massinger some 400 lines generally ascribed to Fletcher. The "em-them" test has strengthened the probability of the Fletcher and Shakspere divisions; and a critic who can make hay of these as does Mr. Boyle must have an extraordinary notion of Massinger's faculty of varying his style.

Mr. Oliphant and Mr. Fleay are no more convincing in their assignments to Massinger. The former (*Englische Studien*, 15, 326), gives Massinger II, 1, 137–end; IV, 1, 1–36; V, 3, 1–96 (or V, 2, 35–129; scenes 2 and 3 should perhaps be connected). In these 162 lines he assigns 7 'ems and 1 them to Massinger, including such Fletcherian lines as these (V, 3, 22),

> "Pace 'em not in their hands to make 'em gentle.
> But stop their mouths with stubborn bits, and spur 'em."

Mr. Fleay (*Life Shaks.*, pp. 250, 251) assigns I, 1; III, 2, 1–193; V, 1, to Massinger, thus giving him 3 'ems.

41

Moreover, an examination of the table will reveal considerable evidence that the Shakspere and Fletcher parts are distinct, free from interpretations and revisions. There is only one scene (II, 3,) which contains neither ' 'ems ' nor ' thems;' and in each of the other scenes assigned to Shakspere there is a decided predominance of 'thems,' while in each scene of Fletcher's there is a decided predominance of ' 'ems.' We find no bunching of ' 'ems' after Fletcher's manner in Shakspere's part, and we find only 5 ' 'ems ' in the 1168 lines. This does not disprove the possibility of interpolation or revision, but it does in connection with the other tests point strongly to the probability that we have Shakspere's and Fletcher's work intact.

Collaboration. In the absence of any distinct evidence to the contrary, we may assume this probability as a working hypothesis and see what evidence there is in the play itself of direct collaboration between the two authors.

Let us see what Shakspere wrote. Act I, scene 1, is introductory and expository, presenting four of the leading characters, the King, Wolsey, Buckingham, and Katharine, and carrying the action through the arrest of Buckingham. Act I, scene 2, presents the trial of Buckingham. Act II, scene 3, introduces an old lady and Anne Bullen, who has already been introduced in the Fletcherian part, and represents Anne as the recipient of the King's favors; it also prefaces Katharine's fall. Act II, scene 4, is the trial of Katharine, in which she, the King, and Wolsey play the chief parts. Act III, scene 2, lines 1–203, is expository and introductory of the fall of Wolsey. Act V. scene 1, is expository and introductory to the birth of Elizabeth and the elevation of Cranmer—the two events which occupy the rest of the act.

To return again to Mr. Boyle's theory ; we have seen that his assignment of the date of the play rests in part on the amusing identification of the "strange Indian " and "O'Toole," that his theory rests on the exceedingly questionable assumption that Massinger's style is very similar to that of Shakspere's later dramas, and finally that his division between the two authors is simply untenable. It is hardly necessary to consider his argument farther, but it may be added that his main evidence, that of Massinger's repetition and consequent parallel passages, is at best evidence of a very dangerous and misleading sort and that Mr. Boyle by no means keeps clear of absurdities.

Mr. Boyle himself advanced his theory with hesitation, and probably very few have accepted it in its entirety. The trouble with such a theory is that it gains a partial acceptance from its very intricacy. Critics say ' the theory is nonsense, but it may have a germ of truth, perhaps Massinger did have something to do with the play,' or they are incited to make still another guess at the authorship. Thus Mr. Sidney Lee speaks of "occasional aid from Massinger " (*Life*, p. 262), and Mr. Fleay suggests Beaumont. (*Chr.* II, 193.) There is no evidence for Massinger and about as much likelihood of Beaumont as of Bacon.

Now let us see what Fletcher wrote. Act I, scene 3, is merely a conversation on French fashions between gentlemen of the court on their way to Wolsey's. Act I, scene 4, presents the masque at Wolsey's and for the first time in the play introduces Anne Bullen. Act II, scene 1, presents Buckingham after his trial. Act II, scene 2, is introductory and expository of Katharine's fall and presents the arrival of Campeius. Act III, scene 1, represents the visit of the Cardinals to the forsaken Katharine. Act III, scene 2, from line 203 to the end, represents Wolsey's fall and his farewell scene with Cromwell. Act IV, scene 1, represents the coronation of Anne Bullen. Act IV, scene 2, represents Katharine, sick and forsaken, making her last farewell. Act V, scenes 2 and 3, represent Cranmer's elevation. Act V, scene IV, is devoted to a comic porter and the crowd pressing at the doors. Act V, scene 5, brings the play to the conclusion with the christening of Elizabeth and Cranmer's prophecy.

The play deals with the introduction, fall, and farewell of Buckingham, of Wolsey, and of Katharine; and with the rise, elevation, and farewell of Anne Bullen and of Cranmer. Following this analysis we find that Shakspere introduced Buckingham, Wolsey, and Katharine, and described the downfall of Buckingham and Katharine, while Fletcher described the fall of Wolsey and the farewells of all three. Fletcher introduced the story of Anne Bullen, Shakspere shared in its development, and Fletcher carried it to its spectacular conclusion in the coronation and christening scenes. Fletcher introduced the Cranmer story (IV, 1); Shakspere developed it up to the point of the main situation, which with Cranmer's farewell was written by Fletcher.

Thus each writer shared in each of the five main actions. Shakspere's work, though largely expository, includes the trial scene of Katharine; Fletcher's work, while including the main scenes and situations, also includes introductory matter for which Shakspere supplied the dramatic development. On the whole, then, it seems improbable that Shakspere would have written parts of the five main stories and left them all unfinished. On the contrary, it seems probable that he had the general course of each of the main actions well in mind when he wrote. The most natural conjecture, it seems to me, is that a historical and spectacular play was planned (perhaps by Shakspere) dealing with these five main events. The play was undertaken in collaboration between Shakspere and Fletcher; each, after the manner of Elizabethan collaborators, undertaking certain scenes. Shakspere may have intended

---

[1] Compare *Maid's Tragedy:* I, 2, (noted by Boyle) and *Four Plays.* Induction.

43

to do more than he did do, he may have been prevented by some cause from carrying on a situation which he had introduced and may, therefore, have turned that work over to Fletcher; but I see no reason to suppose that Shakspere first wrote his part as we have it and stopped there. It seems to me unlikely that any dramatist should begin a play in that way—beginning three different actions, taking up two in the middle, and finishing none.

In this instance I am at odds with the weight of authority; but on the other hand there is, as we have seen, a *priori* a likelihood of direct collaboration. To my mind the distinct separation between the Fletcherian and Shaksperean parts, the probability that there is little or no revision of Shakspere by Fletcher, and the content of each man's work, all argue against the theory that Fletcher finished a play which Shakspere began [1] and support the *a priori* probability of collaboration pure and simple.

To sum up the conclusions of our discussion : *Henry VIII* was probably first acted at the Globe theater June 29, 1813, and was probably written shortly before that time by Shakspere and Fletcher. The ''em-them' test corroborates the usual verse-tests in separating their work distinctly, and the most natural conclusion from an examination of their shares seems to be that they worked in direct collaboration.

THE TWO NOBLE KINSMEN.

Date. First quarto, 1634. '' Presented at the Blackfriars by the King's Maiesties servants, with great applause: written by the memorable worthies of their time, Mr. *John Fletcher*, and Mr. William Shakspeare, Gent.'' It was entered S. R. April 3, 1634 for John Waterson.

Mr. Fleay, who formerly had an elaborate theory dating the play in 1625,[2] notes in his *Chronicle of the Drama* that the play must date about 1610.

The date seems to me fixed with reasonable certainty from the borrowing of an anti-masque from Beaumont's *Masque of the Inner Temple and Gray's Inn*, presented Feb. 20, 1613.[3]

The description of this dance in the *Masque* is as follows: '' The second Anti-masque rush in, dance their measure, and '' as rudely depart; consisting of a Pedant, May Lord, May '' Lady; Servingman, Chambermaid; a Country Clown or '' Shepherd, Country Wench; an Host, Hostess; a He-Baboon, '' She-Baboon; a He-Fool, She-Fool, ushering them in. All

---

[1] See Mr. Spedding's ingenious theory to this effect. N. S. S. *Transactions*, 1874.
[2] *Life of Shaks.* p. 189, seq.
[3] See *The Two Noble Kinsmen*, ed. Harold Littledale, N. S. S. Series II, 1, 8, 15. London, 1876–1885. Introduction, pp. 54, 55.

"these persons, apparelled to the life, Men issuing out of one
"side of the boscage, and the Women from the other.   The
"music was extremely well-fitted, having such a spirit of
"country jollity, as can hardly be imagined; but the perpetual
"laughter and applause was above the music." [1]

Now this masque was exceedingly well received.   "The
"dance likewise was of the same strain; and the dancers, or
"rather actors, expressed every one their part so naturally
"and aptly, as when a man's eye was caught with this one,
"and then passed on to the other, he could not satisfy himself
"which did best.   It pleased his Majesty to call for it again
"at the end, as he did likewise for the first Anti-masque; but
"one of the Statues by that time was undressed."

Moreover, this anti-masque was a decided innovation.[2]   In
preceding anti-masques, which had been in vogue only since
1608, the costumes of the dancers had all been of one sort, as
in the dance of satyrs in Jonson's *Masque of Oberon*.   Beaumont first introduced the fashion of having various characters
and costumes.   Moreover, as Dr. Soergel has also pointed out,
instead of mere "antic gesticulation" the dancers also in their
mimickery now showed a kind of dramatic action; thus they
are called "dancers, or rather actors."   The innovation in
varying characters and costumes is alluded to in the introduction to the *Masque*[3] and in a description of it in Stow's *Annals*.[4]

In *the Two Noble Kinsmen* (III. 5) this anti-masque is repeated.   The schoolmaster and his troop are introduced into
the action, they meet the mad daughter of the jailor and they
dance before Theseus and his lords and ladies.   The connection with Beaumont's anti-masque is, however, unmistakable.

The schoolmaster thus introduces the dancers:

"I first appeare, though rude, and raw, and muddy,
To speake before thy noble grace, this tenner
At whose great feete I offer up my penner.

---

[1] *Works of Beaumont and Fletcher.*   Ed. Routledge, II, 688.

[2] *Die Englischen Maskenspiele.*   Soergel, 1882, p. 52.

[3] "Then Mercury for his part, brings forth an anti-masque all of
spirits or divine; but yet not of one kind or livery (because that had
been so much in use heretofore) but, as it were, in consort, like to
broken music" . . . [this dance] giveth fit occasion to new and
strange varieties both in the music and paces."   This was the first
anti-masque (four Naiades, five Hyades, four Cupids, and four statues
of gold and silver).   The dance copied in the play is described as "a
May dance, or rural dance, consisting likewise not of any suited persons, but of a confusion or commixture of all such persons as are
natural and proper for country sports.   This is the second anti-masque."

[4] *Stow.* p. 917.   The first anti-masque is described as "of a strange
and different fashion from the others, both in habit and manners, and
very delectable;" and the second, "a rurall or country mask, consisting of many persons, men and women, being all in sundry habits, being
likewise as strange, variable, and delightful."

The next the Lord of May, and Lady bright,
The Chambermaid, and Servingman by night
That seeke out silent hanging ; Then mine Host
And his fat Spouse, that welcomes to their cost
The gauled Traveller, and with a beckning
Informes the Tapster to inflame the reckning ;
Then the beast eating Clowne, and next the foole,
The Bavian[1] with long tayle, and eke long toole.
Cum multis aliijs that make a dance
Say I, and all shall presently advance.''[2]

Not only are all these the same personages which appear in Beaumont's *Masque;* in the play as in the masque they perform a country May-dance.[3]

There can be but one conclusion from this resemblance. The anti-masque, probably performed by actors from the public companies, was an entirely novel and very successful part of Beaumont's *Masque of the Inner Temple;* and it is inconceivable that this anti-masque should have been introduced into that notable court entertainment after having been staled at the public theaters. On the contrary, it is entirely probable that Fletcher introduced into his play a variation of a dance which had won a great success in a court masque. It is also probable that he used this anti-masque shortly after the court entertainment while the novelty and success of this dance were common talk. A few years later, other anti-masques would have been performed at the theater.[4]

There is no evidence to contradict this evidence for a 1613 date.[5] Mr. Fleay notes that "from 1626 to 1639 Waterson [publisher of the first quarto of 1634] published plays, and whenever he enters the author's name does so correctly,"[6] and

---

[1] "Bavian. Babion (*Cynthia's Revels*, I. 1), or Babian, a man dressed up as a baboon." Littledale. "Bavian, a figure in Morris dance dressed as baboon." Dyce. The comparison between this passage and the masque, of course indicates that 'Bavian' is the baboon. Yet Mr. Fleay (*Chr.* I, 192) says : "the Bavian (Batavian) of III, 5, is surely the same as "the strange Indian" of *Henry 8*, V, 3, 1613, and the 'Cataian of strange nature' of *Ram Alley*, c 1609."

[2] III, 5. Littledale's reprint of the quarto.

[3] The schoolmaster calls the dance a Morris and asks for a May pole.

[4] The actors, too, who performed at court were probably utilized in the performance at the theater.

[5] In Emilia's speech over the two pictures, she says of Arcite, (IV, 2, 43)

"Thou art a changling to him, a mere gipsy."

This, Mr. Fleay says (*Chr.* I, 191) "surely was written after *The Changling* and *The Spanish Gipsy* were produced in 1621." So he thinks the line points to a late revision. It seems improbable that there is any reference to the plays.

[6] Waterson entered ten plays in these years and assigned plays to Fletcher, Massinger, and Davenant correctly. See Fleay. *Life Shaks.* p. 328, seq.

therefore concludes that "he honestly repeated the information given him." Whether this information was correct or not, it indicates that the play was thought to have been written before Shakspere's retirement from London. If the inscription on the title page is correct, 1613 is the most probable date for Shakspere's work and it is also a probable date for Fletcher's collaboration since Beaumont apparently, ceased writing with him in 1611–12.[1]

Mr. Littledale's conjecture, then, that the play dates shortly after the performance of the masque (Feb. 20, 1613), is almost certainly correct.[2]

Authorship. The only external evidence that Shakspere and Fletcher wrote the play is the explicit statement of the quarto of 1634. The publisher Waterson seems to have been trustworthy, and there is no reason to think that in 1634 Shakspere's name would have helped to sell a play of Fletcher's whose plays had not then been collected in a folio. The main external evidence against Shakspere's authorship is the fact that the play does not appear in the folio of 1623, but *Pericles* was also omitted and *Troilus and Cressida* irregularly inserted. In 1691, Langbaine gave the authorship as stated in the quarto of 1634, and there is no direct external evidence against it.

No one now questions Fletcher's authorship,[3] but the authorship of the non-Fletcherian portion of the play is still a much vexed question. It is a question which probably will always remain a matter of opinion, for it does not admit of complete demonstration. So far as Shakspere's authorship can be demonstrated, Mr. Littledale has accomplished the task, and one's opinion on the subject can rest on no better authority.

Proceeding on the hypothesis that Shakspere and Fletcher were the authors, we find that the division of the play between

---

[1] Mr. Oliphant has an astonishing comment on this point. *Englische Studien*, 15, p. 326. " If, as is likely, Fletcher's

" sure he cannot
Be so unmanly as to leave me here!
If he do, maids will not so easily
Trust men again." T. N. K. II, 5.

be a gird at Beaumont's

"if he deceive me thus
A woman will not easily trust a man."
Coxcomb, I, 5.

it is not improbable that Fletcher's alliance with Shakspere followed a quarrel with his old friend." One may safely assure Mr. Oliphant that it is not a gird.

[2] The borrowing of the anti-masque and the consequent determination of the date of the play are important in connection with my conjecture in regard to the dance of satyrs in the *Winter's Tale*. See p. 32.

[3] Delius (Jahrbuch, XIII) attributed the play to an unknown author.

47

the two presents many difficulties. Confident though we may be that many passages are by Shakspere, there are other passages, as in the case of almost any of his plays, which are not saliently characteristic. Moreover the parts are by no means as distinct as in *Henry VIII;* but in the Shaksperean scenes there are sometimes indubitable bits of Fletcher's work, and in the Fletcherian scenes one sometimes suspects Shakspere's touch.

Nevertheless, the different verse-tests have shown that certain scenes possess the metrical characteristics of Shakspere's later work and certain other scenes, the entirely different characteristics of Fletcher's versification. The ''em-them' test also confirms the generally accepted division. In applying this test I have followed Mr. Littledale's division, but some details must be noted. The last forty lines of Act V, scene 3, Mr. Littledale thinks Fletcher had a hand in,[1] and there can be little question of it; these lines, therefore, I have not included in Shakspere's part. The last twenty lines of Act I, scene 4, are credited by Mr. Littledale, together with the rest of the scene, to Shakspere; but in these lines there seem to be sure indications of Fletcher.

> '' Then like men use 'em
> The very lees of such, millions of rates
> Exceeds the wine of others: all our surgions
> Convent in their behoofs, our richest balmes,
> Rather than niggard, wast: Theire lives concerne us
> Much more than Thebs is worth; rather than have 'em
> Freed of this plight, and in their morning state,
> Sound and at liberty, I would 'em dead;
> But, forty thousand fold, we had rather have 'em
> Prisoners to us than death.''[2]

The use of 'em in this passage is a sure indication of Fletcher, and the versification looks as if he had a hand in it. The remaining dozen lines sound more like Shakspere, but the whole passage seems at least retouched or interpolated by Fletcher.

These two passages which show definite signs of Fletcher's manner will be kept from Shakspere's part.[3] The two prose scenes will also be noted apart; for, although they are generally assigned to Shakspere, there are of course, no scientific tests as in the case of verse. Other scenes, in which Mr. Littledale thinks Shakspere's work has been retouched by Fletcher, or in which (I, 2,) Mr. Hickson thinks that Fletcher's work was revised by Shakspere, are left intact as in Mr. Littledale's

---

[1] See Littledale. Introduction, p. 66.

[2] I, 4, 28–37.

[3] The first 17 lines of V, 1, are almost surely by Fletcher, and so assigned by Littledale. There are also some evidence of Fletcher in ll 1–37 of I, 1.

table. This is necessary because the critics have not settled on definite passages as interpolations or divisions.

Shakspere's Part.

	THEM.	LINES.	'EM.	LINES.	TOTAL LINES.
I. 1.	4	50, 76, 146, 195	2	59, 114	235
I. 2.	1	32	1	34	116
I. 3.	2	21, 41	1	22	97
I. 4a.	3	7, 17, 20	0		28 1-28
III. 1.	2	52, 52	0		123
III. 2.	1	15	0		38
V. 1b.	2	105, 108	0		156 17-173
V. 3a.	0		0		104
V. 4.	0		1	12	137
Total.	15		5		1034

Fletcher's Part.

	THEM.	LINES.	'EM.	LINES.	NUMBER LINES IN SCENE.
I. 5.	0		0		6 Fl. (?)
II. 2.	0		10	12, 13, 17, 24, 34, 65, 129, 251, 265, 274.	279
II. 3.	0		1	2.	83
II. 4.	0		0		33
II. 5.	0		0		64
II. 6.	0		0		39
III. 3.	1	23	0		54
III. 4.	0		0		26
III. 5.	0		1	152.	159
III. 6.	0		10	183, 189, 190, 213, 219, 223, 251, 253, 277, 288.	308
IV. 1.	2	12, 102	3	89, 100, 124.	150
IV. 2.	1	72	11	25, 40, 65, 66, 69, 114, 133, 134, 143, 149, 152.	156
V. 1a.	0		2	1, 7.	17 ll 1-17
V. 2.	0		0		112
Total.	4		38		1486

Passages retouched by Fletcher.

	THEM.	LINES.	'EM.	LINES.	NUMBER LINES IN SCENE.
I. 4b.	1	38	5	29, 33, 35, 36, 37.	21 ll 28-49
V. 3b.	0		2	128, 133.	42 ll 104-146

Prose Scenes.

	THEM.	LINES.	'EM.	LINES.
II. 1.	3	28, 40, 53	3	23, 26, 44.
IV. 3.	0		0	

Summary. The two passages retouched by Fletcher ought, perhaps, to be added to his part, and the two prose scenes to Shakspere's. With the prose scenes Shakspere's part would contain 18 thems, 8 'ems; without the prose scenes 15 thems, 5 'ems. In the Shaksperean part of *Henry VIII* (1168 lines) there are 17 thems and 5 'ems.[1] In the Fletcherian part of the *Two Noble Kinsmen* with the added passages, there are 5 thems and 45 'ems; without those two passages 4 thems and 38 'ems. In *Henry VIII*, there are 4 thems and 57 'ems.[2]

The ''em-them' test thus confirms the assignment of the play to Shakspere and Fletcher and the approximate accuracy of its division between the two. The test does not, however, indicate that the division by scenes is as exact as in *Henry VIII*. The 'ems and thems do not happen to be distributed evenly through the play, and often none occur in a scene. A division entirely by scenes, including the prose scenes and the passages revised or rewritten by Fletcher in the Shaksperean part, would give Shakspere 19 thems and 15 'ems. This large number of 'ems at once suggests Fletcher's hand; and furthermore, the presence of 'ems offers a specific basis for my conjecture that I, 4, 28–49 is retouched by Fletcher and confirms Mr. Littledale's suggestions that IV, 3, 1–17 is entirely by Fletcher and V, 3, 104–146 at least revised by him. Doubtless, as Mr. Littledale suspects, other passages show traces of Shakspere's revision. The ''em-them' test is also serviceable in disproving the theory that Massinger wrote the non-Fletcherian part,[3] and there is no evidence for any other author except Shakspere.[4]

---

[1] In *Winter's Tale* 37 thems, 8 'ems. In the *Tempest* 38 thems, 13 'ems.

[2] In *Bonduca* 6 thems, 83 'ems.

[3] See Mr. Boyle's papers. *Englische Studien*, IV, 34, and N. S. S. *Transactions* 1880–86, p. 371; The non-Fletcherian part which Mr. Boyle gives to Massinger is as follows: I, 1, 4 thems, 2 'ems; I, 2, 34–84, 1 'em; I, 3, 2 thems, 1 'em; I, 4 and 5, 4 thems and 5 'ems; II, 1, 77–118 (including part of II, 2, according to our notation), 3 thems, 4 'ems; III, 1, 2 thems; III, 2, 1 them; IV, 3, none; V, 1, 2 thems, 2 'ems; V, 3, 2 'ems; V, 4, 1 'em. Total 18 thems, 16 'ems. There are 'ems in almost every scene. The presence of so many 'ems is enough to disprove Massinger's authorship, unless Mr. Boyle's argument from parallel passages appeals with very much more force to others than it does to me. The fixing of the date at 1613, in fact, destroys the main basis for the Massinger argument which depended on an assumed date of about 1626.

[4] Mr. Fleay advances one argument for Beaumont (*Chr.* I, 191,) from the use of *carve* which is paralleled in Beaumont's *Remedy of Love*.

IV, 5. "Carve her, drink to her," etc.

Remedy of Love. "Drink to him, carve him, give him compliment." "This use of carve is not common," says Mr. Fleay, but it seems to have been a regular Elizabethan idiom. Schmidt's *Lexicon* gives two examples in Shakspere of this meaning—"to show great courtesy and affability."

See also *Hamlet* I, 3, 20, and *Othello* II, 3, 173, and Lyly's *Euphues*, ed. Arber, p. 55. "I mean not to be mine owne carver."

Collaboration. In conjecturing that the play was written in direct collaboration between Shakspere and Fletcher, we cannot avail ourselves, as in *Henry VIII*, of the argument that the two parts are distinctly separated. At the same time the division is fairly distinct. The great majority of Fletcher's scenes were almost certainly written by him alone, and Shakspere's scenes show definite additions only at the beginnings or ends. They show no evidence of general revision by another writer. Eleven of the scenes as marked in the quarto of 1634, seem to have been mainly composed by Shakspere; and thirteen scenes, as marked in the quarto, seem to have been almost entirely the work of Fletcher.

Moreover, the strong probability that the play was first acted in 1613 makes the *prima facie* likelihood of direct collaboration the same as in the case of *Henry VIII*. In 1612–13 Shakspere seems to have been occupied with other affairs as well as play-writing, but there is no evidence that he had left London or severed his connection with the King's men. Fletcher had by that time achieved eminent success through his plays written in collaboration with Beaumont for the King's men and by 1612 was apparently no longer writing with Beaumont. On the face of things collaboration between Shakspere and Fletcher is not at all improbable.

Before looking directly at the separate scenes for evidence, we must note one objection often urged against collaboration. If Shakspere had seen the finished play, he would not—so some urge—have tolerated the trash of the underplot.[1] It is at least probable that Shakspere did see the finished play in 1613; but this probability aside, the underplot is certainly no greater trash than that of *Pericles* which he managed to endure. The conception that Shakspere acted as a schoolmaster and Fletcher as a pupil, has no foundation whatever. Even if Shakspere planned the play, there is no reason to suppose that he would have dictated to the younger poet.

The feeling that Shakspere would not have tolerated the underplot is, however, accentuated by the supposition that this underplot contains imitations, and very poor ones, of Holofernes in *Love's Labour's Lost*[2] and Ophelia in *Hamlet*.[3] In respect to Holofernes, I do not think there was any imitation in mind. The scene exhibiting the schoolmaster and his troop of entertainers received its suggestion from the *Masque of the Inner Temple*, as we have seen, and probably not at all from so old a play as *Love's Labour's Lost*. In fact, if we want to go back to the original of the situation of a schoolmaster arranging a May-day entertainment, we must go back at least as early as

---

[1] See Littledale. Introduction.
[2] T. N. K. III, 5.
[3] See the scenes in which the jailer's daughter appears.

Sir Philip Sidney's *May Lady*, 1578, when the pedant Rombus appears. In the same way, the mad girl with her songs and childish talk was a conventional stage character, appearing in Lyly's the *Woman in the Moon*, the original *Hamlet*, and *Hoffman* as well as the final *Hamlet*.

The case here, however, is different from that of the schoolmaster. *Hamlet* was a popular play, and the situation of Ophelia must have suggested the description of the mad girl floating on the water amid the flowers and speaking love posies and singing "willow, willow, willow."[1] We must, however, note that there is no imitation of Ophelia's character, the only distinct imitation is of the circumstances of her death. Now, this imitation, so far from being an objection to collaboration seems to me readily explainable on the supposition of collaboration. Shakspere, with his usual economy of invention[2] may have determined in planning the play to introduce a mad girl; and Fletcher working out the suggestion was fully capable of doing the rest—trash and all. In spite of the trash, the conversation of V, 2, was probably very pleasing to both the groundlings and lordlings of Blackfriars.

Returning to the evidence for collaboration, we must examine the work of each author. In the underplot dealing with the jailer's daughter, Shakspere is assigned three and Fletcher seven scenes. Act II, scene 1, by Shakspere introduces the jailer, the wooer, and the daughter, who shows that she is already a little in love with the prisoner Palamon. The next scene by Shakspere (III, 2,) is a soliloquy by the daughter who has freed Palamon and is seeking him. She is alone in the woods and fears lest she go mad. The last scene of the underplot by Shakspere (IV, 3,) represents the jailer, wooer, and doctor consulting over a cure for the girl who, it now appears, is insane. The scene also introduces the girl with mad talk and songs.

In Fletcher's part of the underplot, Act II, scene 3, introduces a crowd of country people a-maying. Act II, scene 4, is a soliloquy by the jailer's daughter (introduced earlier by Shakspere) who is not yet mad and who resolves to free Palamon. Act II, scene 5, is another soliloquy from which it appears that she is about to free him. In Act III, scene 4, she is insane (first suggested in Shakspere's part). Act III, scene 5, includes the morris dance and another appearance of the mad girl. Act IV, scene 1, includes the description of the girl's escape from a watery grave and another appearance of the mad girl. Act V, scene 2, represents the wooer curing the

---

[1] T. N. K. IV, I.

[2] See *William Shakspere* by Barrett Wendell, 1894, pp. 87, 422 *et passim*.

girl of her madness after the manner prescribed by the doctor in Shakspere's scene.

Two things are plain from this analysis. First, each writer understood the outline of the plot, for scenes in each part depend on scenes in the other. Second, it is almost impossible that Shakspere should have written his three scenes first and left the underplot in that shape, for the scenes have neither connection with each other nor importance by themselves. The most natural conclusion seems to be that the two parts were written by two dramatists who had the plot well outlined and each of whom took certain scenes to write.

In the development of the main plot, Shakspere is assigned eight scenes and Fletcher five.[1] Of Shakspere's part the first four scenes of the first act deal largely with the widowed queens and Theseus. They serve also as an introduction to the main action, presenting all the leading characters including Palamon and Arcite. This act, however, with the kneeling queens, the wedding masque, and the "funerall solempnity," is from a stage point of view good as a spectacle rather than as an introduction to the action. In Act III, scene 1, Arcite (who has been freed from prison in Fletcher's part) and Palamon (who has escaped in Fletcher's part) meet and arrange to fight. In Act V, scene 1, there are the prayers of the two kinsmen and Emilia before the final tournament (the action having gone on to this point in Fletcher's scenes). Here again the scene is spectacular. In Act V, scene 3, the fight goes on behind the arras while Emilia awaits her fate; this scene presenting the culmination of the main action. In the next scene (V, 4,) the play is brought to an end with the rescue of Palamon, the death of Arcite, and the closing speech of Theseus.

Of Fletcher's scenes, Act II, scene 2, represents Palamon and Arcite in prison, the entrance of Emilia in the garden, the quarrel of the two lovers, and the removal of Arcite. This is the real beginning of the main action. In Act II, scene 3, Arcite is free and about to go to court. In Act II, scene 5, he attains success there. In Act III, scene 3, Arcite brings food and files to Palamon (according to the agreement made in the Shaksperean part). In Act III, scene 6, the two kinsmen arm each other and fight, whereupon they are interrupted by Theseus and his train, exposed to death by Palamon's confession, and saved by Emilia's intercession. This is, perhaps, the most effective stage situation of the play. In Act IV, scene 2, Emilia debates over the pictures of her two lovers, and a messenger describes the combatants; this scene preparing the way for the main action of the last act by Shakspere.

---

[1] I omit I, 5, (only 6 lines and a song) because the authorship is very doubtful. II, 3, (Fletcher) deals with both the main and the underplot.

From this analysis of the main action it will be seen that the scenes by one author depend closely on those by the other. So intimate is this inter-relation of the two parts that we safely conclude that each author was well acquainted with the plan of the whole action and the arrangement by scenes and situations. As in the case of the underplot, it is almost impossible that the Shaksperean part was written before and independently of the Fletcherian part.

On that supposition we should have to believe that after Shakspere had planned the play in detail and written a whole introductory act with some elaboration, he then wrote a few disconnected and relatively unimportant scenes for the underplot and one scene of the main plot, the meeting of Palamon and Arcite in the forest, but left the opening and development of the main action untouched. Then, leaving the further development of the main action still untouched, we are to suppose, that he went on to finish with manifest elaboration the final act in the play. Two or three bits of the underplot, the first act, the last act, and one intermediate scene of the main action—however else the play may have been written, one feels fairly certain that it was not begun in this way.

The date, 1613, indeed destroys one conjecture often adopted that the play was left unfinished by Shakspere at his death and was finished by Fletcher at a late date in his career.[1] Our examination of Shakspere's share of the play makes it equally improbable that Shakspere planned and began the play about 1610, and for some reason turned it over in its incomplete form to Fletcher who completed it. Fletcher does, indeed, seem to have made some additions and in some places to have retouched Shakspere's work. He may, probably enough, have given the final touches to the play. Moreover in a play which was still popular in 1634 and which had therefore been in the stock of the King's men for twelve years of Fletcher's life and for nine years after his death, there is a manifest possibility that the text was subject to some alteration and revision.

The part assigned to Shakspere is, however, with the exceptions of these possible alterations, definitely marked off by the scenes of the first quarto. The scenes which Shakspere wrote show a knowledge of the whole course of the dramatic action. They are, however, entirely disconnected by themselves but are closely connected with some of Fletcher's scenes. Still further, each scene by itself is complete and elaborate, utterly unlike unfinished work. It does not seem possible, therefore, that these scenes represent a play which he had begun and left thus unfinished. Fletcher's scenes in the same way are disconnected except when taken in connection with Shakspere's; and each one in itself is complete and well elabo-

[1] See Dyce.

54

rated. These considerations make it probable that, after having made a fairly detailed outline of the play, each writer took certain scenes and, to all intents, completed those scenes after his own fashion. As in *Henry VIII*, the method of composition seems to have been collaboration, pure and simple.

CARDENIO.

It was entered S. R. Sept. 9, 1653, by Humphrey Moseley and described as "by Fletcher and Shakspere." It was not printed.

It was on Warburton's list, but nothing is certainly known of it.[1] The ascription to Shakspere, whether correct or not, indicates that it was an old play, dating before his death. In May, 1613, Hemings was paid for a performance at court by the King's men of *Cardenno*, and in June, 1613, for *Cardenna*. These three, *Cardenio—Cardenno—Cardenna* are probably the same play, and all the evidence we have of authorship is Moseley's assignment to Fletcher and Shakspere.

We have, then, three plays—two probably acted for the first time in 1613, and the third certainly as early as 1613—for which there is evidence that they were written by Shakspere and Fletcher. In the case of the two extant plays this evidence has seemed reasonably conclusive, and the evidence for direct collaboration hardly less so. The evidence on these matters in one play corroborates the evidence in the case of the other; and the evidence in the case of *Cardenio*, though slight, is in harmony with our conclusions in the cases of *Henry VIII* and the *Two Noble Kinsmen*. On the whole it seems decidedly probable that in the course of the years 1611–1613 Shakspere and Fletcher were writing plays in collaboration for the King's men.

The important bearing of this conclusion on our main investigation is at once evident. We are trying to demonstrate that in the years 1608–11 Shakspere was influenced by the romances of Beaumont and Fletcher; and in the years 1611–1613 we find that Shakspere wrote two and possibly three plays in collaboration with Fletcher. If Shakspere was influenced by any one in the last years of his dramatic career, it was most likely by Fletcher.

A fairly strong case, too, might be made for saying that in *Henry VIII* and the *Two Noble Kinsmen*, Fletcher's influence rather than Shakspere's is predominant. It may at least be noted that while *Henry VIII* is a chronicle history more in

---

[1] For a refutation of Mr. Fleay's theory that the play was identical with *Love's Pilgrimage*, see the discussion of the date of that play. Attempts have also been made to identify it with *A Very Woman* and *the Double Falsehood*.

Shakspere's than Fletcher's method, Fletcher's best scenes both in stage effectiveness and dramatic power are as notable as Shakspere's. In the *Two Noble Kinsmen*, in spite of the trash of the underplot and the weakness of his characterization, Fletcher seems to have contributed most largely to the dramatic development of the main action. Much has been said of the power of Shakspere's partnership in bringing out Fletcher's best work, but something also might be said of Fletcher's influence in these plays on Shakspere.[1] In a case, however, where our conclusions rest to such an extent on conjecture, it is not worth while to use these conclusions for inductions in regard to the mutual influence of the two collaborators.

Admitting that there is much in the discussion of these two plays which remains conjectural, we shall still insist on the probability of our main conclusion that Shakspere and Fletcher collaborated. We may also again emphasize the fact that the probability of this collaboration greatly strengthens the *prima facie* likelihood that Shakspere was directly influenced by the Beaumont-Fletcher romances.

---

[1] Mr. Sidney Lee is even willing to find a direct Fletcherian influence on Shakspere's style. Speaking of Wolsey's farewell to Cromwell, he says: "It recalls at every point the style of Fletcher, and nowhere that of Shakespeare's. . . . . we are driven to the alternative conclusion that the noble valediction was by Shakespeare, who in it gave proof of his versatility by echoing in a glorified key the habitual strain of Fletcher, his colleague and virtual successor." *Life*, pp. 262, 263.

CHAPTER V.

In arranging a chronology of the plays attributed to Beaumont and Fletcher, we may conveniently divide them in three groups: I, plays produced before the end of 1611; II, plays 1612–1618, inclusive; III, plays produced after 1618. The first group is the important one for us. Shakspere's three romances cannot date later than 1611, so no plays by Beaumont and Fletcher after that date can have influenced Shakspere, but any plays before that may have done so. I have taken Mr. Fleay's examination [1] as the basis of my investigation, and in group I my results differ radically from his. In groups II and III the chronology is by no means so uncertain as in group I, and I have added little to Mr. Fleay's results. My conclusions in regard to plays of those groups are given without discussion, except in a few cases of special significance.

In group I we shall first consider eight plays which date certainly before the close of 1611 and then eight others which are conjecturally placed in that period. In examining *Four Plays in One, Cupid's Revenge*, and *Thierry and Theodoret*, it will be necessary to anticipate some of the matter of Chapter VII on the general character of the Beaumont-Fletcher romances.

When a reference is made to Mr. Fleay's conclusions without page number, it is always to the discussion of the play under consideration in his *Chronicle of the Drama*. In the same way a reference merely to Dyce always refers to his note on the passage under discussion.

I. First Group. Plays Before the End of 1611.

The Woman Hater. Licensed for publication by Sir George Buc, 20 May, 1607. First quarto, 1607, "as it hath been lately acted by the Children of Paules." 1648, quarto "by J. Fletcher." 1649, by F. Beaumont and J. Fletcher.

Although the statement on the title page cannot be taken to prove much concerning the date of the original performance, it would seem to indicate that the play was produced not very long before May, 1607.[2] Eight of the Paul's boys plays were

---

[1] Chr. I, p. 164, seq.
[2] *A Mad World My Masters*, by Middleton; entered 4 Oct., 1608;

licensed in 1607,[1] showing that the company broke up at about that time. The last play which we know that they produced was the *Abuses*, before the King, 30 July, 1606.[2]

Mr. Fleay places the date of the first representation at Easter, April 5, 1607, on account of the two allusions. "A favorite on a sudden" (I, 3), he thinks refers to Robert Carr, afterwards Earl of Somerset, who was first introduced to the King's notice at a tilt which occurred March 24, 1607. Carr was at this time a mere page, brought forward by Sir James Hays, and was accidentally injured. The King was attracted by the boy's beauty and visited him during his confinement from the injury. Carr did not, however, become notorious as a great favorite until a couple of years later; evidently between March 24 and April 5 there could hardly have been occasion for so positive an allusion. Moreover the play contains a number of allusions to favorites and new-made lords, and James had several favorites before Carr.[3]

Mr. Fleay's second allusion, "another inundation" (III, 1), he takes to refer to the rise of the Severn in Somersetshire and Gloucestershire Jan. 20, 1607.[4] The expression seems more likely to refer to Noah's flood. In expressing surprise at Gondarino's sudden change, Oriana says:

> "Sure we shall have store of larks, the skies will
> Not hold up long; I should have look'd as soon
> For frost in the Dog-days, or another inundation,
> As hoped this strange conversion above miracle."

I find only one passage which helps at all to decide the date. Beaumont and Fletcher were friends of Jonson, as we have seen, at least as early as 1607. In 1605–6 the Paul's boys were under the management of E. Kirkham who had been with the Queen's children of the revels and who had apparently left at the time of their trouble over *Eastward Ho*, 1604–5.[5] Chapman's *Bussy D'Ambois* was produced by the Paul's boys, perhaps about 1605.[6] A friend of Jonson's and a writer for the Paul's boys must have been acquainted with the circumstances of the imprisonment of Jonson, Chapman, and Marston,

---

4to 1608—"it hath bin lately in Action by the Children of Paules." It is dated by Fleay in 1606. *The Roaring Girl;* 4to 1611, "lately acted on Fortune Stage, is dated by Fleay 1604–5.

[1] *Northward Ho*, Aug. 6; *Phœnix*, May 9; *Michaelmas Term*, May 15; *Woman Hater*, May 5; *Bussy D'Ambois*, June 5; *Trick to Catch the Old One*, Oct. 7; all in 1607. *Mad World My Masters*, Oct. 4, 1608. *Northward Ho* was published in 1607.

[2] Nichols, IV, p. 1074.

[3] For Carr's early career, *cf.* Nichols, II, p. 411–415, II, 161. III, 1076. Carr was not knighted until Dec. 24, 1607.

[4] Stow, p. 889.

[5] Chr. I, 59, 60.

[6] Chr. I, 60.

and their danger of losing their ears.[1] The following passage
in the prologue seems reminiscent of that; at any rate I know
nothing else it would be so likely to refer to.

" Or if there be any lurking amongst you in corners with
" table-books, who have some hope to find fit matter to feed
" his —— malice on, let them clasp them up and slink away,
" or stay and be converted. For he who made this play means
" to please auditors so, as he may be an auditor himself here-
" after, and not purchase them with the dear loss of his ears."

All through the play there is ridicule of intelligencers and
trumped-up charges of treason; and Fletcher's verses to Jonson's *Volpone* (acted 1605, published 1607) make special mention of Jonson's foes. The above quotation seems to me likely
to have been written at a date near that of the troubles referred
to; and the passage on the title page also fits a date as early as
1605-6.

The play contains several burlesque imitations of *Hamlet*[2]
and in other places apparently parodies contemporary writers.
There is at least nothing in the play to contradict 1605-6 as
the probable date of composition and presentation.

The Knight of the Burning Pestle. First quarto 1613. Walter
Burre, the publisher, in his preface addressed to Robert Keysar,
makes a number of statements about the play. ' It was written in eight days; soon after (perhaps because it was so unlike
its brethren) exposed to the wide world, who utterly rejected
it. It was succoured from perpetual oblivion by Keysar and by
him sent to Burre who had fostered it privately these two years
and now returns it. Perhaps it will be thought to be of the
race of *Don Quixote;* we may both confidently swear it is his
elder above a year.'[3]

Don Quixote must refer to the translation, entered S. R. 1611
and printed 1612. This date and the statement that Burre had
kept the play by him two years seem to fix the date at 1610-11.
Mr. Fleay supports 1610 with several allusions to contemporary
events in the play; an examination of such allusions, however,
leaves me rather inclined to place the date several years earlier.
I shall state first the internal evidence in favor of 1610 and
then that which points to an earlier date.

Several songs in the play[4] are found in Ravenscroft's collections *Deuteromelia* (entered S. R. 1609) and *Pammelia* (entered

---

[1] Chr. I, 81. II, 346. Jonson was also in prison again in connection
with *Sejanus* and was accused of both Popery and treason. See Chr.
II, p. 347.
[2] II, 1, p. 37: III, 1, p. 41 : II, 1, p. 34. See Dyce's notes.
[3] Nevertheless, the indebtedness of K. B. P. to *Don Quixote* is un-
questionable.
[4] I, 4, p. 150, *Deuteromelia*. II, 4, *Deuteromelia*. II, 7, *Pammelia*
(Trowl the Black Bowl). These are all merest snatches.

S. R. 1609). These were, however, collections of songs and snatches already familiar.

"The little child," etc., (III, 2,) seems to be the same as "the boy of six years old," etc., of the *Alchemist* (1610), (V. I,).

"The hermaphrodite" (III, 2,)[1] Mr. Fleay thinks is the monstrous child born July 31, 1601, at Sandwich. This is a very doubtful conjecture.

The above references[2] are at least in harmony with a 1610 date. The following seem to contradict it.

"This seven years there have been plays at this house." (Induction.) Mr. Fleay places the production of the play at Whitefriars, because he thinks the play was acted by the Revels children who were at Whitefriars in 1610. He so placed it in his *History of the Stage* in violence to this passage, for he then believed Whitefriars was first opened January 1610. Later Mr. Greenstreet's papers showed that Whitefriars was occupied 1607–1610; so in the *Chronicle of the Drama*, Mr. Fleay notices this passage and from it concludes that the play-house in Whitefriars must also have been occupied 1604–7. There is no evidence that it was so occupied. Frequent references to the children show that the play was produced by a children's company. If by the Queen's Revels, the seven years can hardly refer to anything except their occupancy of Blackfriars from their organization of 1600 to 1607.[3] If by the Paul's boys, the passage again alludes to a period beginning in 1599[4] and ending 1606–7. Judging from what we know of the stage history, the passage cannot refer to any theater, if spoken in 1610; if spoken in 1607, it can refer to Blackfriars or probably to the house occupied by the Paul's boys.

There is an allusion (IV, 1,)[5] to the *Travails of Three Eng-*

---

[1] "The Great Dutchman" (III, 2), of the same passage has not been identified.

[2] Mr. Fleay also says the statute of Jan. 7, 1609, is referred to in I, 1. I can find no statute of that date. Parliament did not meet in that year.

[3] A glance at the first few lines of the induction will convince any one that there is no reference to an occupancy by previous companies, as Mr. Fleay states. The lease of Blackfriars was taken 1600 (H. of S. p. 184,), but the Revels Company was acting before.

[4] The date of the reinstatement of Paul's boys is 1599, not 1600. See *The Stage Quarrel between Ben Jonson and the so-called Poetasters*.

[5] IV, 1. Citizen. "Why so, sir? go and fetch me him then and let the Sophy of Persia come and christen him a child."
Boy. "Believe me, sir, that will not do so well; 'tis stale; it has been had before at the Red Bull.
Mr. Fleay regards this allusion to the Red Bull, proof of a date as late as 1610 (H. of S. 195), because he thinks the Red Bull was not used until April 15, 1609. His proof of this is the patent granted Queen Anne's players on that day. But the patent (Shak. Soc. Papers IV, p. 44) reads "to shewe and exercise publickly as well within their

lish Brothers, printed 1607 as acted at the Curtain. Mr. Boyle[1] notes the allusion, and since the *Travails* was based on the adventures of the three Shirleys and was only of immediate interest, he thinks a reference to it would be likely to be contemporary. The play[2] was hurriedly written and at once published and must have soon been superseded in favor, and for these reasons Mr. Boyle is inclined to think the reference in the *Knight of the Burning Pestle* fixes the date of that play about 1607.

> "Welcome, sir Knight, into my father's court,
> King of Moldavia, unto me Pomponia." (IV, 2.)

In Nichols (II, 157), we find that in November, 1607, "the Turk and the Prince of Moldavia are now going away (from London). In Jonson's *Epicœne* (acted 1609) there is also an allusion to the Prince of Moldavia (V, 1,), but as Jonson spent a year or two on a play this mention corresponds with that in Nichols. The reference in the *Burning Pestle*, therefore, seems to indicate an earlier date than 1610.

Merrythought, who is constantly singing ditties, recalls Valerius in Heywood's *Rape of Lucrece*, printed 1608, and of course acted earlier.[3] The *Burning Pestle* satirizes Heywood's plays and his company (Queen's men), but perhaps Beaumont in this instance borrowed an idea which had proved a popular innovation, or perhaps Heywood borrowed it from Beaumont. In either case 1607–8 becomes the more likely date for the *Burning Pestle*. This is pure conjecture on my part.

There remain a number of references and allusions which give no definite evidence in regard to the date, although considered cumulatively they favor the earlier rather than the later.

In the Induction the following plays are mentioned: the

"nowe usual houses called the Redd Bull, Clerkenwell and the Curtayne in Hallowell as alsoe within any Towne Hall," etc. It is difficult to conceive how Mr. Fleay concludes from this that on that date the company changed from the Curtain to the Bull. One would naturally infer that the company had used both theaters for some time. There are several references to the Red Bull in the *Knight of the Burning Pestle;* and according to Mr. Fleay's theory they indicate a date later than 1609. From my interpretation of the 1609 patent, they indicate nothing of the kind.

[1] Englische Studien, Vol. IX.

[2] See Chr. II, 277.

[3] Fleay, in curious contradiction with his theory that the Red Bull was not opened until 1609, places *Lucrece* among the plays at the Bull 1609–13 rather than at the Curtain 1607–9. (H. of S. p. 189.) In the *Chronicle* of the *Drama* he gives the date of the first quarto correctly, 1608. *Lucrece* in modern editions is usually said to have been acted at the Red Bull, but I don't know whether the first quarto states this or not, as I have not seen a copy. Fleay (H. of S. p. 201,) says the Red Bull is mentioned for the first time in the 1635 4to.

61

Legend of Whittington,[1] *Life and Death of Sir Thomas Gresham with the building of the Royal Exchange*,[2] the story of *Queen Eleanor*,[3] *Jane Shore*,[4] and *Bold Beauchamps*.[5] These are all old plays, and favorites with the citizen. He asks: "why could you not be contented, as well as others, with these?" The phrase "as well as others" seems to allude to the Queen's men. So far as can be determined these were all plays popular during the first few years of the century.

Musidorus and *Jeronimo* are also alluded to in the Induction.

Heywood's *Four Apprentices* is several times ridiculed. The citizen says (IV, 1), 'Read the play of the *Four Apprentices* where they toss their pikes." The play was printed in 1615, but in the preface Heywood describes it as written fifteen or sixteen years before. The passage quoted seems to point to an earlier edition than that of 1615, but there is no other indication of one. As the citizen is made to speak incorrectly, Dyce thinks the passage does not indicate an earlier edition; Fleay on the contrary thinks there was one.[6] Heywood in the preface to the 1615 edition, alludes to the resumption of artillery practice by the citizens, which took place in 1610; Mr. Fleay, therefore, concludes that the preface was written for a 1610 edition. He also identifies the play with *Godfrey* of *Bulloigne*. All this is extremely doubtful, and to use it to establish a date 1610–11 for the *Burning Pestle* would be a bad case of reasoning in a circle.

There is considerable burlesque of the *Mirrour of Knighthood*, printed 1602 (final part), which is also alluded to in the *Scornful Lady*. (III, 1.) A song[7] is given which occurs with variations and an additional stanza in the *Captain*. Another song[8] is quoted in the *Woman's Prize*, *Monsieur Thomas*, *Blurt Master Constable*, and *Lucrece*. There is an allusion to the battle at Mile End[9] as in *Monsieur Thomas*.

---

[1] S. R. 1604.

[2] Heywood's *If you know not me, you know nobody*, 4to, 1605. See Chr. I, 292.

[3] *The famous chronicle of King Edward I.* (?)

[4] *Edward* IV (1599).

[5] See Chr. I, 287. See also a possible allusion in *A Mad World My Masters* (4to, 1608), Middleton's Works. Ed. Bullen, V, 2, note.

[6] Chr. I, 282.

[7] III, 1. "Tell me, dearest, what is love?" The Captain, II, 2.

[8] III, 5. "Go from my window, love, go!" W. P., I, 3. Mon. T., III, 3. B. M. C., IV, 2. The whole song is one of those added to *Lucrece*.

[9] II, 2. "I can assure thee, Michael, Mile End is a goodly matter; there has been a pitch field, my child, between naughty Spaniards and Englishmen," etc. *Mon. Thomas*, III, 3. A ballad is mentioned of "the Landing of the Spaniards at Bow and bloody battle at Mile End."

There are burlesques of passages in *Henry IV,*[1] *Romeo and Juliet,*[2] and the *Spanish Tragedy.*[3]

One other passage has a slight bearing on the date.   In I, 1, the wife asks: "Were you never none of Master Moncaster's scholars?"[4]   Dr. Richard Mulcaster was head master of St. Paul's school 1596–1608.

This reference to Mulcaster and the songs which occur in other plays hardly point to one date more than the other.   The plays referred to by name and the plays burlesqued are all plays that were familiar early in the century, but references might have been made to them in 1610 as well as 1607.   The similarity of the burlesque of contemporary drama to that in the *Woman Hater* must, however, be noticed; and that play was surely not later than 1607 and probably dates 1605–6.

The evidence which we have seen points definitely to 1607 is not contradicted by anything in the play and gives us a good many difficulties to explain if we adopt the usual 1610–11 date. On the other hand, if we assume a 1607 date, we shall have to assume that Robert Keysar turned the play over to Burre a considerable time after its first production and that Burre knew nothing personally of its first production.   I see no escape from the dilemma, but I am inclined to think the 1607 date the less objectionable.   The play at all events cannot be later than 1611.

The Faithful Shepherdess.   First quarto, undated, but before May 1610, when Sir William Skipwith, one of the three persons to whom it is dedicated, died.

---

[1] Induction.   "By heaven, methinks it were an easy leap,
    To pluck bright honour," etc.
This is an almost verbatim burlesque of Hotspur's speech, 1 *Henry IV*; III, 1.
    V. 3.   To a resolv'd mind his home is everywhere. . .
        * * * "Saint George and on, my hearts!"
—seems reminiscent of Henry's speech before Harfleur, *Henry* V, III, 1; or perhaps of *Antonio's Revenge*, II, 1.
    "A wise man's house is wheresoe'er he is wise," etc.
[2] II, 1.   "Good night, twenty good nights and twenty more,
        And twenty more good nights—that makes three score."
—seems to be a parody of the balcony scene.
[3] The final speech of Ralph's ghost—
        When "I was mortal and my costive corpse
        Did lap up figs and raisins in the strand,"—
is a burlesque of Andrea's ghost.
[4] Mr. Fleay comments on the passage quoted, "*i. e.*, a Paul's boy before 1602."   Dyce notes that Mulcaster was head master of the Merchant Taylor's school, 1561–1586.   He was head master of St. Paul's school 1596–1608, but his term does not fix the date of this reference which might have been made after he had given up teaching or even after his death, 1611.   For an account of the life of this famous schoolmaster, see Dictionary of National Biography.   His name appears several times in connection with the stage history of the period.

Mr. Fleay says that Bonian and Whalley, the publishers, are conjoined in the Stationer's Register from Dec. 22, 1608, to Sept. 1, 1609; and therefore thinks this quarto is to be placed between those dates. Bartholomew Sutter, however, seems to have been added to the two other publishers in entering the *Case is Altered*, July 20, 1609.[1]

In the dedication to Sir Walter Aston, Fletcher speaks of "the infection," which may refer specifically to the prevalence of the plague, 1608–9, or it may be a general reference to the continuance of the plague since the great outbreak in 1603. In his commendatory verses, Field speaks of his muse "in swaddling clouts;" and his first play, says Mr. Fleay,[2] was acted in 1609, but in another place Mr. Fleay gives 1610 as the date of *A Woman is a Weathercock*.[3] Ben Jonson in Drummond's Conversations (1618) is reported to have said, "Fletcher and Beaumont ten years since have written the *Faithful Shepherdess*."

Some of Mr. Fleay's theories which he thinks bear on the date of this play may be left to one side,[4] but the foregoing evidence supports his conclusion that it was first acted (when it was a failure) in 1608.[5]

Philaster: or, Love Lies a Bleeding. First quarto, 1620, "as acted at the Globe by his Majesties Servants." This was apparently a pirated edition.

In the *Scourge of Folly*, by John Davies of Hertford, entered S. R. Oct. 8, 1610, occurs an epigram[6] referring to this play.

Mr. Fleay makes several different statements about the date. In his *Life of Shakspere*,[7] he says: "*Philaster*, which contains some passages suggested by this play [Cymbeline], was written in 1611." In his *History of the Stage*,[8] he

---

[1] Chr. I, 312.
[2] Chr. I, 178.
[3] Chr. I, 185.
[4] The fact that Field, Chapman, and Jonson wrote commendatory verses for this play, seems to Fleay proof that it was written for the Queen's Revels children, because he thinks these men were all connected with the Revels boys 1608–9. He also thinks the play must be dated before July 28, 1608, when he thinks the theaters were closed by the plague. We have already discussed the value of these two kinds of evidence. The play was doubtless acted by a company of children.
[5] There is no certain early limit.
[6] "To the well-deserving, Mr. John Fletcher."

> "Love lies bleeding, if it should not prove
> His utmost act to show why it doth love,
> Thou being the subject (now) it waits upon
> Reign'st in Acte, Judgment, and Invention.
> For this I love thee, and can do no less
> For thine as faire, as faithful Shepherdess."

[7] L. of S., p. 246.
[8] H. of S., p. 203.

places *Philaster* among the plays first produced at the Globe and the Blackfriars by the King's men 1610–13, and again in a foot-note[1], after Dec. 24, 1609. In his *Chronicle of the Drama*,[2] he says it was produced by the King's men at the Globe, before 1610, Oct. 8. Here at last he is on safe ground, but even here he assumes that it was written after Shakspere left the King's men,[3] which we have already seen, even from his own statements, to be impossible.[4]

The statement in the 1620 quarto that the play was acted at the Globe is probably of no value in indicating the place of the first performance,[5] but there is no reason why *Philaster* may not have been produced there before Burbadge took up the Blackfriars lease in 1608. There is, in fact, no early limit that can be set for the date; the final limit is of course, fixed by Davies' Epigram. The *Scourge of Folly* furnishes no further clue in regard to the date of this epigram. The only other play referred to is Marston's *Malcontent* (printed 1604). The epigram preceding the one on Fletcher is addressed to Ostler, "sole king of actors," who joined the King's men when Burbadge took up the lease in 1608.

One passage in the play seems certainly to contain a local allusion, but I have not been able to identify it.

> "So please you, sir, he's gone to see the city
> And the *new platform;* with some gentlemen
> Attending on him."[6]

One passage seems to be an echo of *Hamlet*,[7] and Mr. Macaulay and Dr. Leonhardt[8] have also found other similarities.

The date, 1608, adopted by Dyce, Leonhardt, Macaulay, and students in general, is no more than a conjecture; but on the whole it seems a probable one.

The Maid's Tragedy. First quarto, 1619. "As it hath been divers times acted at the Blackfriars by the King Majesty's Servants." No authors are given.

It was evidently written before Oct. 31, 1611, on which day a play was licensed by Sir George Buc, which he endorsed as "this second maiden's tragedy." This is written on the manu-

---

[1] H. of S., p. 250.
[2] Chr. I, p. 189.
[3] Chr. I, p. 170. Note the order in which he arranges the plays.
[4] See page 21.
[5] Because *Philaster* was a very popular play and was doubtless on the stage in 1620.
[6] *Philaster*, Act. V, sc. 3.
[7] I, 1. Dion: "Mark but the King, how pale he looks with fear!
  Oh, this same whoreson conscience, how it jades us!"
[8] Anglia, Vol. VIII. The plot includes Philaster's revenge on the King, his father's deposer, and hence there are resemblances to the earlier tragedies dealing with "revenge for a father," and of course, to *Hamlet*.

script of that play now in existence, but the title of the play is missing. Mr. Fleay thinks this endorsement shows that the *Maid's Tragedy* was licensed immediately before the play of Oct. 31. This is pure conjecture; the superscription may, on the contrary, be taken to indicate that the *Maid's Tragedy* was well known. The "second maiden's tragedy" has no apparent relation to Beaumont and Fletcher's play, and one can only guess at Sir George Buc's reasons for using the title.

Mr. Fleay thinks that the masque was inserted at the time of the court performance[1] (1612-13), and even conjectures that it was written for a marriage Jan. 29, 1612, and later inserted in the play. The masque is mentioned in the opening lines of the play and several times afterwards in the first act, which would indicate that it was a part of the play from the first. In fact it is an integrant part of the action. It may have been revised, although the irregularities instanced by Mr. Fleay hardly indicate that.[2]

It must be noted that the statement in the 1619 quarto that the play was acted at the Blackfriars cannot be accepted as settling the place of the first performance, so even the purchase of the Blackfriars' lease in 1608 cannot be certainly taken as fixing an early limit. Mr. Fleay finds the date 1611 in conformity with his theories of the stage history; the usual conjecture has been 1609 or 1610. So far as I can find, there is no early limit for the date, 1609 is an unobjectionable conjecture, and the latest limit is certainly Oct. 31, 1611.

The Coxcomb. First printed in folio 1647. Acted at court by Rossiter's Company before Lady Elizabeth and Prince Palatine Oct., 1612;[3] also acted before the King March, 1613.[4]

There is a list of actors given in the second folio (1679). In the *History of the Stage*[5] Mr. Fleay assigns this list to the presentation before the King 1613. In the *Chronicle of the Drama*[6] he decides that the list "must date before August 29, 1611, for Cary and Barkstead, who appear on it, and who had always,

---

[1] See ante, p. 29.

[2] Mr. Fleay is at so much trouble to prove that the masque was a later insertion because he thinks the lines—

"You shall have many floods fuller and higher
Than you have wished for; and no ebb shall dare
To let the day see where your dwellings are."

can hardly refer to the floods of 1607, and must, therefore, refer to those of 1612, Oct.-Dec., *i. e.*, the allusion must have been made in the revision for the court performance. The allusion is very doubtful at best, but there is no reason why the play may not date early enough to make the allusion to the floods of 1607.

[3] H. of S., p. 175.

[4] Oldys' ms. notes to Langbaine.

[5] H. of S., p. 187.

[6] Chr., I, 185.

till then, been Revels boys, at that date joined the Lady Elizabeth's men under Foster." He also decides that the date must be later than Mar. 30, 1610, because Joseph Taylor, who is on the list, was on that date with the Duke of York's men. The first statement is correct, but the last is a surprising inference. The Duke of York's Company was just established on March 30, 1610;[1] so that Fleay conjectures that Taylor at once left this newly formed men's company to play with Rossiter's children. The natural inference is that Taylor[2] had been with the Revels children and left them in March, 1610, to join the newly formed men's company, just as Cary and Barkstead did in 1611. Taylor was evidently a prominent actor by 1610-12, for he is second on the list of Lady Elizabeth's Company, Aug., 1611 (which he joined with Cary and Barkstead), and is acting as manager in 1612-13[3] in the list of court payments. If we take the natural inference in regard to him the *Coxcomb* must date not after but before March 30, 1610.[4]

Now, Jonson's *Epicœne* was performed by the Revels children in 1609, and we have a list of the actors. Rossiter's Company, it will be remembered, was a continuation of the Revels (first Queen's). The question arises did the *Coxcomb* precede or follow *Epicœne*? A comparison of the two lists leaves the question in doubt: five names are the same on both lists. I give them, with numbers denoting their order:

	Cox.	Epic.
Nathan Field,	1	1
Giles Carey,	3	3
Rich. Allin,	5	6
Hugh Attawell,	6	5
Will Barkstead,	8	2

Three names are different on each list. I give them, with the dates and companies with which they are known to have been playing after these lists. No one of the six is found on any earlier list.

Coxcomb. Joseph Taylor (2) Mar. 30, 1610, Duke of York's. Aug. 29, 1611, Forster's Lady Elizabeth's.

Emanuel Read (4) 1613, the reorganized Lady Elizabeth's Company, to which Field also went. 1617, Queen Anne's.

Robt. Benfield (7) 1613, Lady Elizabeth's. 1619, King's men.

Epicœne. Will Pen (4) 20 May, 1616, Prince's men.

John Smitth (7) 20 May, 1616, Prince's men.

John Blaney (8) 1617, Queen Anne's.

---

[1] H. of S., p. 188. Patent is quoted, which was granted Mar. 30, 1610, to the Duke of York's men.

[2] Mr. Oliphant also comes to this conclusion. See Eng. Studien, XV, p. 322.

[3] H. of S., p. 175.

[4] So Mr. Oliphant decides. Eng. Studien, XV, p. 322.

There is no evidence which of the lists is older, both may date at about the same time. There is no reason why the *Coxcomb* list may not apply to an earlier presentation than that of *Epicæne;* possibly, then, to a first presentation at Blackfriars, 1605-8.

Other evidences of date are slight. Ostend is alluded to,[1] and also the pamphlet of Nicholas Breton, printed 1600-1602.[2]

The source of the plot which gives the play its name is Cervantes' *Curioso Impertinente;* first printed with *Don Quixote,* 1605; translated into French and published 1608, as *Le Curieux Impertinente.*[3] This fixes the earliest limit for *The Coxcomb* at 1605. It is certainly earlier than Aug. 29, 1611; almost as certainly earlier than March 30, 1610; and, possibly enough, earlier than 1609.[4]

Cupid's Revenge. First quarto, 1615. "By John Fletcher," "As it hath been divers times acted by the Children of her Majestie's Revels." The printer in an address to the reader declares that he is not acquainted with the author and ends: "I once again dedicate this book to the judicious, some whereof "I have heard commend it to be excellent—who because they "saw it acted and knew whereof they spoke are the better to "be believed,—and for my part, I censure thus—that I have "never read a better."

It was acted before Prince Henry and Princess Elizabeth, the Sunday following New Year's 1612, by the Children of Whitefriars, and again at court, according to Oldys, in 1613.

All critics agree in assigning shares to both Beaumont and Fletcher. There are evidences of alteration, and Mr. Fleay thinks it was worked over for the court presentation; Mr. Boyle also finds indications of a third hand; and Mr. Oliphant of a third and fourth.

Mr. Fleay fixes the date at 1610, because Rossiter's company of Revels was then at Whitefriars and because he thinks Beaumont and Fletcher stopped writing for the Revels children and went to the King's men in the fall of 1610. This last statement, we have seen, to be contrary to evidence.[5] The

---

[1] II, 2. "When they take a thief, I'll take Ostend again."
Ostend was taken Sept. 8, 1604. Such an allusion as this might date a number of years after the event. Ostend is also alluded to in *Woman's Prize,* I, 3, and *Love's Cure,* I, 1 (both probably acted before 1608).
[2] V, 4. "Mother, do you read Madcap still?" *Cf.* Dyce. *Cf.,* also, the *Scornful Lady,* II, 1.
[3] *Cf.* Koeppel, p. 83. *Don Quixote* seems to have been known to Beaumont and Fletcher in Spanish. This plot from the *Curioso Impertinente* is also used in Field's *Amends for Ladies* (1611?) and the *Second Maiden's Tragedy* (1611).
[4] The country scenes (especially III, 3) suggest the conjecture that the *Coxcomb* may be one of the comedies written at the time of Beaumont's stay in the country, referred to in his *Poetical Epistle to Ben Jonson* (about 1606).
[5] See ante, Chap. II.

play may have been written for the earlier Revels and handed over by them to Rossiter's company, or it may have been written for Rossiter's company in 1610–11, while Beaumont and Fletcher were also writing for the King's men. The play, as in all cases of which we have evidence, was doubtless acted in public before the court performance; therefore its date cannot be later than the last of 1611.

The plot requires some consideration because it throws open an opportunity for conjectures in respect to the date and because it illustrates the dramatic methods of Beaumont and Fletcher. It is taken from Sidney's *Arcadia*.[1] Two stories are combined more closely than in the *Arcadia*, and the prosy narrative of the novel is developed into a series of lively situations with a new melodramatic dénouement, quite after the style of that in *Thierry* and *Theodoret*. Some of the other alterations are worth noting. (1) The repugnant dwarf Zoilus is substituted for the nurse's son, with whom the Princess is enamoured. This "Cupid's revenge" recalls Oberon's revenge in *Midsummer Night's Dream* as Koeppel suggests, but the change is obviously due to a desire for a 'strong' stage situation. (2) The machinery of Cupid, who descends and ascends, is added; this with the dance and songs supplies the first two acts with a masque-like element. (3) The queen, Bacha, is a very bad woman of the Megra-Brunhalt type; her portrait is, however, distinctly sketched in *Arcadia*. (4) Timantus, the coward and poltroon of the Bessus-Protaldy type is developed from a very slight allusion in the novel to the "queen's wicked counsellors." (5) Ismenus, the faithful friend of the Melantius-Mardonius type, is added. (6) Urania, the girl of the Aspatia-Bellario type, who dons boy's clothes and follows her lover, is also added. These last two characters are not so much as suggested in the *Arcadia*. (7) Leucippus, the hero, is of the Philaster-Amintor sort, or as Mr. Oliphant styles the type, "the Beaumontesque lily-livered order of men." This character is hardly suggested in the novel.[2]

Now the types represented by these last five characters appear in *Philaster*, the *Maid's Tragedy*, *Thierry and Theodoret*, and *A King and No King*. We shall have occasion to discuss them later, but their appearance here shows that when Beaumont and Fletcher wrote *Cupid's Revenge* they had the main features of their characteristic romances clearly in mind. They followed the plot given them rather closely at times but always

---

[1] Works, ed. 1725. Vol. I, 264 ff, 276 ff. *Cf.* Dyce, Vol. II, 331, and Koeppel, p. 41.

[2] It may be noted that the mob which rescues Leucippus is developed from a brief reference in the *Arcadia*. It recalls the mob in *Philaster*.

with an eye to startling and vigorous situations and with the addition of a dénouement similar to one used in another play. To this plot they added a little spectacular business and five types of characters familiar in their other plays. There is no indefiniteness in the character-drawing, little sign of experimentation. There is little masterly poetry in the play, but the "lily-livered prince," the evil, passionate woman, the blunt soldier-friend, the poltroon, and the childishly loving girl are all delineated with a completeness that indicates practice.

The play is such a one as might have been hastily written by men who merely drew from their dramatic stock in trade—it looks like an attempt to repeat the success of *Philaster*. So it seems to me, but one must not rest much on conjectures of this sort. Whatever its date may be in relation to the other romances, *Cupid's Revenge* affords an interesting opportunity to study the methods of construction and the stock characters of the Beaumont and Fletcher romances.

A King and No King. First quarto, entered S. R. Aug. 7, 1618. It was licensed by Buck in 1611, and performed at court Dec. 1611 and again 1612–13. This is the only play acted before 1612, the year of whose production is fixed.

We have now examined the dates of eight plays certainly acted by the end of 1611, we shall next consider the dates of eight others which may be conjecturally assigned to the same period.

The Woman's Prize, or the Tamer Tamed. First printed in folio 1647. Revived in 1633; described in Herbert's licensing book as "an old play by Fletcher;" suppressed by Herbert and the *Scornful Lady* acted instead. Acted before the King and Queen Nov. 28, 1633 by the King's men and "very well liked." Two days before, the *Taming of the Shrew* was acted and only "liked."

The play is a sequel to the *Taming of the Shrew* and introduces Petruchio with a second wife who tames him. Mr. Fleay is in doubt whether to date it 1612 or 1615, preferring the latter and conjecturing that the play was originally produced by the Lady Elizabeth's men. Mr. Oliphant gives reasons for thinking it was an early play of 1606–7, or possibly 1604, and revised about 1613–14.[1]

Mr. Oliphant points out that Dekker's *Medicine for a Curst Wife*[2] was acted by the Admiral's men July 1602, Heywood's *A Woman Killed with Kindness*,[2] Feb.–March, 1603, and the *Taming of the Shrew* by the King's men in 1603,[3] and that *Patient Grissil* was published in 1603. Fletcher's play on a

---

[1] Englische Studien, XV, pp. 388, 389.
[2] See Henslow's Diary.
[3] Fleay, Shaks., p. 224.

similar theme he thinks may have been suggested by these; or, as he thinks more likely, it may be connected with the publication of *A Woman Killed with Kindness*, in 1607, and the re-entry of the old *Taming of the Shrew* in the same year.

The play contains the following allusions (I, 3) to the siege of Ostend (July 5, 1601, to Sept. 8, 1604).

> "Colonel Bianca. She commands the works
> Spinola's but a ditcher to her."
> "The chamber's nothing but a mere Ostend."

The fortification metaphor, moreover, runs throughout the scene. The most natural and, I think, a safe conclusion[1] is that the play was written during or shortly after the siege of Ostend.

There is another allusion (II, 2) which points to an early date.

> "his infliction
> That killed the Prince of Orange, will be sport
> To what we purpose."

The Prince of Orange was murdered in 1584; a very vivid account of the punishments inflicted upon the murderer is given in *A True Discourse Historical of the Succeeding Governors of the Netherlands*, etc., 4to, 1602.[2] This account would seem to have been in the writer's mind when he wrote the above passage.

There is an allusion to the *Spanish Tragedy* (II, 6) and a burlesque on *Hamlet* (V, 3).[3] A ballad is given (I, 3) which is also quoted in the *Burning Pestle* (III, 5) and *Monsieur Thomas* (III, 3).

Valid reasons for dating this and other plays as early as 1604-5 might be adduced from the complete blank in Fletcher's career, 1604-7, and the large number of important plays usually assigned, 1607-11, but consideration of such evidence may well be postponed until we attempt to form a chronology of all the plays together. In this case there is sufficient internal evidence to determine the date. There is nothing in the play to

---

[1] It is possible that the reference may have been written eight or ten years after the event, but it sounds like a contemporaneous allusion. The siege of Ostend was, to be sure, a very famous event, but it is alluded to in only two other of Beaumont and Fletcher's collected plays, *Coxcomb*, II, 2, Dyce, III, p. 154, and *Love's Cure*, I, 1, Dyce, X, p. 112. Both of these, we shall find reason to think, date before 1609, and both of the allusions distinctly refer to the siege as a past event. *A true history of the Memorable Siege of Ostend*, etc., 4 to, was published in 1604.

[2] See Works, ed. Dyce, VII, p. 113.

[3] Mr. Oliphant also finds a parody on *Lear* (II, 5) and an allusion to a *Woman Killed with Kindness* (III, 4). The latter speaks of a husband "killed with kindness," and has no reference to Heywood's play.

71

contradict the early date;[1] and the references to Ostend and the murderer of the Prince of Orange, and, less surely, the plays on similar themes of about 1603, seem to fix the date at 1604.

Love's Cure or the Martial Maid. First printed in folio 1647; without an actors' list, therefore probably not acted by the King's men.

The date was formerly supposed to be fixed by the allusion to the cold Muscovite[2] at 1622 or a little later. Mr. Fleay, however, has shown reasons for thinking that the first production was much earlier and that the reference to the cold Muscovite belongs to a late revision by Massinger of the original play by Beaumont and Fletcher. At the start it is necessary to show some evidence of such a revision. Fleay, Boyle, and Oliphant are all agreed that a large part of the play as it now stands is to be accredited to Massinger. No one finds any very conclusive evidence of Fletcher's work; the probability, therefore, of an original unrevised play rests on the question of Beaumont's authorship.

The prologue at a late revival, subsequent to 1625, mentions Beaumont and Fletcher as the authors, which rather implies that the play was written in Beaumont's life-time. Moreover, Beaumont's hand seems to me distinctly traceable. Two scenes in particular seem to me Beaumont's in entirety. On looking at their divisions, I find that Fleay and Oliphant also assign these scenes among others to Beaumont. Boyle assigns them to an unknown author, but an examination of his tables[3] shows that these scenes must be assigned by verse tests to Beaumont. The table shows the tests for the two scenes in *Love's Cure* and compares the results with the percentages of other of Beaumont's plays.

This is as near as you can come to proving authorship by verse-tests.[4] We are justified, then, in concluding that as

---

[1] Mr. Oliphant finds an allusion to Jonson's *Silent Woman* (III, 1), and also says he finds comparisons with half a dozen of Beaumont and Fletcher's plays. He only gives two of these, and they do not tempt one to search farther. They are:

Woman's Prize, II, 1. " My nose blown to my hand."
Woman Hater, III, 1. " My nose blow'd to my hand."
Woman's Prize, II, 2. " Put up your pipes."
Woman Hater, III, 1. " Put up thy pipes."

Obviously, Mr. Oliphant has a very keen scent for these similarities, and he thinks a good many of them belong to the conjectured revision of 1613-14. The two titles and the fact that the scene is London, while the characters have Italian names, are the only definite evidences of this revision. No one has detected any author except Fletcher.

[2] II, 2. See Dyce.
[3] Englische Studien. V, p. 74, seq. The figures in the table are Boyle's.
[4] The ' 'em-them ' test is worth noting in this connection, although it is not helpful in deciding the authorship. There are 17 thems and 21 'ems in the play: according to Boyle's division there are 13 thems

	VERSE LINES	DOUBLE ENDINGS	RUN-OVER LINES	LIGHT END-INGS	WEAK END-INGS	RHYMES
Love's Cure, III, 3,	123	14	41	3	0	4
" " V, 3,	217	40	60	7	1	8
" " two scenes,	340	54	101	10	1	12
" " Percentage,		15.9	29.7	3-	0	3.5
Beaumont's share Triumph of Love (entire),	628	15.6	25.	3.	—	9.
Beaumont's share Philaster,	1,730	15.2	26.2	2.4	—	1.2
" " A King and No King,	1,650	11.9	27.8	1.8	.7	1.

Beaumont had a share in the play it must have been written before 1616 and revised by Massinger after 1622. This hypothesis is more plausible than the old one fixing the date of the first production in 1622, for then we should have a play accredited to Beaumont and Fletcher in which neither had a share. A part of the original play may have been written by Fletcher, but his work is hardly discernible through Massinger's revision; Beaumont's work is discernible in my opinion in much that has been revised as well as in a number of scenes where it seems preserved in its entirety.

We come now to internal evidence which fixes the date of the original play. Mr. Fleay has pointed out a number of references. Alvarez[1] (I, 3) has had twenty years of exile; Lucio, born just after the departure of Alvarez into exile is twenty years old;[2] Alvarez had been exiled sixteen years[3] before he brought Clara to Ostend (June, 1661—Aug., 1604). The date of the action of the play, then, is four years later, 1605–1608; which, Mr. Fleay adds, "is no doubt, as usual in plays where such chronological calculations are introduced, the date of writing." Certainly it is natural for the date of action in such cases to coincide with the date of writing, but the time of action

and 1 'em in Massinger's half of the play and 4 thems and 20 'ems in the half assigned to the unknown author. In Oliphant's division there are 13 thems and 1 'em in Massinger's part, 3 'ems in Beaumont and Massinger's, and 4 thems and 17 'ems in Beaumont's part. Even a single 'em in Massinger is suspicious; the 'ems furnish no conclusive evidence of Fletcher's hand; and the proportion of 'ems and thems neither counts for nor against Beaumont.

I. 1.	1 them.	III. 5.	1 them (prose).
I. 3.	1 them (prose).	IV. 2.	1 'em.
II. 1.	1 them 5 'ems (all prose).	IV. 3.	7 thems.
II. 2.	1 them 3 'ems.	V. 1.	4 thems.
III. 2.	3 'ems.	V. 3.	5 'ems (2 in prose).
III. 3.	3 'ems.		
III. 4.	1 them 1 'em.	Total 17 thems 21 'ems.

[1] I, 3, p. 121. "My twenty years of sorrow but a dream."
 I, 3, p. 123. "Have you been twenty years a stranger to it?"
[2] I, 2, p. 116. "For twenty years, which is ever since you were born."
[3] I, 1, p. 112.

is stated directly in the first lines of the play without any chronological calculations. The lines are spoken of Alvarez.

> "As if by his command alone, and fortune,
> Holland, with those low Provinces that hold out
> Against the Arch-duke, were again compell'd
> With their obedience to give up their lives
> To be at his devotion."

These lines and the other allusions in the first scene to the Arch-duke and Ostend can only refer to the war between Spain and the Netherlands in which the Cardinal Arch-duke Albert was governor of the Netherlands and which ended in a truce April 9, 1609. The Arch-duke was given special powers to bring about a truce Jan. 10, 1608,[1] and from that time on negotiations were in progress; perhaps the references in *Love's Cure*, then, may be taken to indicate a period earlier than 1608. At all events, they fix the time of the action, and I think unquestionably the time of the writing between 1605 and 1609.

Mr. Fleay has also noticed "the use of the name Lazarillo as in the *Woman Hater*." Not only is the name the same, but this Lazarillo, like the fellow in the *Woman Hater*, is a glutton, interested in nothing but eating. Thus when he comes to hanging he says: "I have no stomach for it, but I'll endeavor," and again when he is sent to the galleys, "Well, though I herrings want, I shall have rows." The similarity between the two Lazarillos points to Beaumont's authorship of *Love's Cure* and a date not very distant from that of the *Woman Hater*.

Mr. Fleay also says that the "miraculous maid" (II, 1,) is the maid of Confolens, 1604. I haven't identified this.

The other references which he cites as evidences of an early date are very doubtful.[2]

There is one other passage which bears on the date. "Why I but taught her a Spanish trick in charity and holp the King

---

[1] There was a seven months truce beginning April 24, 1607. For an account of the Siege of Ostend, etc., see Motley's *Uuited Netherlands*, Vol. IV.

[2] III, 1, p. 142. "You, politic Diego with your face of wisdom! Don Blirt!"

Fleay thinks that this refers to Middleton's play, *Blurt Master Constable* (4to, 1602). Don Diego, a famous and unsavory character, is mentioned in that play and in the *Famous History of Sir Thomas Wyatt* (1602), but he is frequently alluded to in the later dramatists, *e. g., Maid of the Mill* (licensed 1623), so the allusion does not indicate an early date.

V, 3, end. Alquazier. "You have married a whore, may she prove honest."

Perrato. "It is better, my Lord, than to marry
An honest woman that may prove whore."

Considerable ingenuity is required to find here, as does Fleay, an allusion to Dekker's play.

74

to a subject that may live to take Grave Maurice prisoner" (I, 2). This passage would most likely have been written when Maurice was at war with Spain. He was at war up to 1609, and then, after a truce of twelve years, again from 1621 to his death in 1625. So far the passage might have been written either at the time of the original or the revised version of the play; but Graf Maurice of Nassau became Prince of Orange in 1618, and if the passage was written in 1622 the latter title would naturally have been used. The passage, then, still farther proves that the date of writing of the original version corresponds with the date of the action, and that this date is before 1609 and probably 1605-8.

Thierry and Theodoret. First quarto, 1621; "As it was divers times acted at the Black Friers by the King's Majesties Servants:" no authors given. Quarto, 1648, "by John Fletcher." Quarto, 1649, "by F. Beaumont and J. Fletcher."

The quarto in 1621 was printed by T. Walkley, who, in 1620, printed an apparently pirated edition of *Philaster*, and in 1619 a quarto of *A King and No King*.[1] In a preface to the latter, Walkley addresses Sir Henry Neville, from whom he says he had received the manuscript, and he speaks of both authors as living. Beaumont had been dead three years, and Walkley evidently had no intercourse with Fletcher. The testimony of the quartos is as usual untrustworthy, but it is worth noting that as far as quartos go *Thierry and Theodoret* has practically as good evidence for an early date as *Philaster* and *A King and No King* and the same testimony to Beaumont's authorship as the *Woman Hater*.[2]

Mr. Fleay places the date about 1617, because he thinks the play a satire on the French court at that period. Mr. Fleay and Mr. Boyle think the play written by Fletcher, Massinger, and a third writer concerning whose identity they are in doubt.[3] Dyce and Macaulay find evidences of Beaumont's authorship which would require an early date; and Mr. Oliphant thinks the play was first written by Beaumont and Fletcher about 1607–8 and revised 1617 by Fletcher and Massinger. I shall try to show that there is good reason, apart from Mr. Oliphant's analysis, to conclude that the play was originally written at an early date and revised at a later date by Massinger. The proof of this proposition will depend mainly on an examination of the sources of the plot and a comparison of the play with the other romances by Beaumont and Fletcher; but at the start we must look at the authorship tests to see what warrant they give for

---

[1] In these two quartos Beaumont and Fletcher were named.

[2] *Woman Hater*, 4to, 1607, no author: 4to, 1648, "by J. Fletcher;" 4to, 1649, by F. Beaumont and J. Fletcher.

[3] Mr. A. H. Bullen adopts this analysis. Dict. Nat. Biog.

supposing that Massinger was a late reviser and Beaumont one of the original authors.

Besides the scenes which are variously assigned, four scenes (I, 1; II, 2; IV, 1; V, 2,) are assigned by every one to Fletcher; three others are assigned to Massinger by Fleay, Oliphant, and Boyle in his *Englische Studien* papers [1] (I, 2; II, 1; IV, 2). Two of the three remaining verse scenes are selected by Macaulay as most plainly Beaumont's, are assigned in large part by Oliphant to Beaumont, were assigned to Beaumont by Fleay before he had fixed on 1617 for the date, and are now assigned by Fleay and Boyle rather doubtfully to Field and Daborne, respectively. From an examination of Mr. Boyle's own verse tests, it will be seen that there is no great difficulty in accrediting these scenes to Beaumont; indeed a comparison with the verse tests of the two plays most probably wholly his entirely removes the difficulty.

	VERSE LINES	DOUBLE ENDINGS	RUN-OVER LINES	WEAK END-INGS	LIGHT END-INGS	RHYMES
Th. and Th. III, 1,	296	67	69	5	2	16
Th. and Th. III, 2,	70	15	17	2	1	2
Percentage,		22.4	23.6	1.9	0.9	4.9
Knight of the B. P.,		23.2	18.	0.7	—	23.4
Woman Hater,		17.	22.7	2.	0.5	6.8
Philaster (Beaumont's share),		15.2	26.2	2.4	—	1.2

So much for verse tests and Beaumont's authorship; Massinger's share in the play is not denied, and if Beaumont was one of the original authors Massinger must be counted a reviser. Mr. Oliphant, in fact, finds portions of scenes in which he thinks Massinger's revision of Beaumont's work is apparent, and there is one scene (II, 3) in which Mr. Boyle finds Massinger where the others find only Fletcher. Moreover, in a scene assigned by all three critics to Massinger (II, 1), there are two 'ems and eleven thems.[2] Even these two 'ems rather indicate that

---

[1] Eng. Studien, Vol. V.

[2] The 'ems and thems occur as follows :

I. 1.	6 'ems.	1 them.	F.	IV. 1.	1 'em.	2 them.	F.
I. 2.	0 'ems.	1 them.	M.	IV. 2.	0 'ems.	2 thems.	M.
II. 1.	2 'ems.	11 thems.	M.	V. 1.	1 'em.	8 thems.	B.? prose
II. 2.	5 'ems.	1 them.	F.	V. 2.	0 'ems.	2 thems.	F.
II. 3.	0 'ems.	2 thems.	?		—	—	
III. 1.	1 'em.	1 them.	B?	Total	16 'ems.	31 thems.	
III. 2.	0 'ems.	0 them.	B.?				

In the four scenes generally assigned to Fletcher there are 12 'ems 6 thems in 735 lines. In the three scenes assigned generally to Massinger, 2 'ems 13 thems (728 lines). In the two verse scenes assigned to Beaumont 1 'em 1 them (366 lines). The 'em-them test thus indicates that the division between Massinger and Fletcher is roughly

some one besides Massinger had a hand in the scene. Still further, in another scene assigned to Massinger (I, 2), there seems to me a noticeable difference in the style before and after the entrance of De Vitry. An application of the verse tests confirms my opinion.[1] Throughout the play, both in Fletcher's and Beaumont's parts, Massinger's work will similarly, I suspect, be found to be that of a reviser and completer.[2]

The sources of the plot were stated by Langbaine to be the chronicles of the time of Clotaire II: Fredegarius, Aimonius, Crispin, De Serres, and Mezeray. This statement has been frequently quoted by later writers, but an examination of the sources seems never to have to have been attempted. Mezeray[3] did not write until towards the end of the century, long after *Thierry and Theodoret;* the chronicles of Fredegarius and Aimonius[4] do contain the sources of the plot; but the immediate source seems to have been a work based on the chronicles. *Lez Antiquitez et Histoires Gauloises et Françoises,*[5] by M. Claude Fauchet was published as appears by the dedicatory letter, in 1599. This work may very readily have come to the hands of Beaumont and Fletcher and seems to have supplied all the historical matter they used. It follows the chronicles so closely that one cannot say certainly whether they used it or the chronicles, but its existence and vogue (several editions) at

---

accurate; but the 'ems in Massinger's part, and the large proportion of thems in Fletcher's, hint that the separation of the two authors is not exact.

1	VERSE LINES	DOUBLE ENDINGS	RUN-OVER LINES	WEAK END-INGS.	LIGHT END-INGS	RHYMES
I, 2, a, to De Vitry's entry,	78	18	41	6	4	2
Percentage,		23.1	52.6	7.7	5.	
I, 2, b, after De Vitry's entry,	54	23.	18.	1.	1.	2
Percentage,		51.9	33.3	—	—	—

The second part of the scene answers pretty well to the Fletcher canon though the number of run-over lines is a trifle large. The first part suits the Massinger canon better than the second, but the double endings are rather few and the run-over lines rather many. Add the two parts together and you get percentages which correspond fairly well with Massinger's work; which shows how easily verse tests may conceal rather than disclose double authorship. The verse tests I have given don't prove double authorship, but in substantiation of an opinion formed merely in reading the lines they are rather striking.

[2] This will have to rest on opinion; verse tests, at least, offer no sure help.

[3] Born 1610.

[4] I have not examined De Serres or Crispin.

[5] I have used an edition of *Les Oeuvres* de Fev M. Claude Fauchet, Paris, 1610; described as the "dernière édition"—"révisées et corrigées "—"supplées et augmentées.

this time make the probability great that Beaumont and Fletcher drew from it alone.[1]

The principal events which form the historical basis of the play are as follows:

1.[2] The kingdom is divided between Thierry and Theodoret, and Brunhalt (Brunhaud), having outraged the Austrasians by her cruelty, is expelled from the court of Theodoret and goes to that of Thierry. Historically, she is the grandmother of the two kings.

2.[3] The characters of Brunhalt and Thierry and their respective amours are distinctly outlined.

3.[4] Protaldy (Protand or Protadius), Brunhalt's minion, is elevated to the office of master of the palace. He is later killed by the nobles while seated in the tent of King Thierry, "jouant aux tables avec Pierre, premier médecin du Roy."

4.[5] This civil war between Thierry and Theodoret, thus prevented by the death of the leader, Protaldy, is urged on anew by Brunhalt. She incites Thierry by declaring that Theodoret is the son of a gardener, not of the king.

5.[6] Theodoret is defeated in battle, captured by Thierry, and put to death by Brunhalt.

6.[7] Thierry marries Ermemberge, daughter of the King of Spain, but he is prevented by Brunhalt[8] and her sister from ever living with his bride as husband, and Ermemberge is sent back to Spain.

7.[9] Thierry wishes to marry the daughter of Theodoret (who in the play is named Memberge, evidently suggested by Ermemberge), but Brunhalt opposes and now declares that Theodoret really was his brother. She finally poisons Thierry. This account[10] may be quoted in full to show how the historical narrative is made dramatic.

"Thiebert, Roy d'Austrasie auvit, comme i'ay dit laissé une tres belle fille, de l'excellente beauté de laquelle Thierry vaincu, desira l'auoir pour femme, contre la volonté de son ayeule; laquelle n'ayant fait difficulté d'espouser Merouée neueu de

---

[1] Apart from the dependence of the plot of *Thierry and Theodoret* on the historical narrative, there is evidence that Beaumont and Fletcher used either the chronicles or Fauchet. The name, Pharamond, in *Philaster* seems to be taken from Fauchet, it is the name of the first king of France. In Henry VIII, I, 3, l 10, (Fletcher's part) there is an allusion to Pepin and Clotaire.

[2] Book V, ch. 2, p. 151.

[3] Bk. V, ch. 2.

[4] Bk. V, ch. 2, p. 153.

[5] B. V, ch. 3, p. 153.

[6] B. V, ch. 4, p. 156.

[7] B. V, ch. 3, p. 154.

[8] In the translation of Mezeray "by the witchcraft of Brunhalt," etc.

[9] B. V, ch. 5, p. 157.

[10] *Ibid.*

Sigisbert son mary, maintenant se monstroit plus conscientieuse
à l'endroit de Thierry, & luiz mettoit deuant les yeux, que
ceste Damoiselle estant fille de son frere, il ne la pouuoit raison-
nablement espouser. Sur quoy Thierry presque forcené d'amour,
luy respondit; mechante ennemie de Dieu, ne m'as tu pas dit
qu'il n'estoit point mon frere? Pourquoy donc, si ceste cy est
ma niepce, m'as tu fait commettre un si detestable parricide? Je
t'assure que tu en mourras; & mettant la main à l'espee, sur
l'heure s'en alloit tuer son ayeule, qui ne la luy eust oster.
Toutesfois elle fut portee en sa maison, ayant eschappé la mort
toute certaine: mais retenant en son courage vn appetit de
vengeance qu'elle ne point longuement garder. Car à l'issué
d'un bain, elle fit presenter à ce Roy vn beuuage empoisonné
duquel il mourut aussi meschautement qu'il s'estoit desordon-
nément porté la reste de sa vie.''

Throughout the play as well as in the dramatization of this
chapter, the historical narrative is much changed, the chronological order is avoided, and many new situations are added.
We shall return later to a consideration of some of these
changes and additions; for the present we are to note that the
indebtedness of the play to the historical account is certainly
very considerable.[1] Any political references to the contemporary
French court made in Massinger's revision of the play would
not interfere with our hypothesis of an early date; but there
is no evidence of any satire on the court of Mary de Medici.

Mr. Fleay's evidence is: "The astrology of Lacure and the
name De Vitry distinctly point to the condemnation of Concini
in 1617 for treason and sorcery. Vitri arrested the Marechal
d'Ancre, and on his resistance killed him.''

Lecure, Protaldy's associate in villainy, is described as physi-
cian to Brunhalt and is obviously suggested by Protaldy's
companion in the chronicles, the "premier médecin du Roy.''
His astrology and the drugs by which he renders Thierry incapable seem, also, to have been derived from the actual practices
of Brunhalt in frustrating the marriage of Thierry and Her-
meric. For a contemporary prototype of Lecure there is no
need of going to France and the Concini case; a much better
example is to be found in the notorious Dr. Simon Forman, of
London, who was at the height of his quackery for the ten years
preceding his death, in 1611. Forman's practices,[2] exactly re-

---

[1] *Brunhowlte*, an old play of 1597, mentioned in Henslow's diary,
may have been at the basis of *Thierry and Theodoret*, but the latter's
obligation to the historical narrative is sometimes so minute, and the
development of the material so characteristic of Beaumont and Fletcher,
that I don't imagine they used the old play at all.

[2] *State Trials*, I, p. 339, seq. *Kennett*, Vol. II, p. 667. Forman was
consulted by Lady Essex (Frances Howard) and Mrs. Turner "how
they might stop the current of the Earl's affection toward his wife.''
"He made many little pictures of brass and wax '' . . . . "and

sembling those of Lecure upon Thierry, are related in the state trials and seventeenth century accounts of the career and trial of Frances Howard. Forman was well known and he was only one of many; such astrologers as Lecure and such practices as his were common enough. Their exploitation in this play can have no specific reference to Concini, but is clearly only the natural development of the direct suggestions of the historical narrative.

As to the name De Vitry, it is too common to point very closely at the Vitri who arrested Marechal d'Ancre. We learn from the letters of the French minister, Beaumont,[1] that there was a M. de Vitry in England 1603–5, "a perfect master of the science of the chase," sent by Henry to insinuate himself into James' favor. Moreover this name may have been derived directly from the chronicles on Fauchet. In Gregory of Tours[2]— of whose chronicle Fredegarius is a continuation—in an account of an expedition by Brunhalt and her husband against Chilperic, there is mention of a village "de nom de Vitry." In Fauchet[3] the village is à Vitry.

So much for Mr. Fleay's conjectures in the light of the play's sources; returning now to the dramatic development of the historical material, I find additional evidences of Beaumont's workmanship. Among the most notable situations added to the historical plot are (1) those involving Protaldy and (2) those involving Ordella. The Protaldy scenes have a very close resemblance to the Bessus scenes in *A King and No King*. In one scene[4] Protaldy, the braggart-coward, is kicked and deprived of his sword by Martell just as Bessus, a similar braggart and coward, is kicked and deprived of his sword by Bacurius.[5] In another scene[6] Protaldy is again disgraced and beaten by de Vitry as Bessus is beaten by Lygones.[7] Of the Ordella scenes, the final one,[8] a highly melodramatic dénouement, quite after the style of Beaumont and Fletcher's romances, closely resembles the dénoument of *Cupid's Revenge*. The hero dies by the hand of the wicked queen-mother; the heroine dies apparently simply for the sake of dying with her beloved; the

---

then with philters, powders, and such drugs, he works upon their persons." His powders, according to accounts, proved successful with the Earl and also with Mrs. Turner's lover. Forman was in great demand among the court people of the day, as his papers discovered at his death made evident.

[1] Translation of *von Raumer*, II, 201.
[2] Guizot's edition, Book IV, p. 231.
[3] B. III, ch. XVI.
[4] II, 2 (Fletcher).
[5] A King and N. K., III, 2.
[6] III, 1 (Beaumont?)
[7] A. K. N. K., V, 1.
[8] V, 2 (Fletcher). For other Ordella Scenes, see III, 1; IV, 1.

wicked queen-mother commits suicide; and the faithful friend is left to curse her and to lament his friend.

The development of the characterization even more closely resembles that of the other Beaumont and Fletcher romances. Ordella is merely named in the history; in the play she becomes another of the devoted, sacrificing, idyllic maidens so familiar in Beaumont and Fletcher. Martell, the blunt and faithful friend, and De Vitry, a sort of understudy, are not so much as hinted at in the history but are of a type familiar in the other romances and perhaps most highly developed in Mardonius of *A King and No King*. Protaldy in the chronicles is the par- amour of Brunhalt, but a man "subtil et habile en toutes actions;"[1] in the play he is developed into the utter poltroon and supplies the comic element. He reminds one very closely of Bessus in *A King and No King*. Brunhalt and Thierry are at least outlined in the history, but in the play they are developed much as their prototypes are developed in *Cupid's Revenge* from a similar outline in the *Arcadia*. Thierry resembles most closely Arbaces of *A King and No King*.[2]

These five types of character are the same five types that we find in *Philaster*, the *Maid's Tragedy*,[3] *A King and No King*, and *Cupid's Revenge*. The first three of these romances were probably written mainly by Beaumont, and he had a share of the fourth. These five types of character, on whose development the plays depend for their characteristic qualities, are certainly among the most salient features of Beaumont and Fletcher's work. They appear in every romance in which Beaumont had a share and they appear together in no play written by Fletcher alone and in no play of Massinger's. They are characteristic of the four plays mentioned above and of *Thierry and Theo- doret* and of no other.[4] The evidence, then, is strong that Beaumont had a share with Fletcher in creating *Thierry and Theodoret*.

Not only do these resemblances to the other romances point to Beaumont's authorship, they point in a still more definite way to an early date. In the method of dramatizing a short narrative, in the construction of the dénouement, and in the addition and development of certain fixed types of character; we have seen that the play resembles *Cupid's Revenge*. Still more specifically in the character types and distinctly in the braggart- soldier scenes, we have noted its resemblance to *A King and*

---

[1] Fauchet: B. V., ch. 3, p. 153.

[2] Thierry and Arbaces form a species by themselves, differing con- siderably from the other heroes. The Bauder and the rest are the ordinary comic people of the stage and readily suggested by the ac- counts of the amours of Brunhalt and of Thierry.

[3] Except the poltroon.

[4] *Four Plays* ought perhaps to be added to make the case even stronger, but all the five types do not appear there together.

No King. Furthermore I venture to conjecture that in the narrative passage quoted above from Fauchet and the situation developed from it in *Thierry and Theodoret*, we have the source of *A King and No King*.

No other source is known. The story of Tigranes and Aspatia is merely a variation of the Philaster-Bellario and Amintor-Aspatia situations, and the story of Bessus may well be a development of the Protaldy situations; but the main plot, the story of Arbace's love for his supposed sister, has no parallel in the plays of Beaumont and Fletcher unless it be the story of Thierry's love for his niece Memberge. In the history and in *Thierry and Theodoret* the situation is the same: the queen has two sons; she tells number one that number two is not her son and has him killed; then when number one is about to marry number two's daughter, the queen-mother declares that number two really was her son and that number one will commit incest if he marries the girl. In *A King and No King* the wicked queen pretends that she has a son; he falls violently in love with his supposed sister; the queen, who hates him and has tried to kill him, finally removes his fear of incest by declaring that really he is not her son. The actors are the same and the motives are the same as in *Thierry and Theodoret*, but the situation is exactly opposite. In *Thierry and Theodoret*, in order to prevent incest, the man who is supposed to be no king is shown by the queen to be a king and her son; in *A King and No King*, in order to prevent incest, the man supposed to be a king is shown by the queen to be no king and not her son.

I conjecture, therefore, that Beaumont and Fletcher, having taken the Thierry-Memberge situation from Fauchet and used it in the play, later developed that situation into the Arbaces-Panthea plot, changed it so as to have a happy ending, and thus created *A King and No King*. The other resemblances between the two plays—the two kings in each play, one of whom in each case is a somewhat furious ranter, the queen-mother who loathes her son, the cowardly soldier and the comic scenes—all these add to the plausibility of a direct connection between the two such as I have conjectured. Furthermore the elaboration of a slightly outlined motive into a series of effective situations and the addition of a happy dénouement are characteristic of the authors' dramatic methods and mark *A King and No King* as the later play. If, however, my conjecture seems to any one fantastic rather than plausible, it at least detracts nothing from the rest of our evidence.

Without relying on a conjecture so insusceptible of proof, we have no small accumulation of reasons for assigning the play in its original form to Beaumont and Fletcher and to a date earlier than 1611. The evidence of the quartos and folio is, so far as it goes, in harmony with this hypothesis. The opinions of critics and the evidence of verse tests point to Beaumont as one of the authors and to Massinger as a reviser. An examination of the sources shows that the authors probably drew their material from a history well known in the first decade of the century and enables us to decide that there is no evidence for the date 1617. Not only had Beaumont and Fletcher known the same source as early as *Philaster*, our examination further shows that *Thierry and Theodoret* was constructed from a narrative in much the same way as *Cupid's Revenge* and that in its most salient characteristics it is of the same type as the romances which Beaumont and Fletcher were writing prior to 1611. Beaumont's large share in these romances is a further indication of his share in this play, which is still further shown by its strong likeness to *A King and No King*. In this likeness I found ground for a conjecture in regard to the origin of *A King and No King* which indicates that *Thierry and Theodoret* preceded it. Even without this conjecture, the nature of our main hypothesis leads us to assign a somewhat early date; for if Massinger revised a play of Beaumont's at some time before 1619, the probability is strong that the play was an old and not very satisfactory one. The probability that Beaumont and Fletcher had read Fauchet when they wrote *Philaster* adds a little to the probability of an early date which we may fix conjecturally at 1607.[1]

Monsieur Thomas. First quarto, 1639. "Acted at the Private House in Black Fryers." "The author, John Fletcher, Gent." There is a dedication by Rich. Brome who speaks of the play as Fletcher's whose it undoubtedly is.

Mr. Fleay conjectures that this is *the Father's own Son*[2] on the 1639 list of the Queen's men. Brome was writing for the Queen's men at that date, and the play, therefore, seems to have been in their possession. Mr. Fleay concludes that it was not acted by the King's men, but must have come down to the Queen's men from the Revels children and must, therefore, have been acted about 1609, *i. e.*, before the Revels children left Blackfriars according to his theory. The only certain date for their removal from Blackfriars, however, is August, 1608; and if we adopt the rest of Mr. Fleay's plausible conjecture, the date is about 1607–8. There are bits of songs[3] which are

---

[1] The only allusion bearing on the date is in harmony with a very early date.

"Where would I wish myself now? in the Isle of Dogs, so I might escape scratching." III, 2.

This seems to be on allusion to Nash's *Isle of Dogs*, acted 1597 (Fleay, Chr. II, 149).

[2] See Fleay's comment on Halliwell-Phillips reprint of a droll of this name.

[3] III, 3. "Go from my window," etc. K. B. P., III, 5. III, 3, mention of the ballad of Mile End. K. B. P., II, 2.

also found in *the Knight of the Burning Pestle* which indicate that this date is approximately correct. Mr. Oliphant has also noticed that "come from Tripoli" occurs in Jonson's *Epicœne* (acted 1609), and as Jonson was some time in writing a play, this harmonizes with a 1607–8 date.[1]

Four Plays in One. First printed in folio of 1647. No list of actors is given in the second folio, so the presumption is that it was not acted by the King's men.

The critics are generally agreed in assigning the induction and the first two plays to Beaumont and the last two to Fletcher.[2]

The play is decidedly spectacular. There is the machinery of the scaffolding filled with spectators, and the place where "the mist ariseth, the rocks remove." Numerous gods descend, and there are many processions and dumb shows. The *Four Plays* are given in the form of an entertainment before a king and his bride, and the *Triumph of Time* has unmistakably the form of a court masque. Theme, spectacle, and dances, all follow the recognized fashion. Mercury and Time appear; "one half of a cloud [is] drawn," "singers are discovered," then the other half is drawn and Jupiter seen in his glory." The main masque is danced by Delight, Pleasure, Lucre, Craft, Vanity, etc., and there is also an anti-masque of a "Troop of Indians, singing and dancing wildly about Plutus." We have not merely an introduction of masque-like pageantry but a skillful effort to combine romantic drama and a court masque.[3]

The spectacular business with Cupids and deities and allegorical personages recalls *Cupid's Revenge* and makes it probable that the *Four Plays* were presented by a children's company.

The play has many correspondences with other of Beaumont and Fletcher's plays. In the induction the satire on the citizens suggests the *Knight of the Burning Pestle*, and a similar representation of citizens crowding to see a court pageant occurs in the *Maid's Tragedy*.[4] In the *Triumph of Death*, Gabriella's murder of Lavall recalls Evadne's murder of the king in the *Maid's Tragedy;*[5] in the *Triumph of Fortune*, the opening dialogue between Marius and Sophocles recalls the one between Arbaces and Tigranes in a *A King and No King;*[6] and in the *Triumph of Love*, Violante is of the Bellario-Aspatia type—a sort of half finished sketch.[7]

---

[1] *Englische Studien*, XV, 351.
[2] Mr. Oliphant also sees signs of Field.
[3] For discussion of the influence of the masque on drama, see Chap. VII.
[4] I, 2.   [5] V, 2.   [6] I, 1.
[7] For example, see her prattle at child-birth and in the scene where Ferdinand comes with the poison.

In one respect the *Triumph of Death* differs from Fletcher's other plays; it contains traces of the tragedy of ghosts and revenge which both Beaumont and Fletcher discarded.[1] The plot centers on the revenge upon Lavall, and a ghost appears and prophesies his fate. Further, the business of throwing down his heart is quite like the style of the tragedy of blood; and Perolot's advice—

"No; take him dead-drunk now, without repentance,
His lechery inseamed upon him."

—sounds like a bit from an old revenge play. Now Fletcher never elsewhere brings a ghost on the stage except in the *Humourous Lieutenant*,[2] and there in the form of a set of dancing spirits conjured up by a magician; the presence of a ghost here, then, seems to indicate that this was one of his earliest tragedies, written at a time when he was still slightly influenced by the ghost-revenge plays that we find so common from 1600 to 1607.

The probability that the play was presented by one of the children's companies for whom Beaumont and Fletcher were writing 1606–1611; the resemblance to other plays dating before 1611; and the agreement that Beaumont who probably retired about 1611, had a share in the composition; all make the date almost certainly earlier than 1611.

Owing to the presence of the ghost and the resemblances to the other romances and the somewhat less matured treatment in comparison with them, I conjecture a date several years earlier. The use of the anti-masque, however, fixes the early limit at the time of the introduction of anti-masques into the court masques, 1608.[3] I do not think the *Four Plays* much later than 1608.[4]

The Scornful Lady. First quarto, entered S. R., March 19, 1616. "As it was acted with great applause by the children

---

[1] There is the motive of revenge for a father in *Philaster*.

[2] There is a ghost in *the Lover's Progress* (III, 5) and there are spirits in the *Prophetess*, but both of these plays are in very large part by Massinger; in neither have we an admonishing, revengeful spirit as in the *Triumph of Death*.

[3] See p. 28 ante.

[4] Mr. Fleay fixes the date at 1608, because "the *Yorkshire Tragedy* was published 1608 (S. R., May 21) as 'one of the *Four Plays in One*,' as if to delude the unwary purchaser into the belief that he was buying one of the plays then being performed." All the other authorities that I have consulted (W. C. Hazlitt's Manual, 1892. Hans W. Singer, *Das Bürgerlich Trauerspiel*, 1891; Knight's and Malone's Editions of Shakspere) agree in stating that the reference to the *Four Plays in One*, is not in the 1608 quarto of the *Yorkshire Tragedy*, but only in the 1619 quarto. I have not been able to examine the 1608 quarto and so cannot be sure of the facts; the 1619 quarto is as described by Hazlitt and the others. Fleay's conjecture, even if based on fact, is by no means certain.

of her Maiestie's Revels in the Blackfriers.'' Beaumont and Fletcher are both named as authors, which is doubtless correct.

Mr. Fleay thinks it was acted not later than December, 1609, for then, according to his theory, the Revels children left Blackfriars, nor earlier than 1609, for then began the Cleve wars referred to in act V, scene 3. Since he thinks that the theaters did not open until after the deaths from the plague dropped below forty a week (they exceeded forty up to Nov. 30, 1609), and since he thinks the King's men occupied the theater December 25, he has the date of the play fixed within about two weeks. We have already seen that the theories by which he reaches this conclusion are groundless.

There are a couple of difficulties apart from his theories which he has not noticed. In the first place, it is by no means certain that the statement in the quarto of 1616 refers to the play's first presentation. The play was a popular one, and the reference may quite as plausibly be to the 1616 performance. Rossiter's company was also known as her Majesty's Revels and played in Whitefriars 1610–15, but in 1615–17 was attempting to build a new theater in Blackfriars. The play may have been given there. *Amends for Ladies*, 1618, was published as acted at the Blackfriars both by the Prince's servants and the Lady Elizabeth's, and may, as Fleay suggests, have also been acted at this new Blackfriars.[1] More plausibly, perhaps, the allusion to Blackfriars may indicate that the old theater was sometimes temporarily occupied by other companies than the King's men.

In the second place, it is very doubtful if the passages referring to the Cleve wars were written as early as 1609. The facts about the Cleve wars are as follows:[2] John William, Duke of Cleves, died March 25, 1609. A quarrel ensued in regard to the succession, and Leopold of Austria took possession of the capitol, Juliers. The assassination of Henry IV of France (April, 1610), interrupted his plans against Austria, but on Sept. 1, 1610, Prince Maurice of Orange took Juliers with the aid of troops supplied by France and the English forces then in the service of the States under Sir Edward Cecil. The "cast Cleve captain"[3] in the play must refer to these English auxiliaries, but they took no part in the war earlier than 1610, and there was in fact no fighting until 1610. So, although the passages may date any time up to 1614, when the wars closed, they could hardly have been written as early as December, 1609.

There is still further evidence in this matter in several allusions to Cleve wars in Field's *Woman is a Weathercock*[4] where

---

[1] Chr. I, 201.
[2] *The Life and Death of John of Barnevelt.* J. L. Motley. Vol. I, 60–66. *Rapin*, Vol. IX, p. 324.
[3] V, 4.   [4] I, 2.

one of the characters is about to start for Cleveland. This play dates between Jan. 1610 and Nov. 1611.[1] The reference in the *Scornful Lady* may well enough date at about that time.

Other allusions in the play are indecisive as to date, but on the whole class it with plays at least as early as 1610–11. "Knights of the Sun, Rosicleer,"[2] refers to the *Mirrour of Knighthood* (1602), also alluded to in the *Knight of the Burning Pestle*. There is also an allusion to Madcap,[3] a pamphlet by Nicholas Breton, also alluded to in the *Coxcomb*.[4] A reference to building a hospital recalls a similar one in the *Woman Hater*.[5] There is one certain[6] and one possible[7] slur at *Hamlet*. The reference to the Apocrypha[8] probably cannot refer to a discussion about the authorized edition as Mr. Fleay thinks.

On the whole, while the allusion in the quarto to Blackfriars is puzzling, there is little question that the play is as early as 1611.

Wit at Several Weapons. First printed in folio of 1647. No actor-list. A passage in the epilogue at a late revival refers to Fletcher as the author and rather implies that he only wrote a part of the play.

Mr. Fleay identifies it with the *Devil of Dowgate*, licensed 1623, but his reasoning does not enable me to see the slightest connection between the two titles. All the critics discover the work of one or more writers besides Fletcher: Mr. A. W. Ward, Mr. Macaulay, and Mr. Oliphant giving a share to Beaumont. Mr. Fleay assigns the play to Fletcher and Rowley, Mr. Boyle to Fletcher and an unknown; Mr. Bullen is reminded of Middleton and Rowley. Admitting the possibility of a revision, I think it probable that a part of the original play was by Beaumont.

A good deal of the play is in prose, where the determination of authorship is very precarious, but the Pompey part is much like the burlesque in the *Knight of the Burning Pestle* and the *Woman Hater* and seems probably by Beaumont. In the verse scenes generally assigned to another author than Fletcher, the verse tests also agree with those for the *Knight of the Burning*

---

[1] Fleay, Chr. I, 185.
[2] IV, 1.
[3] II, 1.
[4] I, 4.
[5] IV, 2.
[6] II, 1.
[7] III, End.
[8] I, 2. "I'll hear no more of this Apocrypha; bind it by itself, steward." The Apocrypha was generally separated from the rest of the bible in English bibles, and the passage has only a general reference.

Pestle.[1] The proportion of double endings is a little large and of run-on lines a little small for the averages set up by the verse analyzers of Beaumont's other plays, but even in comparison with these there is no great discrepancy, particularly in the case of the first scene of the last act. If we remember that his work may be present only in an altered form, there is no improbability in assigning a portion of the play to Beaumont. If there is any evidence of a date as early as 1611–12, the evidence of his hand becomes convincing.

The internal evidence, although not convincing, seems to favor such an early date. In I, 2. Priscian, a pretended soldier is introduced as a veteran of twenty years service. He then goes on to state that his first battle was " Alcazar in Barbary, where Stukely fell and royal Sebastian." This was in August, 1578. He then goes on to tell of Sebastian's rumored escape and various journeyings, which were matters of common report,[2] and next to describe his last battle, " that memorable skirmish at Newport" with special praise of the Scotch forces. This was July 22, 1600. The details given of the battle and the account of Sebastian make it probable that they were written not very long after 1600. Such a reference might have been made as late as 1620, but in thus padding his dialogue, a writer for the stage would be much more likely to refer to events still familiar to the public.

In I, 2, the puppet show of Ninevah is alluded to as also in the *Knight of the Burning Pestle*,[3] *Bartholomew Fair*,[4] and

---

[1] The *Woman Hater* is generally assigned to Beaumont alone, the *Knight of the Burning Pestle* seems to me also his in the main.

	VERSE LINES	DOUBLE ENDINGS	RUN-OVER LINES	
Wit at Several Weapons, II, 2,	221	57	43	
" " " " II, 4,	89	25	19	
" " " " V, 1,	151	27	26	
Total,	461	109	88	
Percentage,		21.1	19.1	
Woman Hater,		17	22.7	
Knight of Burning Pestle,		23.2	18	
Philaster,		15.2	26.2	Philaster serves fairly for Beaumont canon.
Percentage of V, 1 (Wit at Several Weapons) alone,		18	17.2	

Mr. Boyle, whose figures I have taken in the above table, strangely assigns IV, 2 and IV, 3 to the second author (not Fletcher.) They seem to me clearly Fletcher's, as the verse tests strongly indicate.

[2] See Dyce.
[3] III, 2.
[4] V, 1, (1614).

88

Every Woman in Her Humour.[1] There is also an allusion[2] to "a play at the Bull t'other day," but the date of the opening of the Red Bull is uncertain. The scoff is similar to those in the *Burning Pestle.* An allusion to the two exchanges[3] must date after the erection of the new exchange. It was begun in 1608 and finished in 1609. This may be an addition of the late revisers; it is in the Rowley part as assigned by both Fleay and Oliphant. If in the first form of the play, that cannot be earlier than 1609.

These last allusions would fit in well enough with a 1609–10 date, although the speeches of the soldier would fit better a date several years earlier.

The Captain. First printed in folio of 1647. Played at court by King's men in winter 1612–13.[4]

In the folio of 1679 the scenes are marked and the following list of actors given: Richard Burbage, Henry Condell, William Ostler, Alexander Cooke. All four played in Jonson's *Alchemist,* acted by the King's men, 1610, and in *Catiline,* 1611. Ostler joined the King's men from the Revels children probably in 1608;[5] Cooke died Feb. 25, 1614, and was 'sick of body' Jan. 30, 1614.[6] The date of the play is thus fixed 1608—Jan.–March, 1613, date of court presentation.

Mr. Fleay thinks the present version with the "scene, Venice, Spain," is an altered version made for the court performance. Fleay, Macaulay, Boyle, and Oliphant, all give Beaumont a share in the play, though they all think his share slight.[7]

The song "Tell me dearest what is love?" is found in part in the *Knight of the Burning Pestle;* the allusions to Lusty Lawrence and Don Diego are common in plays of this period and indicate nothing definitely in regard to the date. A passage closely resembling one in the *Faithful Shepherdess* has been noted by Mr. Boyle.[8]

The play cannot be later than 1612, and a reasonable conjecture is 1611.

Second Group. Plays from 1612 to 1618, inclusive.

There is no convincing evidence that Beaumont had a share

---

[1] 4to, 1609, acted 1602? (Fleay.)
[2] II, 2. See note p. 60 for date of opening Red Bull.
[3] V, 1.
[4] So Fleay ; according to Oldy's Ms. note in Langbaine, May 20, 1613, but this date doubtless applies to the payment not the performance.
[5] See p. 19 ante.
[6] See *Memoirs of Principal Actors in the Plays of Shakespeare.* J. P. Collier. Shaks. Soc., 1846, p. 187.
[7] This play furnishes a good example of Mr. Oliphant's subtle analysis. He divides it between Fletcher, Fletcher and Beaumont, Beaumont, Fletcher and Massinger, Beaumont and Massinger, Rowley.
[8] *Englische Studien*, VIII, 40, Act I, sc. 3.

in any of these plays. They were written by Fletcher or by Fletcher in collaboration with other authors. In three plays, *Henry VIII*, the *Two Noble Kinsmen*, and *Cardenio*, there is evidence that he collaborated with Shakspere, and these plays have been discussed in connection with Shakspere's plays of this period. Six of the remaining plays were acted by the King's men and have lists of actors in the 1679 folio, so their dates are determinable with some certainty. Of the remaining plays, several afford no clue in respect to their date. They have no lists of actors and are possibly by other companies than the King's men, and are, therefore, assigned by Mr. Fleay to 1613–16, when he thinks Fletcher was writing for the Lady Elizabeth's men. We have seen how little evidence this supposition affords. I assign these plays to the 1612–1618 period, because the 1619–1625 period is fully provided for, and because there is no evidence for dating them earlier than 1612. I present notes only in the case of plays where Fleay's conclusions require important modification.

Four of the plays are of very doubtful date.

The Bloody Brother; or Rollo, Duke of Normandy. The play has sometimes been dated after Jonson's *Neptune's Triumph*, Jan. 6, 1624, because of a supposed imitation in Act II, scene 2; but it is doubtful if there is any imitation, and if there is, who was the imitator. Fletcher undoubtedly had a share in the play, and there is some ground for Mr. Oliphant's suggestion that the play was re-written more than once, but the exact authorship and the approximate date are both apparently insoluble.

The Nice Valour; or the Passionate Madman in its present form is probably a revision, dating after 1624. Mr. Fleay dates the original play 1613, but his evidence is extremely doubtful.

The Nightwalker; or the Little Thief was licensed in 1633 "as corrected by Shirley." Fleay's conclusion, that it was originally an early play for some other company than the King's men, is reasonable. A number of allusions to books (III, 3,) have not been identified, but may not "a new Book of Fools" be Armin's Nest of Ninnies, 1608?

The Beggar's Bush. Dekker's *Bellman of London* (1608) was evidently used by the authors, and this is the only safe clue to the date.

The remaining plays of the group may be dated with more confidence.

Love's Pilgrimage. Folio, 1647; no actor-list. Mr. Fleay attempts to identify it with *Cardenio* (S. R., 1653) and *Cardenno*, acted at court, 1612–13. Not only does he advance no evidence to support this theory; he unwittingly disproves it. "That the date of the original play was 1612, I have no doubt," he says, and then goes on to state that it is founded on Cervantes *Las das Doncellas* one of the *Novelas Exemplares*, but these were first printed in 1613. The play, therefore, cannot be *Cardenio* and must date after 1613.

Bonduca. Folio, 1643: list of actors in second folio. Field, who apparently joined the King's men about 1616, is not on the list. Ostler is on the list, and his name appears in none of the 1616–19 plays. For these reasons Fleay dates the play before 1616. All of the eight actors on the list acted in *Catiline*, 1611, and all but two, Ostler and Robinson, in the *Loyal Subject*, 1618. The date, then, may be as early as 1611 or as late as 1616. William Eggleston, whose name is on the three lists, seems to have left the King's men for a period including 1613, when he acted in the *Honest Man's Revenge* with the Lady Elizabeth's men. Cooke and Hemings acted in *Catiline* but not in *Bonduca;* Cooke died Feb. 25, 1614. Thus it seems probable that *Bonduca* was first played after Cooke's retirement and after Eggleston's return from the Lady Elizabeth's company: *i. e.*, 1614–1616.

Valentinian. The actor-list points to a date very close to that of Bonduca.

The Knight of Malta. There can be no doubt that this play like others which have both Field and Burbadge on the list, dates 1616–19. Mr. Macaulay and Mr. Boyle, however, both found evidence of Beaumont. They did this in ignorance of the late date of the play; Mr. Fleay gives their Beaumont portion to Field. Mr. Oliphant is in doubt between Field and Beaumont and gets out of the difficulty by considering the play a revised version by Fletcher, Massinger and Field of an old play by Beaumont. Some parts of the play certainly remind one of Beaumont, but there is no safe ground for Mr. Oliphant's hypothesis.

Third Group. Plays from 1619 to 1625, inclusive.

In this group we are able to determine the dates with certainty and definiteness. Moreover, so many plays must be assigned to these seven years, there is small probability that any other plays belong here. I have added nothing to Mr. Fleay's results and substracted little. The dates before 1622 are determined by the actor-lists or court presentations; from 1622 on, we have the dates of licensing in Herbert's office book.

The Wandering Lovers, licensed Dec. 6, 1623, is reasonably identified by Mr. Fleay with the *Lover's Progress.* Two other non-extant plays, *The Devil of Dowgate* and the *Unfortunate Piety*, he identifies with *Wit at Several Weapons* and *the Double Marriage*, respectively; but these identifications seem to me very doubtful. The *Coronation*, one of a number of plays not licensed until after Fletcher's death, was printed as his in

91

1640 and again in the 1679 folio, but was claimed by Shirley. *The Wild Goose Chase* was first printed in 1652, and *Sir John van Olden Barnaveldt* in 1883. All the other plays were first printed in the folio of 1647.

Conclusion.

The following list gives the plays by groups and in a conjecturally chronological order. The exact date of many of the plays cannot be determined. All plays in which either Beaumont or Fletcher had a share are included.

First Period.

Woman's Prize; or, The Tamer Tamed.	1604?
Wit at Several Weapons. First version.	1605?
The Woman Hater.	1606?
Love's Cure, or The Martial Maid.	1606?
Thierry and Theodoret.	1607?
Monsieur Thomas.	1607–8?
The Knight of The Burning Pestle.	1607–8?
Four Plays in One.	1608?
The Faithful Shepherdess.	1608?
Philaster; or Love lies a-bleeding.	1608?
The Coxcomb.	1609?
The Maid's Tragedy.	1609?
Cupid's Revenge.	1609–10?
The Scornful Lady.	1610–11?
A King and No King.	1611
The Captain.	1611?

Second Period.

The Nice Valour; or the Passionate Madman.	1612??
The Night Walker; or the Little Thief.	1612??
The Beggar's Bush.	1612??
Cardenio.	1612–13
The Mask of The Inner Temple.	1613
The Two Noble Kinsmen.	1613?
Henry VIII.	1613?
The Honest Man's Fortune.	1613
Wit Without Money.	1614?
Love's Pilgrimage.	1614?
The Faithful Friends.	1614?
The Chances.	1615?
Bonduca.	1615?
Valentinian.	1615–16?
The Jeweller of Amsterdam.	1616–17?
The Bloody Brother; or Rollo, Duke of Normandy.	1617??
The Queen of Corinth.	c 1617
The Loyal Subject.	1618

The Mad Lover.   c 1618
The Knight of Malta.   c 1618

Third Period.

The Humourous Lieutenant.   c 1619?
Sir John van Olden Barnaveldt.   1619?
The Custom of the Country.   c 1619
The Double Marriage.   c 1619
The Laws of Candy.   c 1619
The Little French Lawyer.   c 1620
The False One.   c 1620
Woman Pleased.   c 1620
The Island Princess.   c 1620
The Pilgrim.   c 1621
The Wild Goose Chase.   c 1621
The Prophetess.   1622
The Sea Voyage.   1622
The Spanish Curate.   1622
The Maid in The Mill.   1623
The Lover's Progress (The Wandering Lovers).   1623
The Fair Maid of The Inn.   1623-4
A Wife for a Month.   1624
Rule a Wife and Have a Wife.   1624
The Noble Gentleman.   1625?
Coronation.   1625??
The Elder Brother.   1624-5??

   The Devil of Dowgate and The Unfortunate Piety are non-
extant, and it is not certain that Fletcher had any share in
them.
   In the eight years covered by the first group I have assigned
sixteen plays; in the seven years of the second group, twenty
plays (including one masque); in the seven years of the
third group twenty plays and probably two others left unfinished. In the third group where the dates are fixed, Fletcher
on the average wrote the whole or parts of three plays a year.
The second period shows about the same average production,
and the first considerably less. An examination of the entire
chronology thus does not diminish the possibility of assigning
other plays to the first period. The dates of a number of the
plays in the second group are purely conjectural, and some of
them might as well be assigned to the first period. The first
versions of some of the later plays may also belong, as Mr.
Oliphant thinks, in the first period. At all events the entire
chronology strengthens rather than weakens the probability that
sixteen plays at least can be dated before 1612.
   Of the plays of the first group, without considering the
eight I have conjecturally placed there, the eight certainly

acted before the end of 1611 present such variety of theme and method that a considerable period must be allowed for their production. It is a long way, for example, from the immature burlesque and the experimenting in Jonson's manner of the *Woman Hater* to such an original and brilliant comedy as the *Scornful Lady*. Beaumont's poetic development was certainly remarkably rapid, but when we consider that the plays which have given him a high rank among English poets and won him an immediate contemporary reputation among the first dramatists were probably all written by the close of 1611, it is impossible to believe that his first play was produced so late as 1607. When we consider the range of plays written by Beaumont and Fletcher in collaboration, the success they attained, and the fame of their partnership, it is impossible to limit the period of their collaboration to four years.[1] Judging merely from their eight plays certainly acted before 1612, we might feel confident that Beaumont and Fletcher began writing earlier than 1607. In considering the few facts known of the lives of these two friends, we found a number of indications that they commenced their dramatic careers earlier than has generally been stated; and there was absolutely no reason to believe they had not commenced as early as the production in 1605 of *Volpone* to which each contributed verses. A study of their lives and plays amply substantiates the definite evidence furnished by the *Woman's Prize, Love's Cure*, and the *Woman Hater* that Beaumont and Fletcher were writing plays 1604–1606.

Among the plays surely acted by the end of 1611, we find four—*Philaster*, the *Maid's Tragedy, Cupid's Revenge*, and *A King and No King*—which present a definite type. These, with the *Four Plays in One*, and *Thierry and Theodoret*, which I also assign before 1611, form a series of romances which possess common characteristics. These plays, while showing marked similarities in material, characters, situations, and general treatment, present differences in versification and methods of construction which require more time for their production than Mr. Fleay assigns.[2] Critics, for example, generally note the marked development in Beaumont's style from *Philaster* to the *Maid's Tragedy*. There seems, too, some ground for saying that the *Four Plays* mark the experiment, *Philaster* the development, the *Maid's Tragedy* the perfection, and *Cupid's Revenge* the recapitulation; and similarly that *Thierry and Theodoret* is an experiment in a form of which *A King and No King* is the more highly developed representative. Such conjectures aside, it is important to remember that these romances repre-

---

[1] *Cf.* Fleay who limits it to 1608–1611.
[2] Fleay places *Philaster*, the *Maid's Tragedy, Cupid's Revenge*, and *A King and No King* in the years 1610–11.

sent practically the whole of Beaumont's life work. While we must make due allowance for the precocity of his genius and of Fletcher's, we may safely conclude that their romances did not have their origin, development and perfection all within a year or two. An examination of those six plays must convince any one that our chronology is conservative in assigning early dates.[1] Plays like the *Maid's Tragedy* and *A King and No King* are not written without some experimenting ; the six romances must cover a period of several years preceding 1611.

This conclusion is of particular importance with reference to the date of *Philaster*. According to Dryden it was the first play of its authors that was popular, and no one questions that it preceded the *Maid's Tragedy* and *A King and No King*. We have also seen reasons to think it earlier than *Cupid's Revenge*. These considerations support the generally accepted conjecture that the date of *Philaster* is as early as 1608.

At all events, Beaumont and Fletcher had produced four, and probably six romances, by the time that Shakspere had written three, and they had written at least four, and probably ten, other plays by the end of the same period. They were then recognized as leading dramatists of the day. There is no certain early limit for the date of any of these sixteen plays except *A King and No King* and the *Scornful Lady*. Some of them were probably acted as early as 1604–5 ; and of the romances, *Philaster* is certainly not one of the latest.

While we cannot be certain about the date of *Cymbeline*, the *Winter's Tale* and the *Tempest* were not acted until after *Philaster*. That play was certainly acted by the King's men while Shakspere was still writing for the company. So, probably, were others of Beaumont and Fletcher's plays ; their fame was certainly high before he retired from the theater. Our investigation makes it probable that *Philaster* and other of their romances preceded any one of his. The bare facts make it clear, that, so far as the chronology is concerned there was opportunity for direct influence between Beaumont and Fletcher and Shakspere.

---

[1] *Cf*. Mr. Oliphant's Chronology.

CHAPTER VI.

THE DRAMA, 1601–1611.

Before proceeding to examine and compare the romances of Beaumont and Fletcher and those of Shakspere, it is necessary to understand the condition of the drama when they were written. Only by a comparison with contemporary plays can we determine in what respects the romances of either Beaumont and Fletcher or Shakspere represent a distinct dramatic type. Certainly these romances were not complete innovations. By 1609 very little will be found in plots, situations, or types of character which had not been tried before. In the thirty preceding years, a host of ingenious play-wrights had been experimenting with new forms and developing old ones; and by 1609 the dramatists had a valuable fund of both experimental and successful work by which they were quick to profit. The romances of Beaumont and Fletcher belong to an advanced stage in the rapid development of the Elizabethan drama; they naturally owe much to all that had gone before; but we can judge of their novelty from a study of their immediate contemporaries.

A glance at the kinds of plays which prevailed on the stage when Beaumont and Fletcher began to write will also help us in answering other questions. Even if their plays form a distinct class, were they not the natural outcome of manifest dramatic tendencies of the time? Supposing that their romances are found to resemble Shakspere's, may not this similarity be due to the fact that romantic plays were common at the time, that many dramatists were experimenting in the field, that romance was in the air? If the resemblance between the two sets of romances can be established, can we argue that one must have been the cause and the other the effect? Evidently such questions can be convincingly answered only by reference to the plays acted before and during the years of the romances.

From 1601 to 1609, from *Twelfth Night* to *Cymbeline*, we know that Shakspere was writing plays very different in most respects from his romances. During that period Beaumont and Fletcher were beginning their dramatic careers and trying various kinds of plays. Possibly as early as 1607 they produced their first romance; by the end of 1611, they had produced the six plays which for our purpose exemplify the type. By this time Beaumont had apparently finished his dramatic work, and the reputation of both men before the public and among their fellow-poets was very high. Shakspere's three romances were produced with some certainty in the years 1609–1611. Hence the period which we must examine for plays offering resemblances to the romances and for any influences which might have led to the romances is the decade preceding 1611. That will take us back to the time when Shakspere turned from English histories and romantic comedies to tragedies and to several years before Beaumont and Fletcher began to write for the stage. It is not likely that they were influenced very extensively by plays earlier than 1601. Many of these were to be read in quartos and some still held the stage, but Beaumont and Fletcher shared with some other dramatists of the time in a growing consciousness of the requirements and possibilities of their art and certainly had no intention of returning to the practices of earlier days. They were young men, the avowed disciples of Jonson, and apparently on friendly terms with Chapman, Webster, and Shakspere, and they wrote their most successful plays for a company which was then producing many of Jonson's most carefully wrought dramas and Shakspere's great series of tragedies. They began to write, moreover, just at the culminating time of the Elizabethan drama. The period 1601–1611 is the period of Dekker, Heywood, Middleton, Chapman, Webster, of Jonson's best work, and of the full maturity of Shakspere's genius. An examination of the plays of these years will certainly show various influences which acted on Beaumont and Fletcher and will also include all the data necessary for determining to what extent they produced a new type of romantic drama.

Such an examination to be absolutely thorough would involve a research into the chronology of all the plays of the period. I cannot attempt this and must rely on the investigations of others, especially those of Mr. Fleay. Fortunately, however, we can obtain a practically exhaustive list of the extant plays which were first acted in this decade 1601–1611. Henslow's *Diary* 1601–1603, the lists of plays published on the breaking up of the various children's companies, Jonson's statements in the folio edition of his plays, and the researches of Shaksperean students furnish a good deal of indisputable evidence. Probably the only plays which we shall be in danger of omitting are some which may have been first acted in this period but were greatly revised at a later date. We can certainly obtain a fairly accurate idea of the kinds of plays which prevailed in the decade. Here I shall endeavor to include in a rough classification all the extant plays which were probably acted in these years and such non-extant plays[1] as belong indisputably to any one of the groups. I cannot analyze any of

---

[1]Non-extant plays will be marked n. e.

these plays carefully, but a hasty grouping will be sufficient to indicate the important facts in this decade of the drama, and will show the relation of Shakspere's and Beaumont and Fletcher's romances to the rest of the drama.

Some of the plays which were exceedingly popular had no direct connection with the work of either Shakspere or Beaumont and Fletcher. The latter wrote most of their romances for Shakspere's company, and they have only satire for the rude plays which entertained the audiences of the Curtain or Red Bull. A large number of plays preserved by name in Henslow's *Diary* (1601–1603) and some still later belong, so far as material and construction go, to the earlier days of Hieronimo and Stukely. They cannot, however, be neglected in a summary of the drama's history.

A number of these can be classed as 'plays of adventures.' They were generally dramatic renderings of stories of travels and consisted of rudely connected representations of improbable and stirring adventures. In method they were similar to the chronicle-histories of ten years before. Their popularity and general style can be judged by this list.

The Bold Beauchamps. n. e.

A Christian turned Turk; or the tragicall lives and deaths of the two famous pirates, Ward and Dansiker.

The Conquest of the West Indies. n. e.

Fortune by Land and Sea. (Plot partly from the accounts of the pirates, Clinton and Tom Watson.)

The Four Prentices of London with the Conquest of Jerusalem.

History of Richard Whittington. n. e.

Siege of Dunkirk; with Alleyn the pirate. n. e.

Travels of Three English Brothers.

Beaumont and Fletcher wrote no plays of this class, but *Pericles* offers some notable resemblances to this type.[1]

Chronicle-history plays, dealing generally with events of English history, form another large class. Beaumont and Fletcher together never dealt with a topic from English history, and Shakspere's *Macbeth* and *Lear*, while exhibiting many of the characteristics of the class, must be grouped with tragedies rather than histories. *Henry VIII*, however, belongs with this group. Most of these plays were as rudely constructed as in the days of *Henry VI*.

Cardinal Wolsey's Life. n. e.

Conquest of Spain by John of Gaunt. n. e.

Earl of Harford. n. e.

Honourable Life of the Humourous Earl of Gloster, and his conquest of Portugal. n. e.

---

[1] See Appendix.

If you know not me, you know nobody, or the troubles of Queen Elizabeth. 2 parts.
Life and Death of Lord Cromwell.
Malcolm, King of Scots. n. e.
Mortimer. n. e.
Nobody and Somebody, with the true chronicle-history of Elidure. A revision (?).
Philip of Spain. n. e.
Richard Crookback. alterations. n. e.
Rising of Cardinal Wolsey. n. e.
Sir Thomas Wyatt, Famous History of. 2 parts.
When you See Me, etc. (Henry VIII.)
The Whore of Babylon. (Allegory of the Armada, etc.)

We may also note here several other plays of a historical character.

The Devil's Charter, life and death of Pope Alexander 6.
King Sebastian of Portugal. n. e.
The Unfortunate General, a French History. n. e.

Four other plays may be classed as spectacular entertainments, although Dekker's *If it be not good*—is in part a satirical comedy.

England's Joy.
The Golden Age, with the loves of Jupiter and Saturn.
Necromantes. n. e.
If it be not good, the devil is in't.

We come now to the tragedies of the period. In the years just preceding 1601, domestic tragedies, founded on actual contemporary murders, were very popular. Plays of this type were also presented after 1600, and one of them, the *Yorkshire Tragedy*, has on considerable external evidence sometimes been assigned to Shakspere.

The Bristol Tragedy. n. e.
The Chester Tragedy. (Randal, Earl of Chester.) n. e.
The Miseries of Enforced Marriage.
The Yorkshire Tragedy.

Under the head of 'tragedies of blood,' a large number of Elizabethan plays may be included. One of the most important species of this genus is the tragedy of revenge, generally based on the revenge of a father for a son, like the *Spanish Tragedy*, or the revenge of a son for a father, like the original *Hamlet*. Marston's two plays, *Antonio and Mellida* and *Antonio's Revenge*, in 1599, contributed to this species ; and Shakspere's *Hamlet* may have been produced in response to the stage demand for plays of this sort which was apparently strong in 1600–3. The familiar story of a son's revenge on his father's murderer certainly stirred the imaginations of lesser men as

99

well as Shakspere. Plays based on this plot, all probably before 1604, are:
Jonson's *Additions to the Spanish Tragedy*.
The Atheist's Tragedy.
Hamlet.
Hoffman.
Other tragedies of blood, in which the motive of revenge plays a leading part are:
Bussy D'Ambois. 2 parts.
Byron. 2 parts.
The Duchess of Malfi.
The Revenger's Tragedy.
The White Devil.
These plays contain much intrigue, many physical horrors, and many deaths; and deal with revenge, ghosts, insanity, and utter villainy. The tragedy of blood, then, received development from Tourneur, Chapman, Webster, and Shakspere. It was a very important and a fairly distinct type throughout this period, but it exercised very little influence on Beaumont and Fletcher. Their romances do not exhibit ghosts, churchyard scenes, many assassinations; nor do they elaborate stories of revenge.[1] They do not lack in murder and intrigue, but *Thierry and Theodoret* is the only one which could be placed in the most liberal classification of tragedies of blood. There are practically no signs of that type in *Philaster*, the *Maid's Tragedy*, and *A King and No King*.

Tragedies with subjects from classical history form another class of plays popular in this decade and include among their authors Marston, Jonson, and Shakspere. Fletcher later wrote *Valentinian*, but while working with Beaumont made no contribution to this class.

Antony and Cleopatra.	*Philotas*.
Appius and Virginia.	*Nero*.[2]
Cæsar's Fall. n. e.	*Rape of Lucrece*.
Catiline.	*Sejanus*.
Coriolanus.	*Sophonisba*.
Hannibal and Scipio. n. e.	*Timon of Athens*.
Julius Cæsar.	

These classes nearly exhaust the tragedies of the period. The extant plays which remain unclassified are:
Cynthia's Revenge, or Menander's Ecstasy.
The Insatiate Countess.
Lear.
Macbeth.
Othello.

---

[1] See, however, *Four Plays in One*, p. 85, ante.
[2] Possibly not acted.

The Second Maiden's Tragedy.
The Turk, with the Death of Borgias, etc.
Two of these, the *Insatiate Countess* and *Second Maiden's Tragedy*, were not acted till 1611 or later. Others might have been classed in other groups. *Lear*, for example, might have been placed either with the chronicle-histories or the tragedies of blood. Two other tragedies, probably to be dated later than 1611, were, according to Mr. Fleay, acted in some form in this period: the *Noble Spanish Soldier* and the *Virgin Martyr*. Finally, three non-extant plays on biblical themes should be grouped together.

Jephtha. n. e.
Joshua. n. e.
Samson. n. e.

None of these plays can be suspected of influencing to any extent the romances of Beaumont and Fletcher.

In all the tragedies we find no prototypes of Beaumont and Fletcher's romantic tragedies, but on the contrary the prevailing types, tragedies on classical themes and tragedies of blood, are differentiated in kind from such plays as the *Maid's Tragedy,A King and No King*, and *Philaster*. They also differ in kind from Shakspere's romances. They do not even offer any hint of such combinations of tragic and idyllic elements as we find in both sets of romances. One characteristic which distinguishes most of these tragedies will further illustrate their wide divergence from the romances. Since the time of Marlowe's *Tamberlaine*, English tragedies had generally presented the life and death or the revenge of some central figure who dominated the stage during most of the five acts and who gave his name to the play. This character usually had a part suited to violent action and stirring declamation; about him centered the entire interest of the play. This general form prevailed through the period 1601–1611 as the mere names of Shakspere's tragedies will testify—*King Lear, Macbeth, Othello, Coriolanus*—or the names of most of the tragedies of varying types—*Bussy D'Ambois, Byron, Sejanus, Catiline, Hoffman, Samson*. Even this general characteristic will not be found to distinguish the romances of either Shakspere or Beaumont and Fletcher. Even without a careful analysis of the leading traits of the romances, we may safely call them innovations in the field of tragedy. They did not change or develop the old types. Those continued to exist as recognized dramatic forms for many years. Fletcher himself wrote tragedies dealing with English and classical history as late as 1616, and long afterwards Shirley's *Cardinal* reproduced most of the features of the revenge species of the tragedy of blood. So far as tragedy was concerned, the romances were simply an unexpected departure.

We come now to comedy, in which the most important influence during this decade seems to have been Jonson's. In the well-known prologue to *Every Man in His Humour* (1598), he made open war on the chronicle-history plays and declared his intention to present one play such as other plays should be, with

> "deeds and language, such as men do use,
> And persons such as comedy would choose,
> When she would show an image of the times
> And sport with human follies, not with crimes."

In this play he initiated the comedy of humours which he established in a series of remarkable plays and defended and explained in various prologues and addresses. Most of the comedies written in the first decade of the new century seem to have profited by his precept and example. Their predominant trait is realism.

It is difficult to classify them. Many are mainly satirical in purpose. Some of these, like the *Poetaster*, contain personal satire and are connected with the "war of the theaters" existing at the beginning of our period; others indulge in a more general satire of London manners and morals. Some, like Jonson's plays, are devoted to the elaboration of humours; others might be classed as comedies of intrigue, carrying on the plots inherited from Plautus and Terence, but containing a good deal of humoristic caricature. Others deal less satirically and more sympathetically with domestic scenes and motives. Some few are sentimental comedies. In any arrangement the classes will not be wholly exclusive, but they will show that the comedies of the period were not romantic in character but were satirical, realistic, and domestic.

After Jonson, Middleton is the most important contributor to the comedy of this period, and his career illustrates the prevalence of realistic comedies of manners. About 1600 he was writing comedies more or less romantic, with scenes in foreign places and involving a mixture of tragic and comic events. Of this class are the *Old Law* (1599–1600) and *Blurt, Master Constable* (1600–1601); but even these plays abound in satirical pictures of London manners. From the beginning of our period to its close his comedies are invariably social satires; the *Phœnix*, the only one with a romantic plot, being especially satirical. The others are all comedies of manners with realistic plots of intrigue and with the scenes in London or vicinity. *A Mad World, My Masters*, the *Phœnix, Five Witty Gallants*, the *Family of Love, A Trick to Catch the Old One*, and *Michælmas Term* were all published by 1608 and were acted during the five preceding years by the Pauls or Revels boys. Nor did Middleton's comedies of manners cease then. Two others, *A Chaste Maid of Cheapside*, and *No Wit, no*

Help like a Woman's may be dated somewhere in the ensuing five years. *A Match at Midnight* and the *Puritan*, also comedies of manners with scenes in London, were probably written by Middleton during the years 1601–1611;[1] and The *Roaring Girl*, which he wrote in collaboration with Dekker, is a realistic comedy of London life but treats its theme more sympathetically than any other of Middleton's. His great contributions to the romantic drama come much later. During the years 1601–1611 he was solely occupied with realistic comedies of London life largely satirical in purpose.

There are a dozen other comedies of the period which can be described, like Jonson's and Middleton's, as realistic comedies, largely satirical in purpose. Chapman's comedies, like *Volpone*, treat of English manners under foreign names, but most of the others have their scenes in England. Some are mere comedies of intrigue without much satirical purpose, but none are sympathetic in their description of English life and none have any points of similarity with romantic comedies like *Much Ado* and *Twelfth Night*. Some of Beaumont and Fletcher's early comedies which might be included in this list will be spoken of later; it includes all other satirical and realistic comedies of the decade.

The Alchemist.	*No Wit, no Help like a*
All Fools.	*Woman's.*
A Chaste Maid of Cheapside.[2]	*The Phœnix.*
Cupid's Whirligig.	*The Poetaster.*
The Devil's Law Case.	*The Puritan.*
The Dutch Courtesan.	*Ram Alley.*
Epicœne.	*Satiromastix.*
Every Woman in Her Humour.	*Sir Giles Goosecap.*
The Family of Love.	*Tale of a Tub.*
The Fawn.	*A Trick to Catch the Old One.*
Five Witty Gallants.	*Volpone.*
The Fleire.[3]	*Westward, Ho!*
Greene's Tu Quoque.	*What You Will.*
A Mad World, My Masters.	*The Widow's Tears.*
A Match at Midnight.[2]	*The Wise Woman of*
May Day.	*Hodgsdon.*
Northward, Ho!	

In some other domestic and realistic comedies of the time, the purpose is not at all satirical but rather a sympathetic portrayal of various phases of English life. The best of these

[1] See Fleay *Chr.* and Bullen's edition of Middleton; introduction, lxxix.

[2] Possibly later than 1601.

[3] The classification of this curious play is especially difficult. It is a sort of tragi-comedy, but the scene is London and the purpose, so far as there is any, seems to be largely satirical.

is Heywood's sentimental comedy, *A Woman Killed with Kindness*. Most of the others are less masterly in treatment and are devoted to the exploitation of some trade or of some especial feature of London life. Some, like Dekker's *Honest Whore*, are in a considerable part satirical and contain caricatures like "the humours of the patient man," which form the sub-plot of that play. All are realistic in contents and treatment, and their domestic character separates them entirely from the romantic drama.

Eastward, Ho!
The Fair Maid of Bristow.
The Fair Maid of the Exchange.
The Honest Whore. 2 parts.
How to Choose a Good Wife from a Bad.
The London Prodigal.
The Merry Devil of Edmonton. (Perhaps earlier than 1601.)
The Roaring Girl.
A Shoemaker is a Gentleman.
Six Clothiers. 2 parts. n. e.
Six Yoemen of the West. n. e.
A Woman is a Weathercock.
A Woman Killed with Kindness.

The comedies of the period might be classified in other ways. In the early years of the century there was a series of plays dealing with conflicts between wives and husbands—*A Woman Killed with Kindness*, the *Honest Whore, with the humours of the patient man*, *Patient Grissel* (1599), *Medicine for a Cursed Wife* (n. e.), Shakspere's *Taming of the Shrew* (revised after 1600), and Fletcher's *Woman's Prize*. Another group might be made of plays which are concerned chiefly with satire of citizens' wives; another group from plays presenting scenes in houses of ill fame. There are also some plays which must be classed as romantic and not as realistic comedies. Before passing to these we must note that all the comedies so far mentioned are absolutely distinguished in kind from the romances.

The prevalence of realistic comedy, however, had its effect on Beaumont and Fletcher and also on Shakspere. *Troilus and Cressida*, while dealing with a classical theme like the tragedies, certainly shows signs of the satirical impulses which dominated the poets of the time. *Measure for Measure*, while it must be classed with the tragi-comedies of the period, deals in its comic scenes with the same phases of life as many of Middleton's comedies. According to our chronology the first three plays by Beaumont and Fletcher belong to the class of comedy of manners—the *Woman's Prize, Wit at Several Weapons*, the *Woman Hater*—and the last is decidedly in Jonson's manner. *The Knight of the Burning Pestle*, though of an original species, is certainly in the satirical genus. Three other of their comedies of this period have their scenes in London—*Monsieur Thomas*, the *Scornful Lady*, and the *Coxcomb*. The first two are farces dealing with manners; the last contains a sentimental love-story similar to those in the romances and may be considered with *Love's Cure* and the *Captain* as examples of romantic comedy.

It is among the romantic rather than the realistic comedies that we should naturally look for any influences leading to the romances, but there are almost no romantic comedies in this period. Three of these by John Day form a class by themselves—*Isle of Gulls*, *Humour out of Breath*, *Law Tricks*. They abound in satire, some of which seems to have been personal, but each has a romantic plot with many fantastic elements. Some of the incidents, the wit-combats, and the balancing of lovers and ladies remind us of Lyly's comedies. They are artificial, Arcadian fancies, distinguished by much lively humor and quite unlike any other plays of the time. They are also very different from the romances. Middleton's *Phœnix*, and some of Chapman's realistic comedies have already been mentioned as containing some romantic elements; in two others by Chapman, these elements are sufficient to warrant the term romantic comedy. *Monsieur D'Olive* is a sort of romantic comedy of humours of no interest in connection with the romances, but the *Gentleman Usher* is one of the few plays of the period with sufficient mixture of tragic and comic events to be classed as a tragi-comedy.

The most noticeable thing about the tragi-comedies of this period is their scarcity. There are few to be placed with *Philaster*, *A King and No King*, *Cymbeline*, a *Winter's Tale*, and the *Tempest*. Many of the plays, to be sure, contained some mixture of tragic and comic scenes, and the histories and plays of adventure combined a great variety of incidents, but the tragedies were mostly very tragic and the comedies satirical or farcical in tone. Some of the domestic comedies, notably *A Woman Killed with Kindness*, appealed chiefly to the emotion of pity, and some of the satirical comedies had touches of tragic sentiment; but these are hardly more than the exceptions which prove the rule. There are very few plays which combine tragic and sentimental stories and lead them to a happy ending after the fashion of Shakspere's earlier comedies or of a chronicle history like *James IV*. There are almost no romantic tragi-comedies. In fact, including *Measure for Measure* there are only five which offer the slightest generic resemblance to the heroic tragi-comedies like *Philaster* and the *Winter's Tale*. One of these, *A Poor Man's Comfort*, was probably not acted until after 1611, certainly not early enough to have influenced Beaumont and Fletcher; the others are the

Gentleman Usher, the *Dumb Knight*, and the *Malcontent*. The *Gentleman Usher* contains a mixture of humouristic pictures of manners, of a sentimental love story, and of the tragic accompaniments of the loves of the old duke and his son for the heroine. The ending is happy. The *Dumb Knight* has a by-plot of intrigue with the usual satire on lawyers and the morals of city wives, but the main-plot is heroic and romantic. The long declamations, the two trials by combat, and the general method of construction differentiate it distinctly from Beaumont and Fletcher's work. The *Malcontent* resembles Beaumont and Fletcher's romances in one particular; it deals with events wholly tragical and leading to a tragical conclusion which is unexpectedly changed to a happy ending. The material, however, is that of a tragedy of blood after the style of *Antonio and Mellida* and quite unlike Shakspere's or Beaumont's combination of tragic and idyllic incidents. *Measure for Measure* hardly needs comment; no one would think of finding close resemblances between it and any one of the romances.

We are not to discuss here the characteristics of the romances, and we need not pause to distinguish them further from these tragi-comedies. The few examples of this class show that there was almost no experimenting with romantic material. Even the sentimental love story so prominent in the romances of both Beaumont and Fletcher and Shakspere fell into disuse. Of course there were love stories, but there were not many sentimental heroines who suffered everything for their lovers in the drama from 1601 to 1608. Even girls in boys' clothing were rare, though they were plentiful enough before 1601 and equally common in plays by Fletcher and others after 1611. When a woman does appear in boys' clothes, as in the *Honest Whore*, the *Dumb Knight*, *May Day*, and *Ram Alley*, she bears far less resemblance to the heroines of the romances than do the earlier heroines of Shakspere, or Greene or even Lyly. Shakspere was not alone in abandoning the love-lorn maiden and the romantic incidents attaching to her situation. During the years following 1600, most of the dramatists were engaged on material where the boy and girl love story had no opportunity for prominence. In fact, to find any close resemblance to the material of the romances, we must go to plays acted before 1601. The method of Greene's *James IV* is twenty years behind that of the romances, but its stories of violent passion and sentimental love offer more resemblance to the material of the plots of *Philaster* and *Cymbeline* than anything by contemporary dramatists in the years 1601–1611.

The list of all the plays in this period which can be classified as romantic comedies or tragi-comedies will again emphasize their scarcity.

Alls Well that Ends Well.   (Probably before 1601.)
The Captain.
The Coxcomb.
The Dumb Knight.
The Gentleman Usher.
Humour out of Breath.
The Isle of Gulls.
Law Tricks.
Love's Cure.
A Poor Man's Comfort.   (Probably after 1611.)
The Malcontent.
Measure for Measure.
Monsieur D' Olive.[1]

Of these thirteen plays, two belong outside the period or on its extreme limits, three are a peculiar sort of comedy by Day, four more are by Shakspere or Beaumont and Fletcher. One of these, the *Coxcomb*, is properly a domestic comedy, but is included here because its sentimental story is closer to the romances than any other plays on the list. Four plays remain. They certainly demonstrate the barrenness of the period in any plays which would stimulate or suggest any return to the romantic comedies of the previous century or a development of a new romantic type of heroic tragedies and tragi-comedies.

Our examination of the plays of the central period of the Elizabethan drama reveals several facts of importance for our main investigation. We have found that the important contributions to the drama were either satirical and realistic comedies or thorough-going tragedies of fairly definite classes. In the development of realistic comedy, Dekker, Heywood, Middleton, and Jonson contributed. Chapman, Tourneur, Webster, and Jonson, as well as Shakspere were writing tragedies. There was very little romantic comedy, or tragi-comedy, and almost no plays which could be classed as heroic romances. There are only two or three unimportant plays which have even a few of the most noticeable characteristics of the romances— a mixture of tragic and idyllic events, a series of highly improbable events, heroic and sentimental characters, foreign scenes, happy dénouements. We are justified in concluding that when in 1609 Shakspere turned from tragedy to romance he not only departed from his practice of the past eight years, but also from the practice of his contemporaries during that

---

[1] *Pericles*, which might be included in this list, seems to me to belong rather with the plays of adventure. With this list we have classified all the extant plays of the period with the exception of a few closet dramas which were not acted; Daniel's Queen's *Arcadia* and Fletcher's *Faithful Shepherdess*, pastoral plays on the Italian model; and *Two Maids of Mortclake*, apparently a history, which I have not been able to examine.

period.[1] So far as we can determine, without anticipating our analysis of Beaumont and Fletcher's romances, we may conclude that they also marked a distinct departure from contemporary practice.

The plays of other dramatists than Shakspere and Beaumont and Fletcher indicate no promise of such a departure. With all the romantic plays of the preceding decade to draw upon, the dramatists in this period turned to farces, satires, and tragedies. Their work shows no influences working for a revival of romanticism; in the plays of the masters there is nothing to indicate that they would not continue to write historical tragedies and London comedies of manners for another decade. It seems clear that neither set of romances can be considered the direct result of dramatic forces or fashions existing 1601–1611. So far as they constitute a development of a new type of drama, that development seems to have been the work of Beaumont and Fletcher or Shakspere.

We can now examine the two sets of romances themselves and determine their characteristics and consider the questions how far either constitutes a distinct type and what resemblances exist between them. If we find that Beaumont and Fletcher's do form a definite type similar to Shakspere's, we shall be free to face the further questions—did Shakspere influence Beaumont and Fletcher or did they influence Shakspere? While we must keep in mind the influence of other types, of current fashions, of contemporary methods in which none of our authors may have been inventors, still we may feel confident that the appearance of the nine romances in the years 1607–1611 was due primarily to the innovation of either Shakspere or Beaumont and Fletcher.

---

[1] An equally important conclusion may be drawn concerning his change from romantic comedies and chronicle-histories to tragedies, at about 1601. Here, also, he seems to have been following the general dramatic movement. Our investigation also suggests that his choice of themes from 1601 to 1608, and in some measure his treatment of them, were conditioned by the practice of the dramatists of the period—possibly quite as much as by his own personal experiences. In the light of contemporary plays, *e. g.*, the difference between *Measure for Measure* and *Twelfth Night* certainly seems less significant of Shakspere's emotional experiences than has often been assumed. The fact that while his contemporaries were busy with satirical comedies he kept his plays so free from satire, perhaps affords a safer hint at Shakspere's personality and artistic emotions.

CHAPTER VII.

GENERAL CHARACTERISTICS OF THE ROMANCES OF BEAU-
MONT AND FLETCHER.

Six plays by Beaumont and Fletcher—*Philaster, Four Plays in One, Thierry and Theodoret, The Maid's Tragedy, Cupid's Revenge,* and *A King and No King*[1] possess such marked resemblances that they may fairly be said to constitute a distinct type of drama. This ' romance ' type is exemplified to a less degree in other of their plays; but these best illustrate its characteristics, and, as we have seen, were all probably acted before the close of 1611. We shall examine them in order to discover their common characteristics and to note how these characteristics distinguish them from preceding Elizabethan plays. We shall consider in order their plots, characters, style, and stage effect.

One interesting field of investigation we shall hardly touch upon—their indebtedness in particular scenes or details to preceding plays and especially to Shakspere's. I shall try to show that in their main features they were novel plays, and I shall compare them at every point with Shakspere's romances; but it is manifestly outside of the purpose of this investigation to consider all the debts of Beaumont and Fletcher to their predecessors. They doubtless owed much, particularly to Shakspere. The scene between Melantius and Amintor in the *Maid's Tragedy* (III, 2) seems imitated from passages between Brutus and Cassius, and *Philaster* has some obvious likenesses to *Hamlet.* I shall note such resemblances, however, only when they seem of importance in relation to my hypothesis that the romances form a new type of play. We must grant that Beaumont and Fletcher owed much to their predecessors, but we are particularly concerned with their own contributions to the development of a type. Their indebtedness to Shakspere's preceding plays may be cheerfully admitted to have been considerable, but the purpose of this investigation is to discover whether Shakspere owed anything to them.

A. *Plots.*

Beaumont and Fletcher, like all Elizabethans, took the material of their plots from wherever they could find it. They

---

[1] Beaumont probably had the larger share in these romances, but I shall not attempt to differentiate the work of the two partners.

did not, however, go to English or classical histories [1] nor did they rely on Italian novelle, but, perhaps following Jonson's example, they usually exercised great ingenuity in inventing plots. Thus, their most notable plays, *Philaster*,[2] *the Maid's Tragedy*, and *A King and No King*, have original plots. Even when, as in *Cupid's Revenge* and *Thierry and Theodoret*, they found their material already in narrative form, they developed the action very freely by the addition of a number of incidents to furnish excitement and vicissitude. Often they devised unique and fantastic stories as in *Love's Cure*, where the main action deals with a girl who has been brought up in the wars as a boy and a boy who has been brought up at home as a girl; or as in *Monsieur Thomas* where the hero tries to convince his father, who desires him to be a rake, that he is a prig, and to convince his sweetheart, who desires him to be a prig, that he is a rake. The plots of the romances are equally ingenious and improbable, abounding in violent and unnatural situations.

Even in their comedies Beaumont and Fletcher did not often base their plots on a satire of existing conditions, nor did they attempt to treat motives which should find readiest illustration in incidents of contemporary life. In their romances there is still less of the realism which prevailed on the stage from 1601 to 1611. These have no relationship to comedies of intrigue or satires of London life or to domestic dramas of sentiment like Heywood's *A Woman Killed with Kindness*. They deal with heroic persons and heroic actions, with kings and princes and noble soldiers, with queens and princesses, with conquests, and usurpations and revolutions and passions which ruin kingdoms. But, unlike most Elizabethan plays dealing with similar material, they are not historical; nor do they deal with the well-worn motive of revenge. For tragic stories of royal persons, Beaumont and Fletcher did not go, like so many of their contemporaries, to classical history; they went to the land of romance. They located their plays in any place far enough away to permit of strange happenings: in Angiers, Armenia, Austracia (all these places were scenes of their romances), Lycia, Rhodes, Messina, Milan, Lisbon, and Athens. The actions which go on in these places have little to do with the real life of any historical period, they belong to the land of romance—or rather to a stage which required strangeness and variety.

The plots of the romances, however, have a certain uniformity. A story of pure, sentimental love is always given great

---

[1] This is true only of the plays in which Beaumont had a share. Fletcher used ancient and English history and Spanish novels.

[2] In this play they make use of the familiar story of a son's revenge for his father; but this is slightly developed, and the main plot, so far as is known, is their invention.

prominence, and this is always contrasted with a story of gross, sensual passion. The complications arising from this favorite contrast of love and lust give an opportunity for all kinds of incidents involving jealousy, treachery, intrigue, adultery and murder. Each play has its idyllic scenes in which the pure and love-lorn maiden plays her part, and each play abounds in broils and attempted seductions and assassinations. While all this commotion is being aroused in the passions of individuals, thrones are tottering and revolutions brewing. The two main motives of sentimental love and unbridled sexual passion are, in fact, sometimes drowned out by the succession of violent emotions and the great variety of incidents.

Not only did Beaumont and Fletcher seek after wide variety of action, they sought as well for variety of emotional effect; and this characteristic separates their work from that of contemporary Elizabethan dramatists even more decidedly than does the range of their circumstantial invention. To be sure, the presentation in the same play of unrestrained passion and pretty sentiment, of mental agony and comic buffoonery, was common enough on the Elizabethan stage, but they indulge in such contrasts to a greater extent than preceding writers. In Marston's *Malcontent*, for example, one of the few tragi-comedies acted between 1600 and 1608, we have a tragedy of blood turned into a comedy. All the accompaniments of his tragedies appear : an adulterous woman, villainous men, intrigue, stabbing, poisons, a masque disclosing the villainy, but the disguised duke prevents the intrigues of the villain and in his triumph forgives or refuses to punish instead of taking revenge. The emotions excited have little variety, they are of the kind which usually accompany a tragedy of horrors. In *Thierry and Theodoret*, Beaumont and Fletcher were working with a narrative containing material similar to the *Malcontent*, a story of adultery, poisoning, blood, and horrors. Into this plot they introduced the story of the saintly Ordella, which supplies not only one of their best situations, but is full of sentiment and pathos. In this way they always present a variety of highly contrasted emotions ; they never construct a play about one central passion. Thus, except in the *Triumph of Death* and as a subsidiary motive in *Philaster*, they avoided revenge as a central emotion,[1] although it had been used within a decade by Marston, Tourneur, Chapman, Webster, and Shakspere. They did not write any tragedies after Marlowe's style with a central, predominant passion. None of their romances can be said to be a tragedy of jealousy like *Othello*, or a tragedy of ingratitude like *Lear*, or of ambition like *Macbeth*. Though they all involve contrasted love-stories, each deals with the

---

[1] *Cf.* the number of passages in their plays burlesquing *Hamlet*.

most varied emotional results of these stories and with other emotions almost wholly disconnected. Thus *Philaster* exhibits irresolution of the Hamlet type, jealousy at least as poignant as Leontes: Megra's reckless effrontery, and Euphrasia's idyllic self abnegation, as well as the love of Philaster and Arethusa and the contrasted passion of Pharamond and Megra. In short, Beaumont and Fletcher did not trace out the sequence of emotions which would follow from an actual situation, they sought to contrast as many varying emotions as possible. They never strove to keep on one emotional key; they sought for an emotional medley.

The plots of their romances, then, resemble one another in their two main motives but are for the most part original. In their avoidance of domestic or historical material, in their preference for improbable and varied incidents, and in their preference for intense and varied emotions, their choice of material differs from that of their predecessors and is radically romantic.

In their construction of this material into dramatic form there are also some distinguishing traits. The material of the romances is enough to separate them as a class from the plays acted 1601–1611, and the construction on the whole is likewise divergent from Elizabethan practice. They did not observe the Aristotelian unity of action any more closely than their predecessors, but they did discard some archaic methods and thus secured a greater coherency of action. The old method of the chronicle histories was by no means dead in 1600. Not only does it appear in many of the crude historical plays of the time, it is also discernible in some of the great tragedies. *Hamlet* was described in the quartos as "a tragical history" and *Lear* as "a true chronicle history;" and all of Shakspere's great tragedies follow in their construction the chronological outline of a historical narrative. Shakspere, to be sure, changes the order of events in *Lear*, adds new situations and characters, and arranges a new dénouement; so did Marlowe in *Tamburlaine*, and all the Elizabethans deal very freely with historical facts. In a great tragedy like *Lear*, however, in spite of the advances over the days of *Henry VI*, the method is still that of linking together a number of scenes to represent a period of history or the events of a life. It retains something of the epical character of the construction of *Henry VI* and *Tamburlaine;* moreover, camps, heralds, parleys, and battles supply, as in the early chronicle histories, a semblance of scenic effect and historical atmosphere. Beaumont and Fletcher in their romances utterly disregarded the methods of the chronicle histories. In *Thierry and Theodoret*, for example, all the battles and their accessories, with which the historical narrative is filled, are omitted, and the scenes are pretty closely confined to the palaces of the two kings. In all the romances, in fact, there is not a single battle, no army ever appears, there is but one camp scene,[1] and the action is mostly confined to apartments of the palaces. Beaumont and Fletcher had no thought of following in the least historical events, no intention of imitating history. They sought to present a series of situations, each of which should be interesting of itself and should contrast with its neighbors, and all of which should combine sufficiently to lead up to a startling theatrical climax. There is nothing epical about their construction; it is not truly dramatic like that of Shakspere's tragedies where the action is in part developed from character; but it is skillfully suited to theatrical effectiveness.

Such a method involved great care in the development of separate situations. They are not always developed with truth to life or consistency in characterization, but they always give an opportunity for variety and intensity of action. A girl disguised as a boy is stabbed by the man she loves; a woman convicted of adultery boldly defies her accusers and slanders the princess; a king is in love with his supposed sister; a king is persuaded to kill the first woman coming from a temple and encounters the queen, who is unknown to him—these are examples of situations which Beaumont and Fletcher found sufficiently strong. They enveloped their princes and ladies in a series of bewildering and immensely stirring circumstances, and they developed each improbable circumstance into an effective theatrical situation. Each situation may not promote the main action; I am far from asserting for them absolute unity of action, but each situation has enough action of itself to have made it telling on the Elizabethan stage.

Their by-plots are not very closely connected with the main plots and they frequently indulge in passages of poetic description of the style that Mr. Wendell calls operatic, but both these lyrical interludes and the by-plots usually play a part in heightening the main action. Moreover there are practically no scenes in their plays like Act II scene 4 in *Macbeth* where the old man and Ross and Macduff discourse on the events of the preceding act; nor like the opening of Act III in *Lear* where Kent explains to the gentlemen the progress of the story; nor even like Act V, scene 2 in *Hamlet* where Hamlet narrates to Horatio the experience of his voyage. A comparison of *Philaster* and *Much Ado* will further illustrate Beaumont and Fletcher's development of circumstances into acting situations. In each play an innocent lady is basely slandered by a conscienceless villain. In *Much Ado* we have an expository scene (I, 3) in which Don John confers with his accomplices, explains

---

[1] *A King and No King.* I. 1.

his attitude and starts out in his villainy. In the next scene he appears again and begins his slandering (II, 1, 160–180). The next scene (II, 2,) is wholly expository and explains the villain's scheme. Finally (III, 3), Don John brings his accusation against Hero before Claudio. In *Philaster* there are no expository scenes, Megra is detected in her crime and furiously overwhelms the king with her accusation against his daughter. (II, 4.) Beaumont and Fletcher rarely make use of a scene merely for narrative or expository purposes; in their romances, when once started, the action never stops.

It cannot be asserted that in this respect Beaumont and Fletcher differ absolutely from their predecessors. I think there is, however, a difference in skill. Considered merely as opportunities for variety and intensity of stage action, the situations in the romances can hardly be equalled. There is also a difference in degree. Like Sardou and other romanticists of this century, and to a greater degree than other dramatists of their own time, Beaumont and Fletcher sacrificed atmosphere, characterization, and verisimilitude in their eagerness to secure theatrical effectiveness.

The care which they took to secure an effective dénouement is another important element in their method and, like their care in the development of acting situations, must have contributed to the popularity of their plays. The dénouement is never simple; it never turns out in just the way one would expect; it never has the inevitableness of great tragedy. On the other hand it is never, as in *Measure for Measure*, a long explanation of entanglements which the audience already understands. It usually does exhibit the lively variation of incidents, the succession of sharp surprises that we expect in effective melodrama.

Take, for example, the dénouement of the *Maid's Tragedy*. The climax of the action is reached in the scene where the king is murdered by Evadne, his mistress, whom he had married to Amintor. A single scene[1] serves to unite the stories of Evadne and Aspatia, whom Amintor had forsaken for Evadne, and carry on the action to the final catastrophe. Aspatia, disguised as her brother, comes to Amintor, determined to provoke him to fight and thus to enjoy the sad pleasure of dying by the hand of the man she loves. He refuses to fight the brother of the woman he has wronged and laments his falseness to Aspatia. She goads him to fight and finally charges him with cowardice. Then he draws, and after a pass or two of the swords, she falls, apparently dead. Evadne then enters, "her hands bloody with a knife," and announces to Amintor that she has just killed the king and begs him therefore to grant her his

---

[1] v. 4.

love. Amintor turns away, horrified by the two murders and the reawakened consciousness of his love for this guilty woman, whereupon Evadne stabs herself with the fine acting cry—

> "Amintor, thou shalt love me now again:
> Go; I am calm. Farewell, and peace forever!
> Evadne, whom thou hat'st, will die for thee."

Amintor returning strives in vain to stay her hand, and then soliloquizing over the two bodies, resolves to bear them company, but long sbefore he dies to beg Aspatia's forgiveness. While he is speaking she revives and hears his closing lament. She lives long enough to make herself known and dies in his arms.

> "Give me thy hand; my hands grope up and down,
> And cannot find thee; I am wondrous sick:
> Have I thy hand, Amintor?"

Then, after vainly striving to bring her to life, Amintor stabs himself.

> "Must I talk now? Here's to be with thee, love!"

Here we have a number of situations, some not uncommon on the stage, welded together in a dénouement which is perhaps unequalled by any other in the Elizabethan drama in its power to hold the interest of an audience at fever heat. It holds this interest, moreover, after a scene of the greatest acting power; it solves the difficult dramatic problem of maintaining the interest from the climax to the catastrophe. And yet this is no more than a fair example of the care with which Beaumont and Fletcher invariably heightened their dénouements. While joining and contrasting a large number of situations, involving all sorts of vicissitudes and misfortunes, while infusing each situation with dramatic power and advancing to an intensely powerful climax, they also seem to have been more careful than their contemporaries in the development of a striking stage dénouement.

Another marked characteristic of their romances is their use of tragi-comedy. The term had been in use at least since the days of Edwards's *Damon and Pithias*, "a tragicall comedy," licensed in 1567; and Elizabethan plays had been in general, as Sidney charged, neither right tragedies nor right comedies. There were many plays before 1601 with a mixture of tragic and comic material and many plays like *James IV* or *Much Ado* which introduced a happy dénouement as the end of a tragic action. Few plays of this latter sort, however, are to be found after 1600 and before 1608-9; only four, in fact, are extant that could be classed as romantic tragi-comedies, *the Gentleman Usher, the Dumb Knight, the Malcontent*, and *Measure for Measure*. Beaumont and Fletcher's use of tragi-comedy was something of an innovation and it also involved some development in that type.

This is shown by considering some of the characteristics we have already noted in their material and construction. The excitation of a great variety of emotions, especial skill in developing the chances for powerful action in each situation, care for an effective dénouement—these are traits which mark a development in tragi-comedy as well as tragedy. Tragi-comedy is a term covering so many kinds of plays that it is difficult to differentiate Beaumont and Fletcher's contribution to that kind of drama from their contribution to the drama in general. We may, however, say that their tragi-comedies are especially distinguished from earlier ones by their constant and violent contrast of the varying emotions suited to tragedy with those suited to comedy and by their peculiar handling of the happy ending.

They are constantly joining the emotions arising from sentimental love with those arising from the most tragic circumstances. Now in the tragi-comedies immediately preceding we have the tragic results of villainy converted into happiness, but sentimental love is not prominent. Impending tragedy is not always struggling with sentimental bliss. In Beaumont and Fletcher's hands, for example, Mariana's love-lorn devotion to Angelo would have been highly developed and formed a by-plot of the play, or perhaps Isabella would have been distinguished by a sentimental devotion to some lover in the power of the villain. In Marston's *Malcontent*, the gross passion of Aurelia would have been contrasted with the pure love of some other woman; Malevole might have been accompanied in his retirement by some Bellario instead of being provided with a constant wife who remains in seclusion.

To find a union of sentimental and tragic interest in romantic plays before Beaumont and Fletcher, we shall have to go back before 1600 to plays like *James IV* and *Much Ado*. The romances differ from these in the dramatic heightening of the conflict between the tragic and sentimental emotions. *Much Ado* is a sentimental comedy turned to tragedy by slander and jealousy and then to a comedy again by discovery of villainy. In *James IV*, unrighteous passion seems likely to lead to tragedy, but sentimental love conquers and brings about final happiness. In *Philaster* and *A King and No King*, sentiment has no such simple conflict with evil. Through the five acts pure love is constantly on the rack of tragic circumstances. One element of the plot of Philaster will illustrate the complicated union of the emotions of comedy and tragedy. Philaster is in love with Arethusa, of whom he is jealous on account of Bellario, a page who is really a girl in love with him. This complication gives rise to a constant interchange of varying

116

emotions such as cannot be found in the early comedies or else-where, except, perhaps, in *Cymbeline*. To a degree which cannot be asserted of their predecessors, Beaumont and Fletcher fused together sentimental comedy and heroic tragedy.

In the matter of the dénouement, a comparison of the romances with the preceding tragi-comedies of 1601–9 will illustrate the contribution of Beaumont and Fletcher. The construction of the *Gentleman Usher* and the *Dumb Knight* is too crude to justify comment; in *Measure for Measure* and the *Malcontent* there are some noticeable points of similarity. In each case there is a disguised duke who ferrets out the villains, and the audience understands from the first his disguise and purpose. The main action moves toward a tragic catastrophe, but in each play this is averted by the management of the duke, and the crimes of the villain are exposed and pardoned. In *Measure for Measure* the dénouement is really a long explanation, in the *Malcontent* it is managed somewhat effectively by a masque, but it is also merely an unravelling of an action which the audience understands from the start.

In *Philaster* and *A King and No King* there is no such early divulging of the character of the dénouement. From the varied nature of the situations through which the action is developed, a free chance is left to make it either tragic or happy. Skillfully elaborated after the authors' fashion, its happy character comes as a telling surprise. It becomes the real climax of the action. Instead of a mere explanation with a pardon attached, the happy ending becomes in their hands a particularly effective and surprising culmination of a series of tragic situations.

Up to the last scene their romances are all tragi-comedies in their mixture of contrasting emotions or they are all tragedies in the intensity with which the emotions are worked up to a tragic climax. Then the dénouement follows, highly developed and tragic or happy as the case may be. The style of tragi-comedy which results seems to have been peculiarly their own and seems to have been the result of a more or less deliberate effort for stage-effectiveness.

Now some critical knowledge of dramatic rules and types must be assumed in most of the leading dramatists writing as late as 1607–11. We have already passed over evidence that the romances owe their characteristic traits to no uncritical consideration of dramatic rules and precedents. Fletcher working with Shakspere certainly produced in *Henry VIII* a chronicle history following the methods which he abandoned in the romances, and he also himself wrote historical plays. The freedom of the romances from either the material or the methods of historical plays cannot have been wholly undeliberate. Beaumont early in his career wrote the *Woman Hater*, a satirical comedy, and later that unique burlesque the *Knight of the Burning Pestle*. Fletcher early in his career wrote comedies of intrigue dealing with English manners and a pastoral play on Italian models. The change from such types as these to one so diverse as that of the romances cannot have been critically unconscious. Moreover all the main traits of the romances, like the use of tragi-comedy, seem to have been the result of careful striving for theatrical effect.

That the choice of tragi-comedy was deliberate may be further inferred, I think, from Fletcher's explanation prefixed to the *Faithful Shepherdess*, "a pastoral tragi-comedy."

"A tragi-comedy is not so called in respect of mirth and killing, but in respect it wants deaths, which is enough to make it no tragedy, yet brings some near it which is enough to make it no comedy, which must be a representation of familiar people, with such kind of trouble as no life shall be questioned; so that a god is as lawful in this as in a tragedy and mean people as in a comedy."

This, so far as I know, is the first definition in English of a tragi-comedy. Perhaps, in view of their development of tragi-comedy, it is not straining this passage too far to say that Beaumont and Fletcher were the first to study the type and formulate its rules.

Their style of tragi-comedy seems to have gained instant popularity in *Philaster* and *A King and No King*. It is easy, indeed, to see how popular such plays must have been with audiences who had no prejudices of taste against a mixture of opposite emotions, who demanded a representation of violent passions and tragic events, and who still must have had something of our modern sympathetic interest in the triumph of true love and the final happiness of heroes and heroines. Its popularity was, in fact, long continued. Though it fell into disuse for a number of years following 1600, yet after its revival by Beaumont and Fletcher and Shakspere it maintained its popularity until the closing of the theaters. Fletcher, after Beaumont ceased play writing, Massinger, and Shirley used it freely. After the Restoration it continued on the stage until the complete triumph of pseudo-classicism. Thus Dryden in his *Essay on Dramatick Criticism* declares that the English "have invented, increased and perfected a more pleasing way of writing for the stage than was ever known to the ancients or moderns of any nation—which is tragi-comedy."

While Beaumont and Fletcher were not the inventors of tragi-comedy, they were at least its increasers and perfecters. While here again they made use of the practice of their predecessors, their critical and effective use of the form had its effect on the later history of the drama. However we may estimate the importance of their particular development of the form, they were certainly prominent in bringing about a revival of tragi-comedies and they produced two remarkable for theatrical success.

With this use of tragi-comedy we have finished the important characteristics of the material and construction of the plots of the romances. We have seen that to a considerable degree each of these characteristics was an innovation and that each worked for greater stage effectiveness. Taken together they distinguish the romances from the preceding plays of the decade and go far to explain their popularity. Before going on to discuss their characterization and style, it may not be out of place to refer to the earliest play which exemplifies all these traits of the plots and to suggest that these traits are in themselves enough to vouch for its originality and popularity. In its material, its construction, and its effective happy ending, *Philaster* must have attracted by its novelty and its acting qualities. No plays in the preceding ten years resembled it in these important traits, while these traits do reappear in the succeeding romances and in many other plays of the following thirty years. Like *Tamburlaine* and *Every Man in His Humour*, *Philaster* seems to have introduced a type of play of wide influence in the drama. In it and the other romances we have already found considerable to support the statement of J. Addington Symonds that Beaumont and Fletcher were "the inventors of heroical romance.[1]"

B. *Characterization.*

From the very nature of their plots these romances must lack individualization in their characters. They are not, like the historical tragedies, devoted to the presentation of real people; they are merely collections of situations which give vivid momentary pictures of passions. They do not, like the *Duchess of Malfi* and some other dramatizations of Italian novelle, imbue the bare situations with psychologic realism; they place the whole emphasis on situations and dénouments. Their method of construction, therefore, does not favor consistency in developing character; it merely requires that the various characters be exhibited under exciting circumstances.

Thus Philaster is at one moment confronted with the proffer of a kingdom; at another, confronted with a proffer of love from the woman he adores; at another, brought face to face with proofs of her faithlessness; at another so placed that in spite of his jealousy he will pardon both her and her supposed lover; and at still another, brought to such a pitch of fury that he tries to kill them both. Presented in so great a variety of

---

[1] *The Mermaid Series.* Christopher Marlowe. General introduction, p. xxv.

moods, he necessarily loses individuality. He is at different moments an irresolute prince, a fervent lover, a jealous madman, and a coward who cannot fight; he is never a real individual. In the same way most of the characters are presented as the actors in a series of improbable incidents; Amintor in the *Maid's Tragedy* and Leucippus in *Cupid's Revenge*, in particular, displaying an utter lack of consistency in delineation.

Similarly, when the situations are made of chief importance, there can be no shading in characterization. All the people must be indubitably bad or indubitably good. There must be no doubt or hesitation in regard to their purposes, or the situation will lose some of its effectiveness. They must be from the first far within or far without the pale of our sympathies. Their characters, in brief, must be exaggerated and intensified; and still further, since there is no better way to accomplish such exaggeration than by contrast, we may expect to find the very evil ones set off in sharp contrast with the very good.

Take for example the women of the romances. Each play has one very evil woman and at least one very good one. The evil women, it must be confessed, have more individuality than any other of the characters, Evadne being about as living a piece of human flesh as was ever put upon paper; at the same time they are all extremely bad women. Arethusa, Ordella, Euphrasia and the rest are, on the contrary, extremely good and pure and lovable. In the same way, among the men we find a tendency to intensification and vivid contrast at the expense of all semblance of reality. The heroes like Philaster and Leucippus are very pure and generous and noble, and the bad men like Pharamond, Protaldy, and Timantius are so bad that they are inhumanly repugnant. These furnish, perhaps, the most marked examples of exaggeration and contrast.

Again, the over emphasis placed on the theatrical effectiveness of the situations is likely to involve characterization by description rather than by strictly dramatic means. The writer who is striving after telling situations and who is careless of individualization but desirous of producing intense contrasts in characterization, naturally finds that a character can be most effectively presented by the descriptions and comments of other persons. In this way, the interest of the audience is at once removed from the development of character and is centered on the development of plot. At the same time, the sympathies of the audience are from the first directed to the proper persons. Without pressing too far the natural connection between the tragedy, which depends largely on situations and this method of characterization by description, the latter may certainly be classed as a notable characteristic of Beaumont and Fletcher.

For example, such a character as the love-lorn maiden plainly requires something besides her action and words to gain immediately for her the sentimental sympathies of an audience. So Bellario, before she appears on the stage, is described by Philaster, in a speech of thirty lines, beginning :

> " I have a boy
> Sent by the gods, I hope to this intent,
> Not yet seen in the court." [1]

In the same fashion, at the beginning of the *Maid's Tragedy*, Aspatia is described in the speech :

> " But this lady
> Walks discontented with her watery eyes
> Bent on the earth." [2]

In the first scene of the *Maid's Tragedy*, in fact, not only is Aspatia described by Lysippus in this speech of nineteen lines; Amintor is also described by Melantius in fourteen lines, and Melantius by Lysippus in eight lines. Throughout the play, the characters will be found to be presented not only by stated descriptions but also by frequent comments, eulogistic or denunciatory, from the other actors.

Still another trait of the characterization requires especial notice. All the principal characters are people of the court ; even those who are utterly detestable hold positions of rank. When persons outside of the court are introduced, they are altogether vulgar and insignificant like the woodmen and the leaders of the mob in *Philaster*. This practice is in accordance with the classical dogma that tragedy must deal with people of rank and it is in accordance with general Elizabethan practice ; but it is worth noting that Beaumont and Fletcher had only ridicule for the domestic plays and apprentice comedies of Heywood and Dekker, and that they were long distinguished for their faithful presentation of gentlemen and courtiers.

So far, then, we have noticed a few of the traits which distinguish the characterization of the romances. Keeping these traits in mind—the court rank of the characters, their presentation by description, the over-emphasis of their predominant qualities, and the disregard for individual consistency—we can evidently sum up the result by saying that the characters are not individuals, but types. Remembering, too, that the plots of the romances have a generic similarity, we may expect these types to be repeated until they become conventionalized. In our discussion of the chronology of the plays, we have, in fact, already noticed that several types were repeated.[3] We

---

[1] *Philaster*, I, 2.
[2] *Maid's Tragedy*, I, 1.
[3] *Cf.* ante, pp. 69 and 81.

shall now change our point of view and leave the consideration of specific traits of characterization, in order to examine the conventionalized types which resulted.

First, there are the love-lorn maidens: three of whom, Aspatia, in the *Maid's Tragedy*, Urania, in *Cupid's Revenge*, and Bellario-Euphrasia, in *Philaster*, masquerade in boys' clothing. Spaconia, in *A King and No King*, is of the same sort; and Panthea, in *A King and No King*, Ordella, in *Thierry and Theodoret*, and Arethusa, in *Philaster*, can hardly be distinguished from the others except by their royal birth and consequent suitability for marriage to the heroes. The other four, for some reason, cannot be married and consequently are embellished with all the sentimentality adherent to an unrequited passion.

There had been many maidens of this general type on the stage since Elizabethan poets first began to dramatize Italian novels; and the type had been used very effectively, at least as early as the plays of Robert Greene. Examples from Shakspere's comedies will be at once recalled, and the sentimental boy and girl love story had a place in all kinds of drama. For a number of years, however, before the romances of Beaumont and Fletcher, we have found that neither the sentimental love story nor the love-stricken maiden had been popular in the London theaters. Shakspere scarcely used the type from *Twelfth Night* to *Cymbeline*, and the other leading dramatists of the period likewise abandoned it. After the Beaumont-Fletcher romances, the sentimental maiden had a new and long lease of popularity. Thus, in altering *Romeo and Juliet*, Otway made Lavinia (Juliet) wander from home, lose her way in the woods, meet her lover there, and offer her services, exactly like one of the heroines of Beaumont and Fletcher.[1] They seem to deserve credit for the revival of the sentimental love-lorn maiden.

At all events they developed the type beyond all their predecessors. They intensely sentimentalized the character. They emphasized over and over again the purity, the meekness, the utter self-abnegation of these maidens. They were made eager to serve when they could not marry and supremely devoted under the most discouraging circumstances. Dorothea in *James IV*, who has won some praise for wifely devotion, would have to take lessons from Bellario who sacrifices herself for Philaster or his lady in every scene. For pure sentimentality Viola in *Twelfth Night* is a saucy school girl in comparison with the watery-eyed Aspatia. The type had never before been presented so elaborately and with such exaggeration.

---

[1] *History and Fall of Caius Marius.* IV, 2.

Upon these maidens is expended nearly all the lyrical poetry of the plays. The authors' poetic powers are fairly exhausted in an effort to overwhelm them with sentimental fancy, to present them as ideally perfect. However foreign such an ideal of womanhood may be to our modern taste, we must grant that its poetical presentation was by no means lacking in charm and beauty.

Such presentations of ideal maidens are very different when read and when heard on the stage. They doubtless ministered to a taste for idyllic poetry and they are by no means separate from the principal situations, and the situation itself of a girl in doublet and hose seeking her lover was not then an entirely unreal convention.[1] Just what charm this style of girl exercised on the stage is, however, difficult to explain, nor is it necessary. All we need to remember is that they have little individuality, that they are utterly romantic, utterly removed from life, dependent for their charm almost entirely on the poetry with which they are described; and further, that they form one of the most distinguishing features of the Beaumont-Fletcher romances.

Secondly, there are the evil women: Evadne in the *Maid's Tragedy*, Bacha in *Cupid's Revenge*, Megra in *Philaster* and the two queen-mothers, Brunhalt in *Thierry and Theodoret*, and Arane in *A King and No King*. Four of these brazenly confess adultery, and four attempt or commit murder. They are generally distinguished by an absence of all shame, and utter depravity.

Thirdly, there are the lily-livered heroes, as Mr. Oliphant calls them. Philaster, Amintor, and Leucippus are so absolutely alike that they could, so far as they have any personality, readily be exchanged. They are all very loving, very noble, very generous; otherwise they have no characteristics which outlast a single situation. Thierry and Arbaces present a somewhat different type, in which ungovernable passion is largely emphasized.

Fourthly, there are the faithful friends: Dion in *Philaster*, Melantius in the *Maid's Tragedy*, Martell in *Thierry and Theodoret*, Ismeneus in *Cupid's Revenge*, and Mardonius in *A King and No King*. The men of this type are always blunt counsellors, brave soldiers, and devoted friends. They possess a rough humor, an impatience of deceit, and an eagerness for action. There is scarcely an individual peculiarity among the five.

Fifthly, there are the poltroons: Pharamond in *Philaster*, Protaldy in *Thierry and Theodoret*, Timantius in *Cupid's Revenge*, and Bessus in *A King and No King*. They are all cowards,

[1] See *the English Novel in the Time of Shakespeare*. J.J. Jusserand. London, 1890. pp. 238–9.

scoundrels, and beasts. Their baseness, however, is always a little relieved by humorous treatment.

These five types thus include all the principal persons of the romances. Of course the examples under each type present some individual differences and also vary in vividness of portraiture; Bellario, for example, is much more carefully drawn than Urania, and, as has been stated, Evadne has individuality enough. Nevertheless the resemblance among the examples of each type is unmistakable, and on the stage even more than in print they must have seemed to all intents identical.

For further assurance of the favor in which these five types were regarded by Beaumont and Fletcher we may well recall our examination of *Cupid's Revenge* and *Thierry and Theodoret*. In both plays, it will be remembered, they developed the evil woman and the hero from slight hints in the prose narrative; and in both plays, with scarcely a hint from the narratives, they added distinctly drawn portraitures of the poltroon, the faithful friend, and the love-lorn maiden. Whether such repetition was deliberate or not, it could hardly have taken place unless the types of characters were popular on the stage. That they were, there can be little doubt. In spite of their lack of individuality they are presented with absolute distinctness, their predominant traits are unmistakably emphasized, and by their very lack of individuality they are the better suited for violent acting and romantically impossible situations.

C. Style.

The attempt to separate the work of Beaumont from that of Fletcher has led to so thorough a discussion of the poetic style of each that any treatment on my part must be largely repetition. Without attempting any exhaustive analysis, however, there are a few points which are of importance in distinguishing their styles from those of their predecessors and of interest in connection with the versification of Shakspere's romances. In order to examine these points it will be necessary to consider the two dramatists separately.

Fletcher. The most marked trait of Fletcher's versification is the unparalleled abundance of feminine endings which often occur in a proportion of two out of three. Analogous to this is his use of redundant syllables in the middle of a line. The effect of all this is to conceal the metre and make the verse approach as nearly as verse may to the freedom and naturalness of ordinary speech. He uses little or no prose in his plays, for his blank verse answers the purpose. In comparison with the fixed rhythm of the early Elizabethans, one often wonders, indeed, if Fletcher is writing in metre at all. The change from the old, regularly accented, declamatory lines to his irregular, conversational style is almost like the change from blank verse to prose.

As Mr. Macaulay says: "No mouthing is possible, no rounding off of description or sentence; all must be abrupt and almost spasmodic; the outcome of the moment, untramelled as far as may be by any metre, though metre of some sort there always is. It is an absolute breaking away from the rigidity of the older style."[1]

The second marked characteristic of Fletcher's verse is his avoidance of run-over and use of end-stopt lines. This practice, however, by no means produces anything like the effect of the end-stopt lines of Shakspere's early plays. The effect is again an approach to the fragmentary utterance of ordinary conversation. Thus, rhyme is very rarely used, and periodic sentences are generally avoided. There is rarely an attempt at elaborate, connected description, and never anything like the descriptive set pieces of the early dramatists. Images are merely suggested, never elaborately finished; parentheses are admitted in abundance; and the whole effect is that of unpremeditated and disconnected discourse. To quote Mr. Macaulay again: "Impulses seem to work before the eyes of the spectator, the speakers correct themselves, explain by parentheses hastily thown in, or add after thoughts as they occur to the mind."[2]

This use of parentheses is of enough importance to be marked as the third important trait of Fletcher's style. No trick of his structure so instantly impresses the reader. To the reader, indeed, the abundance of parentheses often makes the sentences confused and unintelligible; spoken on the stage, however, with the aid of gesture, these parentheses must have contributed largely toward procuring the effect of spontaneous speech.

A few lines, taken almost at random, will illustrate to what an extraordinary extent parentheses are used and how they serve to imitate naturalness and spontaneity. In *Thierry and Theodoret*[3] Brunhalt speaks to Protaldy:

"Give me leave!
Or free thyself—think in what place you are—
From the foul imputation that is laid
Upon thy valour—be bold, I'll protect you—
Or here I vow—deny it or forswear it—
These honours which thou wear'st unworthily—
Which, be but impudent enough and keep them—
Shall be torn from thee with thine eyes."

After studying a while for an ingenious defence, Protaldy replies:

"Oh, I remember't now. At the stag's fall
As we to-day were hunting, a poor fellow

---

[1] *Francis Beaumont*, p. 45.
[2] *Francis Beaumont*, p. 45.
[3] II, 3.

(And, now I view you better, I may say
Much of your pitch) this silly wretch I spoke of
With his petition falling at my feet,
(Which much against my will he kissed) desired
That, as a special means for his preferment,
I would vouchsafe to let him use my sword
To cut off the stag's head."

.   .   .   .

"I, ever courteous (a great weakness in me)
Granted his humble suit."

We have here an extravagant use of parentheses; serving,
in one case, the purpose of quick stage asides, and in the other,
the hesitating verboseness of the stage liar. These examples
may indicate the variety of action which the parenthetical
structure can serve; it is used most frequently, of course, in
passages of violent passion and consequently, very broken
and rapid utterance.

A fourth trait of Fletcher's style, perhaps not so distinctly
characteristic as the others but still unmistakably manifest,
is his use of conversational abreviations as 'I'll' for 'I will,'
'he's' for 'he is,' and ''tis' for 'it is.' Of the same sort is his
decided preference for ''em' rather than 'them.' He uses
such abbreviations in great abundance, and the effect of this
practice, like that of the other traits of his verse, is clearly
toward a conversational style.

Now all these traits become mannerisms and prevail to an
unwarrantable degree. The end-stopt lines produce a tedious
monotony, and his redundant syllables a slovenly approach to
prose. Parentheses are often so numerous that they make the
sense difficult, and colloquialisms often give a vulgar effect to
passages otherwise dignified. There are other points, however,
more important for our purpose than his faults.

In the first place his verse shows a divergence from the
practice of his predecessors. Totally unlike Marlowe's
sounding line or the lyrical blank verse of Shakspere's early
plays, it also differs markedly from the blank verse of plays
1601 to 1610. Nor is the difference merely that of individual mannerisms, it is a structural difference which is of
significance in the history of versification of the Elizabethan
drama. That history has never been fully investigated, but
its general outline is clear. The change from the old rigid,
periodic structure to a freer, looser style was not an instanta-
neous one but a gradual advance, of which the development of
Shakspere's versification is the most typical example. The
advance of his verse in dramatic freedom from *Romeo and
Juliet* to *Othello* and *Antony and Cleopatra* is an advance which
can be paralleled by a comparison of the plays of the early
nineties with those ten years later. In this general structural
development, however, Fletcher was more than a contributor;
he was a leader and a revolutionist. From the very first he

wrote a verse which, in the freedom of its metre, not only far surpassed that of the dramatists before 1600 but was unapproached either by his immediate predecessors or followers. From the very first, too, he wrote a verse which in its conversational looseness, not only surpassed the early dramatists but also remained an unapproached limit. This metrical freedom and conversational looseness are found, it must be remembered, not only in comedies of manners but also in heroic dramas. Fletcher marks the breaking down of blank verse, if you will; but he certainly marks the introduction of a revolutionary fashion. In comparison with his immediate predecessors, his style was an innovation, especially in heroic tragedy; and, it can hardly be doubted that his style exercised a strong influence on his contemporaries and successors.

In the second place, the question may be raised whether the adoption of this style was not to some degree deliberate. The fact that in his *Faithful Shepherdess* he wrote a regular tensyllable verse with carefully developed images and with few disconnected phrases and parentheses, at least shows that he could write in a lyric, descriptive style when he chose. The radical nature of his structural innovations also suggests that he could not have made them unconsciously. At its best, however, his verse shows no sign of artificiality, rather it seems more spontaneous than that of his predecessors. Even the marked change from the style of the *Faithful Shepherdess* to that of the romances may have resulted from the nature of the plays. The *Faithful Shepherdess* is full of lyrical descriptions and is, in fact, throughout distinctly lyrical, while the romances are, above all, effective acting plays. Whether or not he definitely planned an innovation in Elizabethan blank verse, he must have formed his style with especial reference to stage-action.

At all events, whether there was conscious purpose or not, the effect of Fletcher's innovations is certain. In the third place, then, we may note that all the traits of his style unite to produce a verse suited to stage action. The early Elizabethan blank-verse, with its long periods and carefully elaborated descriptions, was by turns declamatory or lyrical; it did not lend itself readily to action. Fletcher's verse differs in every respect from that; but in comparison with blank verse as late as 1600, no such sharp distinction can be drawn. The general progress was toward dramatic freedom in style, and Fletcher took part in the general progress. Even in comparison with his contemporaries, however, the qualities noticed in his verse mark it as dramatic. It is not dramatic in the sense that it is especially suited to the speakers and their varying emotions, but in structure it is dramatic in that it is suited to be spoken and acted on the stage. The style of *Othello*, for example, is often instanced as being magnificently responsive to dramatic requirements; "not only is every word in character, but every word also adds to the beauty of a noble tragic poem."[1] No one would think of comparing any of Fletcher's plays with *Othello* in these respects. A few facts, however, will show how Fletcher may sometimes surpass *Othello* in adapting his verse to mere stage action without regard to the representation of character or tragic emotions. In *Othello*, there are 76 speeches of 10 lines or more,[2] comprising 1,144 lines. In *Bonduca* (the nearest in date to *Othello* of any tragedy by Fletcher alone) there are only 48 speeches of ten lines or more, comprising 686 lines. In *Othello* there are 12 speeches of twenty lines or more, comprising 301 lines; in *Bonduca* 6 comprising 148 lines. In Fletcher's tragedy there are fewer long declamations and more rapid dialogue.[3] In this respect his style in *Bonduca* seems more directly designed for utterance on the stage than even the most masterly dramatic verse of Shakspere.

Fletcher wrote a verse which by the freedom of its metre and the looseness of its structure was suited both to the varied play of passion and the lively exchange of repartee. It was a verse neither to be declaimed nor recited, but a verse to be spoken on the stage. We have seen two examples which show how his broken phrases served two specific ends in stage action; and almost any page from Fletcher will exemplify the same thing. Now, however, we are dealing not with specific effects but with the general effect. His style varies, of course, with the situations, but all his innovations in structure must have aided in adapting his plays for stage action. His very faults and mannerisms only emphasize this general tendency. Every line helps to give the effect of unpremeditated speech.

Beaumont. Beaumont's verse differs decidedly from Fletcher's. Although he does not avoid the double ending, he uses it far less frequently. He also uses unstopt lines in profusion and has a marked liking for a periodic structure and extended descriptions. Mr. Macaulay has further endeavored to prove that his style shows traces of Shakspere's influence and that, in general, his style is distinguished by its resemblance to the

---

[1] *William Shakspere.* B. Wendell. p. 286.

[2] Speeches in prose are counted according to the number of lines in the Globe ed.

[3] Fletcher cannot be said always to be sparing of long speeches. In *Wit Without Money,* one of his early comedies, the number of speeches both over ten and over 20 lines is much less than in *Bonduca.* In *Valentinian,* however, there are a great many long speeches, 67 of ten lines and 16 of twenty. The number of long speeches varies with the character of the plays, and no generalization could be made without very extensive examination. On the whole I think it can be said that Fletcher in his tragedies and tragi-comedies uses more dialogue composed of very brief speeches of a line or two than will be found in any other tragedies in his time.

style of Shakspere's middle period, notably that of *Hamlet* and *Twelfth Night.* To my mind, this resemblance is mainly due to the fact that Beaumont's imagination in intensity and originality, more than any of his contemporaries, approaches Shakspere's. In considering versification, we shall keep our attention on the structure.

In respect to Beaumont's structure, its difference from Fletcher's, while noticeable, may for the sake of contrast easily be overestimated. While he is in no respect the innovator that Fletcher is, it must not be thought that his verse has much of the early rigidity or that it is wanting in Fletcher's freedom. If not a radical revolutionist, he is at least a Girondist.

There are many distinctively lyrical passages in the romances where the verse is naturally lyric in structure rather than dramatic; and these passages are usually assigned to Beaumont. In the portraiture of the love-lorn maidens, in particular, there is a good deal of descriptive poetry which is in the old manner rather than in Fletcher's; and this is usually assigned to Beaumont. Moreover, he always keeps more closely to a fixed metre than Fletcher, and he has not mannerisms like Fletcher's which tend directly to give the effect of natural speech. Nevertheless, when Beaumont is not writing purely descriptive poetry but is writing speeches to be acted, his structure is marked by broken phrases, repetitions, and parentheses.

An examination of the parts of *Philaster*, the *Maid's Tragedy*, and *Cupid's Revenge* generally assigned to Beaumont, will indicate, I think, to how great a degree this is true. Since in the effort to distinguish his verse from Fletcher's, this fact has been somewhat overlooked, one or two illustrations may be pardoned. The first shall be from one of Aspatia's long speeches which is purely operatic in character. Here, we should hardly expect verse suited to action; but note:

> "If you needs must love,
> (Forced by ill fate) take to your maiden bosoms
> Two dead-cold aspicks, and of them make lovers:
> They cannot flatter, nor forswear; one kiss
> Makes a long peace for all. But man,
> Oh, that beast man! Come, let's be sad, my girls!
> That down-cast eye of thine, Olympias,
> Shews a fine sorrow. Mark, Antiphila;
> Just such another was the nymph Œnone,
> When Paris brought home Helen. Now, a tear;
> And then thou art a piece expressing fully
> The Carthage queen, when, from a cold sea-rock,
> Full with her sorrow, she tied fast her eyes
> To the fair Trojan ships; and, having lost them,
> Just as thine eyes do, down stole a tear. Antiphila,
> What would this wench do, if she were Aspatia?
> Here she would stand, till some more pitying god
> Turn'd her to marble! 'Tis enough, my wench!
> Shew me the piece of needlework you wrought." [1]

---

[1] *Maid's Tragedy.* II, 2, last of the speech.

The remainder of Aspatia's speeches in the scene will be found to exhibit the same broken structure, the same imitation of natural conversation.

These qualities are still more apparent in passages requiring more action; for example, in the quarrel scene between Melantius and Amintor,[1] or in the following passage from *Philaster*.

> *Bellario.* [aside]   "Oh hear,
> You that have plenty! from that flowing store
> Drop some on dry ground. — See, the lively red
> Is gone to guide her heart! I fear she faints—
> Madam? look up! — She breathes not. — Open once more
> Those rosy twins, and send unto my lord
> Your latest farewell! Oh, she stirs: — How is it,
> Madam? speak comfort."

> *Arethusa.*   " 'T is not gently done,
> To put me in a miserable life,
> And hold me there: I prithee, let me go:
> I shall do best without thee: I am well."

> *[Enter Philaster.]*

> *Philaster.*   " I am to blame to be so much in rage:
> I'll tell her coolly, when and where I heard
> This killing truth. I will be temperate
> In speaking, and as just in hearing. ——
> Oh, monstrous! Tempt me not, ye gods! good gods,
> Tempt not a frail man! What's he, that has a heart,
> But he must ease it here!"[2]

Or take Philaster's speech to Pharamond,[3] or, indeed, any passage in the play, and we find a style that is notably suited to action on the stage.

Beaumont's very freedom from Fletcher's mannerisms removes Fletcher's faults without removing the acting quality. Without stopping at the end of every line, he writes disconnected and broken sentences which give the effect of spontaneity. Without straining his metre out of joint, he writes a verse which is like spoken discourse. While far less revolutionary than Fletcher's, his style is representative of the general advance toward a thoroughly dramatic verse. Indeed, when one reads the first three acts of the *Maid's Tragedy*, omitting perhaps the masque and the idyl of Aspatia, one feels like questioning if poetry was ever written better adapted to stage presentation.

D. Stage Effects.

We have seen that the blank verse of both Beaumont and Fletcher, like their varied situations and exciting dénouements, helped to give their romances stage-effectiveness. All the characteristics of the romances, in fact, serve the same end; whatever

---

[1] *Ibid.* III, 2.
[2] *Philaster.* IV, 3.
[3] *Ibid.* I, 1.

their permanent literary value, they certainly must have acted capitally. Moreover, in addition to this general stage-effectiveness, they were not wanting in stage pageantry but abounded in devices which may fairly be called spectacular.

Almost all of these spectacular devices were borrowed from the court masques. These were very popular in the years 1608–1611,[1] and there can be no doubt that Beaumont and Fletcher turned to them for stage pageantry. In the *Four Plays* there is a "scaffolding full of spectators" and in the *Maid's Tragedy*, a "gallery full of spectators." In these cases there is an obvious attempt to represent the setting of a court masque, and there is considerable jesting at the crowds which thronged to those entertainments. In the *Four Plays*, the various deities that descend and ascend, the numerous processions, and the curious machinery where "the mist ariseth and the rocks remove,"[2] are all like similar performances in the court masques. The *Four Plays* are, in fact, given the form of an entertainment before a king and his bride, and the last, the *Triumph of Time*, has unmistakably the form of a masque. Theme, spectacle, and dances all follow the recognized fashion. Mercury and Time appear; "one-half of a cloud is drawn," "singers are discovered," then "the other half is drawn and Jupiter seen in his glory." The main masque is danced by Delight, Pleasure, Lucre, Craft, Vanity, etc., and there is also an anti-masque of a "Troop of Indians, singing and dancing wildly about Plutus." Here we have not merely an introduction of masque-like pageantry but a complete court masque on the public stage in combination with a romantic drama.

In the *Maid's Tragedy*, there is also a masque, complete and elaborated after the usual manner of court masques. In *Cupid's Revenge* there is the machinery of Cupid's descents and a dance by "four young men and maids."[8] In *Thierry and Theodoret* there is a dance of revellers.[4] In many other plays by Beaumont and Fletcher besides the romances, there are also masques or bits of masque-like pageantry—distinct masque elements occurring in eighteen of their plays.[5]

---

[1] Seven of these elaborate and costly entertainments were given at Whitehall in these years. See Soergel, pp. 72, 73.

[2] *Triumph of Honour.* Sc. II.   [8] I, 2.   [4] III, 1.

[5] The simplest form of the masque appears in the *Coxcomb* (I, 2,) and *Wit at Several Weapons* (V, 2). In the *Nice Valour* there is a dance of masquers led by a lady disguised as Cupid (II, 1); and also an anti-masque of fools, the lady leading again (V, 1). Anti-masques also occur in the *Little French Lawyer* (IV, 5), "Gentlemen, habited like Ruffians;" in the *Queen of Corinth* (II, 1), "six disguised, singing and dancing to a horrid music;" in the *Fair Maid of the Inn* (III, 1), "by Tailor, Dancer, Muletteer, Schoolmaster, etc.," and again (IV, 2,) by "four boys shaped like Frogs;" and in the *Mad Lover* (IV, 1), "the Fool and Servants, disguised in a masque of Beasts and

131

Now, the masque in its simple form—a dance by a group of masked revellers, with or without an introductory speech—was common enough in plays before the time of Beaumont and Fletcher, and the influence of the masque on the drama in a general way has been emphasized by Mr. Fleay and treated at length by Dr. Soergel. The nature of this influence in the reign of James I, however, has not been fully examined. Then, as the court masque grew more elaborate, its machinery, costumes, mythological devices, anti-masques, and, indeed, its general construction, were borrowed or imitated so freely by the dramatists that its influence on the drama was distinctly important. Beaumont and Fletcher were undoubtedly promoting what Ben Jonson, who did not mix his masques and plays, called the "concupiscence of dances and antics,"[1] which in 1612 he declared began to reign on the stage.

There is reason to believe that Beaumont and Fletcher were leaders in this fashion of introducing elements from the court masques on the public stage. Beaumont wrote the very successful court masque of the Inner Temple and Grays Inn; and Jonson told Drummond that "next himself only Fletcher[2] and Chapman could make a mask." Moreover, I know of no other dramatist except Shirley who drew so much from the court masques as did they. Of the dramatists writing 1608–11, Shakspere is the only one who is in this respect comparable with them.

If Beaumont and Fletcher did not set this fashion, they were certainly among the first to follow it; and Jonson's scoffs alone are sufficient proof that this innovation was very popular with the patrons of the theater. In addition, then, to the other distinguishing characteristics of the romances, we must note that in a way quite different from any preceding plays and to an extent greater than other contemporary plays, they possessed a good share of stage pageantry much like that of the fashionable court masques.

Trees." In this last play there is also some masque-like business connected with the priestess of Venus; in the *Prophetess* there is a throne on a cloud drawn by dragons (II, 3), a mist (IV, 1), and "a Dance of Shepherds and Shepherdesses, one disguised as Pan leading the men, another as Ceres, the maids" (V, 3). In the *Humourous Lieutenant* (IV, 3), there is a dance of spirits; in the *Maid in the Mill* (II, 2), a dance of goddesses, nymphs, and a shepherd; in the *Faithful Friends* (IV, 3), a masque danced by the ladies with the gentlemen dressed as furies. There are more elaborate masques with especial poetry attached in *Woman Pleased* (V, 3), when there is also a morris dance (IV, 1); in a *Wife for a Month* (II, 6); and in the *False One* (III, 4). This list, while not including all the masque pageantry and devices is sufficient to indicate their abundance in the plays of the Beaumont-Fletcher folio. For masque elements in *Henry VIII* and the *Two Noble Kinsmen*, see Chap. VIII.

[1] See "Address to the reader," *Alchemist* 4to, 1612. See also the Induction to *Bartholomew Fair*.

[2] Possibly Drummond's mistake for Beaumont?

132

CHAPTER VIII

GENERAL CHARACTERISTICS OF SHAKSPERE'S ROMANCES.

We shall now consider the most important traits of Shakspere's romances. According to my hypothesis these will be
found to distinguish the romances clearly from Shakspere's
earlier plays and will also be found to resemble those traits
which mark the romances of Beaumont and Fletcher.

While the points of difference from Shakspere's early work
will be emphasized, it must not be forgotten that there are
many points of likeness. Shakspere repeated motives, situations and types of character. The romances owe an immense
debt to his preceding plays. All this cannot be constantly
dwelt upon in this investigation, but it must be freely admitted.
I shall treat, however, of the influence of his early work only
when that seems to interfere with the hypothesis of contemporary influence. In the main we are concerned with the traits
which differentiate the romances from his preceding plays.

A. Plots.

The plots of the romances differ decidedly from those which
Shakspere had been using in the preceding eight years. During
those years he had drawn his plots largely from history and
especially from classical history, and with one or two exceptions each plot had dealt with the life and death of some heroic
person who gave his name to the play. In *Cymbeline* he connected several very distinct stories with a historical narrative;
in the *Winter's Tale* he dramatized an old romance by Greene;
and in the *Tempest*, possibly on the basis of an Italian novella,
he built up a marvellous story apparently of his own invention.
Although the cases of Cloten and Jachimo might be cited to
the contrary, he did not use stories of abnormal or gross sexual
passion such as attracted Beaumont and Fletcher. For the
basis of each play he did take a story of pure and sentimental
love. Such sentimental love stories, it will be remembered,
were given a similar prominence in the romances of Beaumont
and Fletcher; and such sentimental love stories, it will also
be remembered, had received no like prominence in Shakspere's
work from 1601 to 1608.

About these love stories he weaves many novel and varied
incidents. The course of Hero's love, or even of Juliet's, is
smooth compared with that of Imogen's. The attempted se-

duction by Jachimo, the results of his over-ingenious villainy, the attempted poisoning by the wicked queen, the idyllic adventures of Imogen in boy's clothes, her supposed death, her resurrection, her repulsion by her lover, their final reconciliation—all these are the sort of incidents which Beaumont and Fletcher used in their romances. Like Beaumont and Fletcher again, are the ingenious plots of the *Tempest* and the *Winter's Tale*—the love story of a girl who had never seen a man, and the changing of an image to a woman. In brief, the material of the plots, never taken from history nor resembling real life, is of a sort that we call romantic, of a sort that gives theatrical novelty and variety.

Particularly noticeable is the mixture of tragic incidents with idyllic. In this respect Shakspere returns to his practice in early comedies like the *Two Gentlemen of Verona* and *Much Ado about Nothing;* and in this respect he also agrees with the contemporary romances of Beaumont and Fletcher. And this last resemblance is much the more marked of the two. There is plenty of idyllic material in the Elizabethan drama, and it is often contrasted with tragic material in Greene, Chettle, and Heywood, as well as in Beaumont and Fletcher and Shakspere; but never before these plays, I think, had Shakspere united events so purely idyllic and events so essentially tragic in so marked contrast as in the story of Imogen. In the eight years preceding the performance of *Cymbeline* and *Philaster* we have found, in fact, that the conjunction of heroic tragedy and a sentimental idyl is practically absent from the work of all the other dramatists as well as Shakspere. In the romances of Shakspere, however, as in those of Beaumont and Fletcher, the tragic and idyllic always appear in heightened contrast.

Still further we may notice the variety of emotions which one of the plots presents. Shakspere was no longer dealing with stories exemplifying one central emotion, he now took plots dealing with every variety of emotion. The emotional unity which characterizes the tragedies and the best of the comedies is no longer present. The emotions described range from the wild jealousy of Leontes to the pretty sentimental love-making of Florizel. There is an evident choice of intense, exaggerated emotions; there is no sign of unity.

Thus in variety of emotions as well as of incidents, in the nature of the central theme, and in the marked contrast of tragic and idyllic scenes, these plots differ from those of Shakspere's preceding plays. In all these particulars they also differ from all plays after 1600 and before *Philaster*, but they resemble the material of the plots of Beaumont and Fletcher.

Not less striking than this change from his earlier practice in the choice of material, is Shakspere's change in the construction of plots. Except in the historical parts of *Cymbeline* he abandons the chronicle-history method which he had used up to *Coriolanus* and adopts the method of romance—the connecting of a series of effective situations so that they will lead up to a telling dénouement. There is nothing epical about these plays, and except in *Cymbeline* there are no camps, battles, parleyings, heralds, trials by combat, and other paraphernalia of the historical tragedies. The heroic romances owe no allegiance to history, they aim solely at theatrical effectiveness. A cursory examination of any one of them, of *Cymbeline* in particular, will show that in every act there is a medley of stage situations affording continual variety and excitement. Such an examination will also show that in comparison with earlier plays there are almost no merely narrative scenes, and almost no scenes which are merely operatic interludes. We shall have occasion to revert to these statements when we come to examine the separate plays; for the present, we may pass to the more definable feature of the construction, the treatment of the dénouement.

Cymbeline may be taken to show the transition from the method of the historical tragedies to that of the romances. Shakspere was nominally writing a chronicle-history, but in constructing the play he was not chiefly concerned, as in *Antony and Cleopatra* and *Coriolanus*, in giving dramatic form to the historical narrative. He was chiefly concerned in supplementing the narrative with a large number of good stage situations. The historical part, in fact, has so little connection with the stories of Imogen, Posthumus and Jachimo, Belarius and his sons, that there is some reason for Mr. Fleay's conjecture[1] that it was written earlier than the rest of the play. At all events the method of construction is clearly that of linking together a series of situations, involving intense and varied action, and preparing for elaborate dénouement.

No earlier play of Shakspere's is so overladen with situations, or places so much emphasis on the dénouement. As Mr. Wendell has stated: "the last scene of *Cymbeline* is among the most notable bits of dramatic structure anywhere. The more one studies it, the more one is astonished at the ingenuity with which dénouement follows dénouement. Nowhere else in Shakspere, certainly, is there anything like so elaborate an untying of knots which seem purposely made intricate to prepare for the final situation. Situation, however, is an inadequate word. Into 485 lines Shakspere has crowded some two dozen situations any one of which would probably have been strong enough to carry a whole act."[2]

This last statement proves, on Mr. Wendell's analysis, to be

[1] *Life of Sh.* p. 246.
[2] *William Shakspere.* p. 358.

literally true. Such a dénouement is evidently not the natural outcome of a tragedy or a comedy; it is the elaborate climax, in preparation for which the preceding situations have been made involved and perplexing. It is the dénouement of the drama of situations so arranged as constantly to excite and vary the attention of the spectators up to the moment of the final unravelling. As a matter of fact, the dénouement of *Cymbeline* is so ingeniously intricate that it is ineffective on the stage and thereby defeats the purpose for which the ingenuity was apparently expended. One feels inclined, indeed, to assert with some positiveness that the artistic skill required in managing so elaborate a scene was not exerted without definite purpose. The new technical achievement bespeaks deliberation. Again one feels inclined to conjecture that this artistic effort may have been exerted for the purpose of rivalling similarly heightened dénouements in Beaumont and Fletcher.

Without insisting too much on deliberate rivalry, we may surely say that, just as in the Beaumont-Fletcher romances, the elaborate dénouement is the most marked characteristic of the construction of *Cymbeline*. In the same way in the *Winter's Tale*, and the *Tempest*, dénouements are prepared for, postponed, and heightened. In each, to quote Mr. Wendell again, "there is a new and bold technical experiment" and "the experiment consists chiefly of a deliberately skillful handling of the dénouement."[1] Entirely unprecedented in the preceding plays of Shakspere, such heightened construction of the dénouement is practically unprecedented in all earlier Elizabethan plays; it has its only parallel in Beaumont and Fletcher.

Finally, these plays all end happily. Essentially tragic as are the incidents of *Cymbeline*, the first three acts of the *Winter's Tale*, and the Italian story at the basis of the *Tempest*, no one of these stories is carried out to its tragic conclusion. In *Cymbeline*, the happy ending is secured by a violation of the most liberal notions of poetic justice; in the *Winter's Tale* the happy ending is deliberately substituted for the tragic one of Greene's novel; and in the *Tempest* the happy ending is expanded into an entire play. In consequence there have been many speculations in regard to Shakspere's forgiving charity, his reconciliatory temper, and his attainment of a serene, calmly philosophical maturity. These speculations are interesting so far as they express to us the emotional components of the artistic moods in which these plays were composed. The feelings which arise in any artist during creative work must, however, be distinguished from the practical objective circumstances which for most artists, as for Shakspere, play an important part

---

[1] *William Shakspere.* p. 377.

in determining the subject and form of production. Shakspere's moods may have had little resemblance to the emotional experiences of Beaumont and Fletcher, but so far as stage representation goes, his romances were tragi-comedies, just as *Philaster* and *A King and No King* were tragi-comedies.

We have seen that those plays marked a development on earlier tragi-comedies. In the same way all the traits which we have noticed in Shakspere's romances differentiate them from any earlier tragi-comedies; and in particular, the heightened contrast of tragic and idyllic circumstances and the treatment of dénouement show that Shakspere was now using tragi-comedy with a fuller realization than before of its theatrical possibilities. In comparison with earlier plays like *Much Ado* and *Measure for Measure*, the romances appeal to more varied and more contrasted emotions and present happy endings which are more ingenious, elaborate, and surprising. Without the archaic abundance of murders, the virtuous people are involved in all sorts of difficulties and entanglements and are brought out in the end triumphantly happy. The emotions of the spectators are intensely stimulated, and at the same time their sympathies are gratified. Shakspere may possibly have written these plays to inculcate forgiveness or serenity of disposition; he certainly did write them to be acted on the stage of the Globe theater. The happy culmination of tragic circumstances seems likely, then, to have had its origin in a desire to gratify the public. At this time, too, it was a new structural experiment for Shakspere and an innovation on the practice of his contemporaries, unless it was an adoption of a fashion already successfully set by *Philaster*.

B. Characterization.

In characterization, no less than in plots, the romances show a marked difference from Shakspere's other plays. The characters[1] show, above all, a surprising loss of individuality. They are less consistent, less subtly drawn, less plausibly human; they are more the creatures of stage situations. Their salient characteristics are exaggerated and emphasized by descriptions placed in the mouths of other persons; and thus they often become such heightened types of perfect virtue or utter depravity as we found in Beaumont and Fletcher.

These wholesale assertions will not be readily accepted by those for whom Shakspere's wonderful phrasing has made vital the romantic atmosphere and the people who breathe it. But these assertions do not detract one whit from one's admiration

---

[1] In discussing characters, I shall rarely refer to the comic characters. They seem to me to resemble closely those in the earlier plays and to have little likeness to Beaumont and Fletcher's. For our purpose, then, they may be disregarded.

and delight in Imogen and Perdita; they merely point to a new method in producing that delight. That this change in method is a real one, may be seen by examining the methods used in the characterization of the romances and comparing them with the methods used in the earlier plays. It is well, however, to remind ourselves again that Shakspere must have created these people with their stage presentation in view. Their poetical qualities have immortalized them; but in studying the methods of their creation, we must keep in mind their stage qualities. It is unsafe to suppose that an Elizabethan audience appreciated poetry in a play more keenly than audiences do to-day; and in studying the stage qualities of the characters, it is advisable to put the poetry in the background. Keeping, then, to the point of view of spectators at an Elizabethan theater, we shall be better able to see what effects Shakspere sought to produce and in what ways his characters resembled those of his fellow playwrights.

Coming now to specific characters we may note the lack of individualization and the subservience to situation in Leontes. It is easy, of course, to find intuitive psychology almost anywhere in Shakspere's phrasing; but one must be something of a casuist, I think, to discover a very real human being in Leontes. His vileness and rage and his subsequent tenderness and repentance do not impress one as the traits of an individual. His feelings are all intensified to suit the situations. He is, on the stage, merely a representative of the common Elizabethan type of the suspicious husband in the presence of imaginary cuckoldom. He is a piece of a play, a convention. He is true to life only as a conventional type is true to life. We have only to recall how Othello wooed and loved and murdered and died, and how every act and every phrase seemed a part of a living man in the face of some of the most intense problems of life—and we shall see how greatly the method of characterization has changed in the *Winter's Tale*.

In the same way as Leontes, Hermione is also a creature of situations. The archness and wit of her repartee in the first act, her noble declamation in the trial scene, and the unforgiving chastity of her sixteen years wait, do not convince one that they belong to the same woman. They belong to the plot.

The bad characters display the same lack of consistency and an extraordinary intensification of their evil traits for the sake of situation. Thus, Iachimo is neither the mere figure-head that Don John is in *Much Ado*, nor the astonishingly human monstrosity that Iago is; he is a stage villain who has a telling acting part in two or three situations and very little else in this world. This exaggeration of salient traits is equally apparent in the Queen in *Cymbeline* and in Sebastian and Antonio in the *Tempest*.

This same method of exaggeration is also apparent in the heroines as well as the other methods of a romantic drama. To substantiate this statement, we may begin with one who, to many people, seems the most delightful of Shakspere's heroines—Imogen.

"Of all his women," says Mrs. Jameson, "considered as individuals rather than as heroines, Imogen is the most perfect." "Imogen, the most lovely and perfect of Shakspere's female characters," is the comment of Nathan Drake. "Of all his heroines," says Charles Cowden Clarke, "no one conveys so fully the ideal of womanly perfection as Imogen." "In the character of Imogen," says Schlegel, "no one feature of female excellence is omitted."

These quotations indicate well enough the impression Imogen gives—she is perfect. Like most perfect people, she is not real, she is idealized, and that is possibly what these critics mean by their perfects. In comparison with the women in the early sentimental comedies, Rosalind, Beatrice, Portia, and Viola, she lacks the details of characterization, the mannerisms which remind us of real persons and suggest the possibility of portraiture. In comparison with these heroines, an analysis of Imogen's character fails to supply really individual traits; one is thrown back on a general statement of her perfectibility. She is extremely idealized, or in other words, the exigencies of the romantic drama required a heroine who should be very, very good; and Shakspere, by the delicacy and purity of his fancy, by the exquisite fitness of his verse, succeeded in doing just what Beaumont and Fletcher were forever trying to do with their Bellarios and Aspatias.

That the methods of characterization are the same, may be seen when one examines *Cymbeline* and notes just what Imogen says and does. She is good and chaste and spirited; she resists an attempt at seduction; she wears boys' clothes; she leaves the court in search of her lover; she remains true to him after he has deserted her and sought to kill her; she dies and is brought back to life again; she passes through all sorts of impossible situations to final reconciliation and happiness. In all this there is little trace of an individual character; all this can be duplicated in the stories of Bellario and Arethusa.

Take, again, what she says. Take for example, her speeches in the dialogue with Iachimo:[1] read the lines by themselves— "What makes your admiration?"—"What is the matter, trow?"—"What, dear sir, thus raps you, are you well?"— "Continues well my lord? His health beseech you?"—and so on. Manifestly, there is no individuality there. What she says is suited admirably to the situation, but Bellario, Are-

---

[1] Act I, 6, 38–210.

139

thusa, or any one of half a dozen of the romantic heroine type might say it just as well. Take again the rest of her dialogue with Iachimo, or with Pisanio on the way to Milford Haven;[1] or take her soliloquy on cruel fate;[2] or the one bemoaning her weakness and fatigue;[3] or her speeches in the final act; consider how these speeches spoken by a boy actor would have appealed to an Elizabethan audience, and you will see how complete the similarity is between these speeches and similar matter in the Elizabethan drama. They are part and parcel of the ordinary situations of the romantic drama.

Moreover, even the intense sentimentalization does not produce consistency. The girl who makes some very spirited replies to her father when he interrupts her parting with her lover,[4] the girl who declaims so oratorically to Pisanio when he delivers her lover's letter,[5] the girl who stains her face in the blood of her supposed lover,[6] and the girl who recovers immediately to follow Lucio as a page,[7] are hardly recognizable as the same individual. Still further, it must be noticed that the character is presented largely by means of comments and descriptions on the part of others. The tributes of Iachimo, Posthumus, Pisanio, Guiderius, Arveragus, do more to create our ideas of Imogen's beauty of character than anything she does or says.

Perdita and Miranda have even less marks of individuality than Imogen. Mrs. Jameson says, to be sure, that "Juliet herself is not more firmly and distinctly drawn than Perdita. The picture is perfectly finished at every point." But when one reads Juliet's balcony speech, full of spontaneous and subtle revelation of character, and then reads Perdita's speech to Florizel,[8] one hardly knows what Mrs. Jameson means. Perdita never says anything which any heroine might not say except this mixture of beautiful poetry and poor gardening.

A further reading of Mrs. Jameson and other critics shows that they gain their notions of the beauty and grace of the character from what others of the dramatis personæ say about her, and their notions of her tenderness and delicacy largely from the fact that she is so often silent. The fact that she says so little has given rise to pages of ecstasy over Shakspere's subtle delineation. In fine, she is a conventional romantic heroine, beautifully described, but she is not a successful piece of purely dramatic characterization. Miranda has still less to say or do and is consequently regarded as more ethereally ideal. On the stage, she must have seemed an even less vital representative of the sentimental type.

---

[1] Act. III, 3, 23–84.
[2] I, 6, 1–9.
[3] III, 6, 1–27.
[4] I, 1, 130–150.
[5] III, 4, 44–108.
[6] IV, 2, 330.
[7] IV, 2, 367, seq.
[8] IV, 4, 110–135.

These three heroines, then, who seem to many to possess the lasting suggestiveness of noble ideal conceptions of human nature, could have appeared on the stage only as ordinary heroines. Idealization in poetry becomes on the stage mere emphasis and description of the salient qualities of purity and winsomeness. On the stage, Shakspere's heroines have few traits to distinguish them from almost any of Beaumont and Fletcher's. The same beardless boy who one day played Bellario might the next day, without change of make-up, appear as the page Fidele. Nor is the resemblance merely one of stage appearance. Beaumont and Fletcher and Shakspere alike seem to have sought to produce a heroine—the personification of ideal womanhood, garnished with beautiful poetry—who should fill the requirements of the romantic situations which they built up out of sentimental love stories. Limited by the same requirements, their methods, too, were similar. In connection with these similarities, it becomes important to remember that the sentimentalized heroine had almost no part in Shakspere's plays during the eight years from *Twelfth Night* to *Cymbeline*.

Our emphasis on the similarities between the heroines must not be misinterpreted to indicate a blindness to their differences. They differ in many ways; they differ just as Beaumont's imagination or Fletcher's phrasing differs from Shakspere's imagination or phrasing. Shakspere's imagination, for example, does not delight to linger over the theme of unrequited love to the extent that Beaumont's did. Beaumont and Fletcher, again, fail to suggest by their phrasing the delicacy of sentiment with which Shakspere's heroines are dressed. We must not forget, either, that there are many heroines of this general type in the Elizabethan drama and that there were some on the stage before Shakspere had established himself as a dramatist or Beaumont had been sent to school.

This type, however, plays little part in the drama for six or seven years before the probable date of *Philaster* and little part in Shakspere's plays from *Twelfth Night* to the romances. Two facts are very significant—a sentimentalized heroine plays an important role in each of the Beaumont-Fletcher romances and a sentimentalized heroine likewise has an important part in each of Shakspere's romances. While Shakspere transformed her into a beautiful idealized being, characteristically his own; on analysis as a stage personage, she still presents the characteristics of Beaumont and Fletcher's ideal maidens. To put the case boldly, even Imogen is no other than Bellario plus Shakspere's poetry.

There are other characters, too, in Shakspere's romances who show resemblances to the Beaumont-Fletcher stock types. Thus the wicked queen in *Cymbeline* is very like the wicked queens of Beaumont and Fletcher. The faithful counsellors,

Gonzalo, Camillo, and the faithful servant Pisanio supply the place on the stage of Beaumont and Fletcher's faithful friends. The king in *Cymbeline* has a close likeness to the king in *Philaster;* and the king in the *Winter's Tale*, something of the royal fury of Arbaces in *A King and No King*.

Exact resemblances are not at all to be expected; but a summary of the characters of the romances shows that Shakspere, like Beaumont and Fletcher, used only a few fairly conventionalized types. The heroines are all of one piece, the villains are of one piece; the heroes can hardly be distinguished from each other except that Posthumus has much more to do; the aged counsellors appear in two plays: and these types include about all the principal characters. To see how great a change these types indicate in Shakspere's method of characterization, we have only to remember that within two years before the time when he probably wrote *Cymbeline*, he was probably writing *Antony and Cleopatra*.

On the whole, then, the characterization of the romances shows little of the immense creative power that distinguishes Shakspere's work from *Romeo and Juliet* through *Antony and Cleopatra*. The characters, on the contrary, are in the main only such conventional types as the romantic situations demand. That this change was conscious cannot, of course, be asserted; but that it had its cause in the immediate demand of the London stage, seems in every way probable. It is, at least, in harmony with the supposition that in his effort to produce plays with varied and intense situations, and with tragic and idyllic contrasts, culminating in elaborate dénouements, Shakspere followed so closely the style of play which Beaumont and Fletcher had made popular that, consciously or unconsciously, he adopted their methods of characterization and even made some use of their conventionalized types.

C. Style.

The romances differ from the rest of Shakspere's plays not only in plots and characters but also in versification. Up to *Cymbeline*, the development of Shakspere's versification is regular enough; the increase in unstopt lines and feminine endings and the decrease of rhyme, mark a gradual development in freedom of versification with a constant increase in mastery. In comparison, however, with the splendid phrasing of *Antony and Cleopatra*, *Cymbeline* shows a puzzling decadence; nor can its characteristic traits readily be explained merely as a stage in the development discoverable in Shakspere and in Elizabethan dramatic versification in general. An examination of these structural traits, which are also manifest in the *Winter's Tale* and the *Tempest*, is necessary in order to distinguish the style from that of the preceding plays and is of interest in connection with the contemporary versification of Fletcher.

In the first place, we find an increase in the proportion of double endings. In addition there seems to be a constant deliberate effort to conceal the metre. The rhythm is often hardly discernible until we piece together the broken lines, count the syllables, and place the accents. The verse constantly borders on prose.

In the second place, the end-stopt line is often carefully avoided; there being, in point of fact, two unstopt for every five end-stopt lines. Here, Shakspere's practice differs decidedly from Fletcher's, but in one particular the effect is much the same. Shakspere's verse, like Fletcher's, clearly tends to imitate the natural, unpremeditated manner of ordinary speech; and in attaining this effect, the broken phrases, avoiding the strict metrical limitations of lines and syllables, largely contribute. The unstopt lines, like Fletcher's stopt lines, imitate the discontinuity of actual speech. Fletcher wrote in disconnected lines; Shakspere in disconnected phrases.

Other than this, their technical methods are similar. Shakspere's use of unstopt lines involves a use of weak and light endings, but his structure in general is like Fletcher's. It is never periodic. On the contrary, the speakers repeat themselves, break off abruptly, correct themselves, and add apparent after-thoughts. The speeches of the actors seem suggested by the action of the moment and are almost necessarily accompanied by action. One image is never fully developed, nor are set descriptions indulged in as in the early plays; but image is piled upon image as if one suggested another. As Mr. Macaulay says: " Point is added to point, each one as it comes being apparently suggested by that which has preceded it. . . . . the whole conveying the impression of thoughts uttered as they passed through the mind rather than of any elaborate composition."

Important in producing this loose structure and of itself one of the most distinguishing traits of Shakspere's late verse, is his use of parentheses. Sometimes the parenthetical structure is used to such a degree that the meaning is almost unintelligible; it usually requires the assistance of gesture and skillful elocution. Even bits of operatic convention take on this form, as Pisanio's comment on Imogen's change of clothing.[1] Parentheses serve also to break the declamatory monotony of the early style, as in Hermione's great speech.[2] They are most often used, however, in cases where violent passions demand confused, ejaculatory speech. Take, for example, Imogen's

---

[1] *Cymbeline*, III, 4, 156–168.
[2] *Winter's Tale*, III, 2, 92–117.

speech on receiving Posthumus' letter,[1] or her dialogue with Pisanio,[2] or Leontes' wild outbreak of jealousy,[3] or his speech to Camillo,[4] or his speech to Antigonous.[5] All these examples indicate how well the parenthetical structure is adapted to stage action.

These examples, which may be multiplied almost at random, also illustrate the other traits of style which have been mentioned and which are, indeed, generally recognized as characteristic of Shakspere's late style. Another trait which seems to me especially characteristic of the romances is the frequent use of colloquialisms, as 'he's' for 'he is,' ''tis' for 'it is,' 'I'll' for 'I will,' and so on.[6] While not of much importance of itself, this trait of phrasing resembles the more important traits of structure in the evident imitation of natural speech.

All these traits of the late style seem aimed at producing an effect of natural and unpremeditated speech which should lend itself readily to action; yet, as a matter of fact, one of the most noticeable results of these changes is the obscurity of the verse. This is due partly to the extreme to which the broken sentence structure is carried, and partly to the overburdening of the verse with thought, and partly to the intensity and rapidity of Shakspere's imagination. In avoiding set descriptions he heaps metaphor upon metaphor, and as a result gains a brevity which is forcible but by no means clear.

In this intensity and rapidity of imagination lies a fundamental difference between his verse and Fletcher's. As Charles Lamb[7] says, '' (Fletcher) lays line upon line, making up one after the other, adding image to image so deliberately that we may see where they join. Shakspere mingles everything; he runs line into line, embarrasses sentences and metaphors; before one idea has burst its shell, another is hatched and clamorous for disclosure.'' Fletcher was not troubled with complexity of thought or exuberance of imagination to such an extent that he had difficulty in fitting them for stage utterance; in

---

[1] *Cymb.*, III, 2, 53-61.
[2] *Cymb.*, III, 4, 72-85, 104-109.
[3] *W. T.*, I, 2, 185, seq.
[4] *W. T.* I, 2, 267, seq.
[5] *W. T.* II, 3, 154-162.
[6] An examination of the first acts of *Merchant of Venice, Antony and Cleopatra*, and the *Winter's Tale* shows the number of abbreviations to be 16, 49, and 89, respectively. In the case of 's for is, I'll for I will, 'tis for it is, 'll for will, the ratios of the abbreviated forms to the total number of abbreviated and unabbreviated were .28, .61, and .74, respectively. This furnishes some evidence that Shakspere's increase in the use of colloquialisms was marked in his latest period. A similar examination of several acts in Fletcher's plays indicates that his preference for similar abbreviations was equally marked.
[7] Lamb's *Specimens of Dramatists*. Second Edition. p. 419.

his late period, at any rate, Shakspere undoubtedly was. To this is due in part the difference in the general impression received from their styles. In total effect they are very unlike. In comparing versifications, however, habits of thought or imagination may well be left out of consideration; we must confine ourselves to resemblance in structure. In his greater use of run-over lines and in his more moderate use of double endings, as well as in traits of his imagery and phrasing, Shakspere's verse is readily distinguished from Fletcher's; but in other technical qualities, its resemblance is worth noting. Shakspere uses feminine endings more frequently than before, he is at pains to conceal the metre, he writes in disconnected phrases, he avoids carefully elaborated images, he uses parentheses to an extraordinary degree, he uses colloquialisms with frequency. In all these respects he seems, like Fletcher, to have been imitating the unpremeditated, disjointed utterance which is best suited to stage action.

It is in these structural changes, also, that the verse is distinguished from that of the earlier plays. How complete its departure is from the old lyric style can at once be seen by comparing it with the first act of so late a play as *Lear*. How marked is the structural transformation can be seen by referring to the still later play of *Antony and Cleopatra*. A comparison of this last play with *Cymbeline* also reveals a decided loss of mastery, an apparently conscious and not quite successful struggle to overcome the difficulties of the new structure. More than in the case of any of the other traits of the romances, one is tempted to suggest that the versification, particularly in *Cymbeline*, indicates effort and deliberation.

The cause of this effort may be sought in various directions. The structural peculiarities may have been the outcome, conscious or unconscious, of the new style of play and of the accompanying mood. The general progress of Shakspere's style toward freedom in metre and structure must be given some share in the production of the style of the late plays. Our examination of the traits of the style does, however, emphasize the important influence of another factor. It does not indicate that there was any direct imitation of Fletcher, even in the structural peculiarities. The resemblances in structure between the two styles were probably not related as cause and effect, but were the results of similar dramatic conditions and similar plays. Shakspere does seem to have used means similar to those used by Fletcher, because he was trying as Fletcher was to suit his verse to stage action. This effort to imitate unpremeditated, disconnected, natural speech seems, in fact, sufficient to account for all the marked variations in structure which *Cymbeline* presents in comparison with earlier plays.

D.   Stage Effects.

In considering the plots, characters, and style of the romances we have reached the conclusion that all the traits which distinguish them from Shakspere's other plays show a common tendency to secure greater stage-effectiveness. In face of the fact that the romances have not since the Restoration proved very effective acting plays, this conclusion may still seem questionable. In the first place, it must be remembered, both Shakspere's and Beaumont and Fletcher's romances lack the unity of construction and still more the verisimilitude demanded by modern audiences. Further, it may be repeated, Shakspere's romances do not show anything like Beaumont and Fletcher's cleverness in constructing startling situations and plots. As Elizabethan plays, however, as series of entertaining situations and elaborate climaxes, they must have ministered to the same taste as the Beaumont-Fletcher romances.

Apart from regular dramatic methods, there are still further evidences of efforts for stage success which appeal even less to modern taste. The extraordinary variety of situations in *Cymbeline*[1] was perhaps sufficient, but in the *Winter's Tale* there are additional devices. There is the bear which chases Antigonous off the stage during the storm,[2] there is the antick dance by the twelve satyrs,[3] the graceful dance of shepherds and shepherdesses,[4] the change of clothes, which may easily have afforded a good piece of comic business,[5] and, finally, there is the transformation of the statue to life.[6] No dramatist introduced any of these into his play without a deliberate effort for stage effect. The day of warring armies and revengeful ghosts was passing, but the audiences' craving for novelty was unceasing, and it is amply cared for both here and in *the Tempest*.

The *Tempest*, to us a beautiful poem full of beneficent idealism, on the Elizabethan stage must have seemed largely an effort to satisfy this craving. Caliban, that immensely taking Elizabethan stage-beast, who has proved so prophetically philosophical, must have been the hit of the play. Then there was the old device borrowed from the *Midsummer Night's Dream* of the invisible Ariel bewildering the courtiers,[7] and the still older business of the vanishing banquet, "accomplished with

---

[1] The curious spectacle of Jupiter and the ghosts in Posthumus' dream (V, 4) must not be overlooked.
[2] III, 3.   See note, p. 34, ante.
[3] IV, 4, 352.   See p. 32.   Compare with the dance of Indians in the *Four Plays*.
[4] IV, 4, 165.
[5] IV, 4, 640–670.
[6] V, 3.   For a transformation of a statue to life, see Lyly's *Gallathea*. For use of statues in court masques, see *the Masque of the Inner Temple*, etc. (1613), and *the Golden Age Restored* (1616).
[7] III, 3.

146

a quaint device."[1] Then there were the drunken scenes, such as Shakspere had used before, but now made especially diverting when the climax was reached and the dogs chased the drenched and filthy boors about the stage while Prospero and Ariel cried on quarry! Prospero himself, with his magician's robes and wand, must have made an imposing spectacular figure.

Prospero and Ariel are, indeed, proper figures for a court masque, and the "strange Shapes," like the satyrs in the *Winter's Tale*, are nothing more nor less than an anti-masque. Note, for proof the stage directions:

III, 3. "Enter several strange Shapes, bringing in a banquet; they dance about it with gentle actions of salutation; and, inviting the king, etc., to eat, they depart."

Again, a little later, after Ariel in the form of a harpy has vanished in thunder:

III, 3, 82. —"then, to soft music, enter the Shapes again, and dance with mocks and mows, and carrying out the table."

Still again—

IV, 1. "A noise of hunters heard. Enter divers Spirits, in shape of dogs and hounds," etc.

The anti-masques at the court often appeared in shape of animals, as goats (*Honour of Wales*, 1619) and bears (*Augurs*, 1622) and monkeys (*Middle Temple and Lincoln's Inn*, 1613).

These grotesque spirits, then, in shape of dogs, and, earlier, with their dancing and mocks and mows, must, just as certainly as the masque proper in the fourth act, have been suggested by the court masques. The antic dances and performance of the Shapes, together with the devices of Prospero and Ariel, make, in fact, an unmistakable masque-setting for the masque proper with its goddesses and graceful dance of nymphs and reapers.[2]

Thus in the *Tempest* Shakspere was combining the construction, pageantry, and devices of the court masque, just as Beaumont and Fletcher did in the *Four Plays*. It is interesting to note, by the way, that Shakspere combined his masque-material with his play much more skillfully than any of his contemporaries. Beaumont and Fletcher's *Four Plays* is a rare instance of a similar attempt to unite the diverse elements. Usually, the anti-masque or the spectacle or the masque proper is dragged into the play. In the *Tempest*, however, the strange shapes and the goddesses suit the atmosphere of the enchanted

---

[1] III, 3.
[2] IV, 1, 138. "Enter certain Reapers, properly habited; they join with the Nymphs in a graceful dance; towards the end whereof Prospero starts suddenly and speaks; after which, to a strange, hollow, and confused noise, they heavily vanish."

island and play a natural part in the magic of Ariel and Prospero.

Very distinctly, then, in the *Tempest*, and at least in the dance of shepherds and anti-masque of satyrs in the *Winter's Tale*, Shakspere was adding to the attractiveness of his plays by the introduction of a good deal of pageantry after the style of the court masques. This fashion of imitating the court masques was certainly a new one at the time, and Beaumont and Fletcher were leaders in it. Shakspere also seems to have been regarded as a leader and prominent offender by Ben Jonson, for in protesting against the "jigs and dances" he especially mentions "those that beget tales, tempests and such like drolleries." [1] Our chronology of the plays indicates that Beaumont and Fletcher preceded Shakspere in the imitation of the court masque, but the question of precedence cannot be certainly settled nor is it very important. The development of the court masque in the reign of James I must inevitably have been followed by an adoption of some of its important and novel features on the public stage. Shakspere was a leader in the same fashion in which Beaumont and Fletcher were leaders and was playing to the same taste to which they played.

Before leaving the subject of the stage pageantry of Shakspere's plays, we must note that it is especially abundant in the two plays in which he probably collaborated with Fletcher. *Henry VIII*, according to Sir Henry Wotton, "was set forth with many extraordinary circumstances of pomp and majesty," [2] and the stage directions amply testify to the fact. The trial scene, the coronation, and the christening make the play a succession of pageants, and in addition there are noticeable masque elements. In Act V, scene 4, there is the porter's scene with the satire on the crowds that thronged to masques and pageants, like similar scenes in the *Four Plays* [3] and the *Maid's Tragedy*. [4] In Act I, scene 4, there is the masque at Wolsey's with the king and others disguised as shepherds. Again, in the vision which appears to Katharine, there is a spectacle and dance decidedly like those of the court masques. [5]

---

[1] *Bartholomew Fair*. Induction, (acted 1614).
[2] See p. 37, ante.
[3] Induction.
[4] I, 2.
[5] IV, 2, 80. "Sad and solemn music." Then after line 82: "The vision. Enter, solemnly tripping one after another, six personages, clad in white robes, wearing on their heads garlands of bays, and golden vizards on their faces; branches of bays or palm in their hands. They first congee unto her, then dance; and, at certain changes, the first two hold a spare garland over her head; at which the other four make reverent curtsies . . . . and so in their dancing vanish, carrying their garland with them. The music continues."

These last two masques or dances occur in scenes by Fletcher, but we can't be quite safe in concluding that he devised them, although this is very probable.

In the *Two Noble Kinsmen*, apart from the pageantry of the "funeral solemnity"[1] and of the prayers in the temple,[2] we have a masque and an anti-masque. The wedding masque[3] is in the approved form and the anti-masque,[4] as we have seen, is borrowed from the court *Masque of the Inner Temple*. With the addition of some action, this forms a whole scene representing a performance by some country folk before Theseus.

In these two plays we thus have additional evidence of Fletcher's use of the court masques in stage plays, and also additional evidence that Shakspere was trying to satisfy the taste for stage pageantry.

E. Summary.

The results of our investigation up to this point may be briefly summarized. The three romances by Shakspere show many common traits and a marked divergence from his plays of the preceding eight years. While in a few particulars they resemble the earlier comedies, they stand together and form a new style of drama. The relation of each play to the general type, its resemblances and variations, have been left to succeeding chapters. So far we have dwelt mainly on common traits and common divergences from the preceding plays.

To emphasize this divergence reference may be profitably made to Coleridge's discussion of the qualities which distinguish Shakspere from all other dramatists. Among the seven characteristics enumerated are the following four: "expectation in preference to surprise;" "independence of the dramatic interest in the plot;" "independence of the dramatic interest in the story as the ground of the plot;" "the characters of the dramatis personæ like those in real life are to be inferred by the reader, they are not told to him."[5] These four characteristics are certainly manifest in most of Shakspere's plays, especially in the tragedies which preceded the romances; in the romances, however, no one of them holds with any exactness. In fact the reverse of each seems generally a noticeable trait.

In our analysis we have found varied and ingenious plots, tragic and idyllic scenes furnishing emotional variety and contrast, telling situations, emphasized dénouements, characteri-

---

[1] I, 5.
[2] V, 3.
[3] I, 1. (Shakspere's part.)
[4] III, 5, by Fletcher.
[5] *Characteristics of Shakspere's Drama.* Complete works of Coleridge. Ed. Professor Shedd. New York, 1854, 7 vols. Vol. 4, p. 61, seq.

zation sacrificed to convention and situation, a versification perceptibly designed for stage effect, and considerable pageantry taken from the court masques. In all these, and in more specific ways as well, the romances not only differ from Shakspere's preceding work, they resemble the contemporary romances of Beaumont and Fletcher.

Moreover, we have found from an examination of all the plays acted 1601–1611 that there are none by other authors which offer marked resemblances to those by either Beaumont and Fletcher or Shakspere. Not only is there no play by another author which possesses in any considerable degree the characteristics of either set of romances; there are few plays which offer any resemblances. Among the plays from 1601–1611 there are few romantic plots, almost no tragi-comedies, little emphasis of sentimental heroines, few idyllic scenes, no full-fledged imitations of court masques. There is, in short, no indication of a revival of romance, to say nothing of the formation of a new type of romantic tragedies and tragi-comedies.

Shakspere's romances seem not only unlike his own preceding plays but also unlike any contemporary plays except those of Beaumont and Fletcher. When we remember that Shakspere's change from historical tragedy to romance was very abrupt, that it was almost exactly contemporaneous with the success of Beaumont and Fletcher's romances, that Shakspere and Fletcher wrote two plays together for the King's men, and that three of Beaumont and Fletcher's romances were acted by the same theatrical company as Shakspere's, then the resemblances between the two sets of plays become very significant. So strong do they seem that we must conclude there was considerable indebtedness from one to the other. The co-existence of two sets of romances closely resembling each other has been established, and a study of contemporary drama indicates that the only possible explanation is that of mutual influence.

The question of which group influenced the other remains to be considered. So far we have been discussing resemblances without dwelling on questions of which was cause and which effect. Some light, however, has been thrown on these questions. In some particulars there seems no way of determining the cause, and in some no reason to suppose that there was any definite relation of cause and effect. Common traits in versification, for example, cannot be held to show direct imitation; at the most they indicate only a common purpose. Resemblances in stage pageantry likewise merely indicate that each was securing similar effects by similar means. While in the absence of a certain chronology it is impossible to say who was the innovator in this respect, we can assert that there may have been conscious rivalry and that there must have been conscious effort to meet the same stage demand. In other traits, like the material of the plots, the emphasis placed on a surprising dénouement, the sentimental heroines, we find reason to expect more definite indebtedness. Questions of indebtedness must, in fact, include methods of construction and characterization and all the defining characteristics of the romance type.

Before considering this whole question of mutual influence we may best turn to an examination of some further resemblances between typical representatives of either class—*Cymbeline* and *Philaster*.

CHAPTER IX.

CYMBELINE AND PHILASTER.

Cymbeline is generally considered the earliest of the romances. In *Cymbeline*, then, if anywhere, we may expect to find specific traces of the Beaumont-Fletcher romances. A study of Shakspere's plays after his earliest period does not lead us to expect to find Shakspere absolutely imitating; but it does show that he was constantly influenced by dramatic conditions and fashions and that he was using and perfecting dramatic types which other men had originated. In the first play in which, if our hypothesis be true, he adapted the Beaumont-Fletcher type, there ought to be some definite resemblances to the original. Such resemblances may be found between *Cymbeline* and *Philaster*.

The majority of these have already been discussed by Dr. B. Leonhardt in an article on the relations of *Philaster* to *Hamlet* and *Cymbeline*.[1] He is so impressed with the many resemblances between *Philaster* and *Cymbeline* that he thinks Beaumont and Fletcher used the Cloten-Imogen plot. Further, he takes 1608 as the date of *Philaster* and is therefore moved to suggest in a foot-note that *Cymbeline* was written before 1608. The idea that Shakspere could have imitated or adapted any one's work does not seem to have occurred to him.

In comparing the two plays, it must be remembered that many resemblances have been instanced in the preceding chapters. All that has been said of the romances of Beaumont and Fletcher applies to *Philaster*, and all that has been said of the romances of Shakspere applies with especial force to *Cymbeline*. Here we are to look for more specific resemblances and we will begin, as usual, with the plots. The historical narrative and the Italian expedition of Posthumus have no parallels in *Philaster*, and most of the Megra affair and the rising of the mob in *Philaster* have no parallels in *Cymbeline*. In the main, however, the plots are strikingly similar.

---

[1] *Anglia*, Vol. 8, p. 424. *Über Beziehungen von Beaumont und Fletcher's Philaster, or Love Lies-a-Bleeding zu Shakespeare's Hamlet und Cymbeline.* B. Leonhardt, 1885. The resemblances, to *Hamlet* have been frequently noticed and may be due to a conscious imitation of that play. The resemblance, however, arises mainly from the use of the common motive of 'revenge for a father;' and the frequent burlesque of *Hamlet* in Beaumont and Fletcher's plays counts against the likelihood of conscious imitation.

Imogen, heiress to the throne, is destined by her royal father to marry his boorish step-son, Cloten; but she is wedded to a noble youth, Leonatus Posthumus.[1] Arethusa, only daughter of the King of Calabria, is likewise destined by her father to marry the boorish Spanish prince, Pharamond, but she is in love with Philaster the rightful heir.[2] Leonatus is favorably contrasted by the courtiers with Cloten,[3] and so Philaster is contrasted with Pharamond.[4] Both Leonatus[5] and Philaster[6] are driven from court by the royal fathers. As he is leaving Arethusa's apartments, Philaster has an encounter with Pharamond,[7] and as Leonatus is leaving Imogen, he has an encounter with Cloten.[8] In the absence of Leonatus, Iachimo tries to seduce Imogen,[9] and Pharamond makes similar proposals to Arethusa.[10] Both are repulsed. Iachimo slanders Imogen to Leonatus,[11] and Arethusa is falsely accused to Philaster by Dion.[12] Imogen is brought to despair by Leonatus' letter charging her with unfaithfulness,[13] and Arethusa is likewise in anguish when similarly upbraided to the face by Philaster.[14] Each lover has a passionate soliloquy in which he denounces his mistress and all woman-kind.[15] [16] Imogen leaves the court in disguise to seek Leonatus and, after dismissing Pisanio, loses her way;[17] and Arethusa parts from the hunting party to wander

"O'er mountains, through brambles, pits, and floods."[18]

Both, because falsely slandered, wish to die.[19] [20] Each king is very much disturbed at his daughter's absence.[21] [22] Cymbeline accuses Pisanio of knowing where she is,[23] and so Calabria accuses Dion.[24] Arethusa is wounded by Philaster,[25] and Imogen is struck down by Leonatus.[26] Finally the disentanglements of the two plots are made in similar ways. In *Philaster*, Bellario explains that in spite of her page's clothes she is a woman, and Megra confesses that she has falsely slandered Arethusa.[27] In *Cymbeline*, Imogen explains and Iachimo confesses.[28] In *Philaster*, all are forgiven, even Megra and Pharamond,[29] so in *Cymbeline* Iachimo is pardoned;[30] and in each play the lovers are happily united under the king's favor.

[1] *Cymb.*, I, 1.
[2] *Phil.*, I, 1.
[3] *Cymb.*, I, 1.
[4] *Phil.*, I, 1.
[5] *Cymb.*, I, 1, 120–130.
[6] *Phil.*, I, 1.
[7] *Phil.*, I, 2.
[8] *Cymb.*, I, 2.
[9] *Cymb.*, I, 6.
[10] *Phil.*, I, 2.
[11] *Cymb.*, II, 4.
[12] *Phil.*, III, 1.
[13] *Cymb.*, III, 4, 20, seq.
[14] *Phil.*, III, 2.
[15] *Cymb.*, II, 5.

[16] *Phil.*, III, 2.
[17] *Cymb.*, III, 6.
[18] *Phil.*, IV, 3.
[19] *Cymb.*, III, 4, 75-95 : IV, 2, 15.
[20] *Phil.*, III, 2 : IV, 3.
[21] *Cymb.*, III, 5, 28-52.
[22] *Phil.*, IV, 2.
[23] *Cymb.*, IV, 3, 1-12.
[24] *Phil.*, IV, 2.
[25] *Phil.*, IV, 3.
[26] *Cymb.*, V, 5, 228.
[27] *Phil.*, V, 5.
[28] *Cymb.*, V, 5.
[29] *Phil.*, V, 5.
[30] *Cymb.*, V, 5.

These parallels indicate a close similarity between the two plots, yet after all the similarity does not lie so much in the stories as in the situations. The basis of the Imogen story is probably the ninth novel of the second day in the Decamerone. This story, the story of Iachimo's trick, forms no part of *Philaster*. To this Iachimo-Imogen story, however, Shakspere added a dozen or so situations which are almost exact counterparts of situations in *Philaster*.

Although the resemblance is not so close, the idyllic scenes in *Cymbeline* have more than a chance likeness to those in *Philaster*. The scenes in the mountains between Belarius and his foster sons, which give an opportunity to display Imogen's character with so much charm, recall a passage in *Philaster*.

> "Oh, that I had been nourished in these woods
> With milk of goats and acorns, and not known
> The right of crowns nor the dissembling trains
> Of women's looks; but digged myself a cave,
> Where I, my fire, my cattle, and my bed,
> Might have been shut together in one shed;
> And then had taken me some mountain girl,
> Beaten with winds, chaste as the hardened rocks
> Whereon she dwelt, that might have strewed my bed
> With leaves and reeds, and with the skins of beasts,
> Our neighbors, and have borne at her big breasts
> My large, coarse issue! This had been a life
> Free from vexation."[1]

The same ideas receive a much greater amplification in *Cymbeline*, where Belarius dwells in a cave and upholds the free, isolated life in a long discussion with his sons.[2] The passage in which Philaster describes his meeting with Bellario:

> "Hunting the buck,
> I found him sitting by a fountain's side," etc.[3]

gives expression to similar idyllic sentiments. The scenic representation of the idyl in *Philaster* is much less notable than in *Cymbeline* but occupies the whole of the fourth act. The four scenes of that act are located in a forest whither come a hunting party, a country fellow, woodmen, and the two maidens wandering forlorn. Into this forest, as in the mountains of Belarius, tragic events press thick and fast.

The idyllic elements in each play have still further similarity in the developments of the stories of Imogen-Fidele and Euphrasia-Bellario. As a princess at court, Imogen resembles Arethusa, but as a page in the country scenes she has a closer likeness to Bellario. As Dr. Leonhardt has shown, the resemblance is also much closer than that between Bellario and Viola. The resemblance between the two latter consists mainly

---

[1] *Phil.*, IV, 2.
[2] *Cymb.*, III, 3.
[3] *Phil.*, I, 2.

in their one common situation, each being the messenger from the man she loves to the woman he loves. Imogen and Bellario, however, are alike in their situations, sentiments, and characters. In noting their likenesses, we may join our discussion of the plots with that of the characterization of the two plays.

They both serve as pages, in their boys' clothes they wander through the woods, they suffer fatigue,[1] they beg for food,[2] they are heart-sick, again and again both wish for death; and throughout all their misfortunes they appeal in every line to the most sentimental sympathies of an audience. Their tenderness, simplicity, and utter devotion to their lords are emphasized over and over again. They are both extremely romantic idealizations of the 'love-lorn maiden' type; and for all the finer shading she receives from the meeting with her unknown brothers, Imogen does not unquestionably present the more exquisite poetry. Dramatically, at least, she says nothing quite so sympathetically effective as Bellario's submission:

> "Alas, my lord, my life is not a thing
> Worthy your noble thoughts! 't is not a life,
> 'T is but a piece of childhood thrown away."[3]

Other characters in the two plays offer points of likeness. The two kings are almost identically the same, except that the king of Calabria receives a certain coarseness from his belief in his daughter's guilt, and Cymbeline a certain importance from the historical narrative. The queen in *Cymbeline* and Megra in *Philaster* at least supply the same dramatic requirement for a wicked woman; and Dion and Pisanio for a faithful friend. Philaster and Leonatus have similar situations in the love stories and resemble each other not only in the general attributes of noble heroes but specifically in the fury of their jealousy, in their freedom from any sensual motives, and in the strongly marked, sentimental character of their love. Cloten and Pharamond are both out-and-out boors, both brutish, and both braggarts. They fill similar situations, and each one serves to supply the comic element in the play. Thus, the persons of the main action of each play may be paired together; and if the resemblance is apparent to the reader, despite the different imaginative development and phrasing given by the different poets, it must have been very marked on the stage where the two representatives of the same type had similar situations, similar action, similar costumes, and very probably the same actors.[4]

---

[1] *Cymb.*, III, 6, I, seq. *Phil.*, IV, 4, I, seq.
[2] *Cymb.*, III, 6, 45, seq. *Phil.*, IV, 3, 8, seq.
[3] *Phil.*, V. 2, 14-17.
[4] Both plays were acted by the King's men.

The general similarity of characters, situations, and sentiments, and even some slight verbal similarities may be further
seen by comparing the following parallel passages. First, take
the opening sixty or seventy lines of each play. Second, compare Arethusa's speech at the end of act III :

"Peace guide thee! Thou hast overthrown me once;" etc.

with Imogen's speech on Leonatus' falseness:

"True honest men being heard, like false Æneas," etc.[1]

Third, compare Posthumus' soliloquy, beginning:

"O, vengeance, vengeance!"[2]

with Philaster's,

"Now you may take that little right I have
To this poor kingdom," etc.[3]

Or the beginning of Posthumus' soliloquy where he dwells on
Imogen's apparent chastity with the opening lines of another
by Philaster:

"Oh, let all women
That love black deeds, learn to dissemble here," etc.[4]

Fourth, compare Philaster's speech after he is hurt by the
country fellow[5] with Iachimo's after he has been overcome by
Posthumus.[6] There is also a similar word play on ' strange '
and ' stranger : '[7] and in connection with the resemblance between the idyllic scenes, it may be noted that the name Bellario in *Philaster* appears in *Cymbeline* as Belarius.

Between *Philaster* and *Cymbeline*, then, there is a closer
resemblance than has been indicated between Beaumont and
Fletcher's and Shakspere's romances. In plot, characters, and
style, each play possesses the distinguishing traits of its class;
but in addition to these there are enough specific similarities
to make it very probable that one play was directly suggested
by the other. When we remember that both plays were written
at nearly the same time, for the same company, and by drama-

---

[1] III, 4, 60-66.
[2] II, 5, 8, seq.
[3] III, 2.
[4] *Phil.*, III, 1.
[5] *Phil.* IV, 3. "The gods take part against me : could this boor
Have held me thus else?"
[6] *Cymb.*, V, 2, 1-6.
[7] *Megra.* "Near me, perhaps : but there's a lady endures no stranger ; and to me you appear a very strange fellow."
Lady. "Methinks he's not so strange; he would quickly be acquainted." [*Philaster*, I, 1.
First Lord. "Did you hear of a stranger that's come to court to-
night?"
Cloten. "A stranger, and I know not on't!"
Second Lord. "He's a strange fellow himself, and knows it not."
[*Cymbeline*, II, 1.

tists who must have been acquainted, the probability approaches certainty.

Our comparison of the two plays thus re-enforces the conclusion already reached that there must have been some direct indebtedness of one set of romances to the other. It also brings us face to face with the question, which was the debtor and which the creditor?

It is not only practically certain that *Philaster* was written for the King's men while Shakspere was still writing for that company; it is also probable that it was written before *Cymbeline*.[1] In that case we could not escape the conclusion that Shakspere was indebted to *Philaster*.

Suppose for a moment that our chronology was certain instead of probable, and let us see what the nature of Shakspere's indebtedness would be. Beaumont and Fletcher had already experimented with several plays when they produced *Philaster*. Acted by the King's men at the Globe and at the more fashionable Blackfriars, the play made an instant and complete success. This was due not only to the skill of the authors in constructing the plot, in developing telling situations, and in writing a verse notably suited to stage action; it was also due to many novel features. There had been no play for seven or eight years at all resembling *Philaster*. During that time, at least, there had been no character like Bellario, no play containing such a contrast of tragic and idyllic scenes, or presenting such a surprising and ingenious dénouement. With all the excitement and pathos of a heroic tragedy, it had all the charm of a sentimental comedy. After the long succession of gloomy tragedies, historical plays with armies and battles, and satirical and realistic comedies of London life, this romance filled the audience with surprise and delight.

During the year or two preceding, Shakspere had been writing *Antony and Cleopatra*, *Timon*, and *Coriolanus*. Perhaps he was growing tired of tragic and classical themes; perhaps his mood was changing and he was beginning to take a more cheerful view of life; perhaps *Timon* and *Coriolanus* had not achieved great success on the stage—at any rate the success of *Philaster* aroused his interest. He may have known of the play before it was acted, and followed its development in the hands of his brilliant young friends; he may have watched their earlier work with a generous appreciation of their talents. As soon as *Philaster* was acted by his company, he must certainly have perceived its dramatic and poetic excellencies, the theatrical value of some of its innovations, and the appeal which its romantic situations made to the audiences. With his usual quickness to take advantage of anything the con-

[1] See p. 95, ante.

temporary drama offered, he at once forsook the themes with which he had been dealing for some seven years and started to write a play in friendly rivalry of *Philaster*. Possibly he already had the historical story of *Cymbeline* partially composed; to this he added other stories and many situations which were like those in *Philaster*. He made his play tragic in many of its circumstances and, recognizing the effectiveness of Beaumont and Fletcher's use of a happy ending, he labored especially over a happy dénouement. He introduced idyllic scenes and developed them more fully than had Beaumont and Fletcher, and he introduced a sentimental heroine that should surpass Bellario. Perhaps the sweetness and tenderness of that maiden touched Shakspere's feeling and harmonized with his new mood of peaceful reconciliation with life; and it may be the clever boy-actor who had made a success in Bellario wanted a similar part. If so, the task proved a congenial one to Shakspere. The part of Imogen seems to have been created with freer fancy and more spontaneous expression than the rest of the play. He recalled the women of his earlier comedies, Julia, Hero, Rosalind, Helena, and Viola, but he also had in mind the traits of Beaumont and Fletcher's heroines. In the case of some of the other characters, in the new structural experiment of the dénouement, and in the versification, he worked with much less spontaneity and with apparent effort. In fact, however much he was moved by thoughts of reconciliation, gentleness, and peace, he was also striving to make a play which should equal in theatrical effectiveness the recent success gained by the skill and innovation of Beaumont and Fletcher. Seeking the same end as they did, he used similar means. When completed, however, *Cymbeline* did not owe a very large share of its total effect to *Philaster*. Shakspere was in possession of all the dramatic mastery which he had learned in twenty years' experience. Whatever changes he made in methods of construction, characterization, or versification, were directed by his own experience. Whatever hints or suggestions he received from Beaumont and Fletcher for situations or traits of character were colored by the plots and people of his own plays and transformed by his genius. But he was trying to produce and did produce a play with many of the specific characteristics and of the same type as *Philaster*.

Some such statement of the influence of *Philaster* on *Cymbeline* could be adopted if we were certain of our chronology. But the evidence for the priority of *Philaster* is not conclusive, and its support cannot be confidently relied on. Leaving aside, then, the question of exact date and only premising the fact that both plays were written at about the same time, we must face the questions—which is more plausible, that Shakspere influenced Beaumont and Fletcher or that they influenced

Shakspere?—which on its face is more likely to be the original, *Cymbeline* or *Philaster*? The question is not which play owes most to other plays, but which was the earliest representative of the 'romance' type? Many situations and characteristics in *Philaster* show the influence of earlier plays, but it represents a type that was new. Beaumont and Fletcher were new writers for the stage; it is one of the earliest of their notable plays; it was followed immediately by five romances of the same style in plot and characters; it possesses all the important traits and is one of the most masterly plays of the class. It presents traits of characterization, style, and plot which mark Fletcher's work for the next twenty years. All these facts create a strong presumption that *Philaster* was the original.

We began this investigation with the premise that Shakspere was as eager as any Elizabethan dramatist for stage success, that he was as likely as any to be influenced by current fashions and the practice of his contemporaries. At every point we have found definite indications that he was striving for stage-effectiveness and no evidence which would make his imitation of *Philaster* seem unplausible. Apart from his relation to Beaumont and Fletcher, our study has revealed several results which illustrate his adaptability to theatrical conditions. The fact that he abandoned romantic comedy for tragedy at the time other dramatists were turning away from romance is significant; and his plays from 1601 to 1609, even on the briefest consideration, reveal an evident observance of current forms and fashions. His collaboration with Fletcher bears further testimony to his subservience to theatrical conditions. It might reasonably be held to justify the inference that he recognized in Fletcher the dramatist best able to satisfy the stage-demand of the day. At all events, *Henry VIII* and the *Two Noble Kinsmen* do not indicate that Fletcher was an imitator of Shakspere; they do indicate that if Shakspere in his late period was influenced by any contemporary dramatist, Fletcher was the man.

We also started with a suggestion that there was an *a priori* likelihood that Shakspere would prove on careful investigation an adapter rather than an inventor of dramatic forms. Since this investigation was undertaken, that hypothesis has received a very striking confirmation in Mr. Sidney Lee's masterly discussion of the sonnets. Of all Shakspere's work they have generally been regarded the most expressive of his personal opinions and experiences. Mr. Lee has shown that they were undoubtedly indebted to preceding sonnet series, and that in them Shakspere frankly adopted many of the conventions and methods of a fashionable literary form. Our examination of his indebtedness to the court masques has shown him in a similar way borrowing and imitating many features of a fashionable dramatic form.

We may, indeed, safely assert that Shakspere almost never invented dramatic types. In his earliest plays he was a versatile imitator of current forms, and in his later work he was constantly adapting dramatic types used by other men. He wrote chronicle-histories, romantic and sentimental comedies, farcical comedies of manners, tragedies based on classical history, a tragedy of blood-revenge. In none of these cases did he originate a dramatic type or first introduce one on the Elizabethan stage; in all these cases he was to a large extent an adapter and transformer. *Cymbeline* differs markedly from any play he had previously written; and its differences prove to be traits similar to those characteristic of the Beaumont-Fletcher romances. These facts create a strong presumption that *Cymbeline* was the copy.

Still further we must remember the well-attested success of *Philaster* and its manifest spontaneity. No play of its day was more warmly praised by its contemporaries; no play by its authors seems more completely their own, more characteristic of their temperaments and .methods. *Cymbeline*, on the contrary, has no such evidence of success as *Romeo and Juliet*, *Hamlet*, or the *Tempest*, nor has it a tithe of their spontaneity. In the opinion of most critics, it shows decided creative effort. It was an experiment in new fields made at the close of his career by a consummate adapter, and made with evident effort. These considerations surely add to the probability that Beaumont and Fletcher were the inventors and Shakspere the adapter.

The final decision must hinge on such considerations as these. If we leave aside the direct evidence in regard to the dates, all our knowledge of the authors of the two plays and of the dramatic conditions of the time seem to me to point to the conclusion that in some such way as has been hypothetically described, *Philaster* influenced *Cymbeline*.

CHAPTER X.

A WINTER'S TALE AND THE TEMPEST.

A Winter's Tale and *The Tempest* do not show so close a relation as *Cymbeline* to the Beaumont-Fletcher romantic type. Neither seems to have been suggested by any one play as *Cymbeline* by *Philaster*; they are both plays, however, which link themselves with *Cymbeline* in separation from the rest of Shakspere's work and which possess, as has already been indicated, many of the characteristics of the Beaumont-Fletcher romances. Which of the two was written first is hardly determinable, but there is general agreement that they both succeeded *Cymbeline*. If this order is the true one; there is no reason for expecting traces of anything like direct imitation to be longer prominent. We may rather expect to find Shakspere transforming the experimental form of *Cymbeline* into something indisputably his own. We may, however, expect to find evidences of the Beaumont-Fletcher methods and fashions and of Shakspere's development of them. At the risk of repetition, we will consider some of the ways in which the two plays show Shakspere's development of the Beaumont-Fletcher romance, which he had first tried in *Cymbeline*.

The *Winter's Tale* gives prominence to a sentimental love story and has an involved plot with decided contrasts of tragic and idyllic incidents. The stories of Leontes' jealousy and fury and of the apparent deaths of Hermione and Perdita occupy the whole of the first three acts. Instead of weaving the idyllic scenes and the sentimental love story into the main plot, Shakspere added them in an almost separate play which occupies the whole of the fourth act. It goes without saying that he has treated this idyllic element with complete originality, and with a reality which Beaumont and Fletcher never approached. This fourth act is, indeed, about the only part of the romances which has an atmosphere of reality. In the fifth act, the two distinct plays are united with due regard for an unexpected and effective dénouement.

The use of a happy ending, it will be remembered, is a change from Greene's novel. This change and the carefully prepared dénouement are general traits of the romances; and so, too, is the construction of the main plot. It is notably a succession of situations. Sometimes, indeed, situations succeed each other with a rapidity which destroys all effect of plausibility, however well it may favor varied and violent action. For example, the first act opens conventionally with a conversation between some gentlemen of the court explaining the circumstances of the succeeding action. Then follows the lively dialogue in which Hermione succeeds in persuading Polixenes to lengthen his visit;[1] Leontes, immediately aroused to jealousy, is left to soliloquize and to talk with the child Mamillius;[2] Hermione and Polixenes return and add a little fresh fuel to his fire; as they retire again, he breaks out in the exceedingly vile and violent speech, beginning:

> " Gone already,
> Inch deep, knee deep, o'er head and ears a fork'd one!"[3]

There is some further accentuation by Mamillius' prattle; then comes the dialogue with Camillo, whose belief in Hermione's innocence furnishes a good acting contrast with the king's impatient jealousy, and who is finally persuaded to agree to poison Polixenes; then Camillo has a soliloquy, one phrase of which seems almost an echo from Beaumont and Fletcher:

> "If I could find example
> Of thousands that had struck annointed kings
> And flourished after," etc.[4]

Polixines next enters: Camillo explains the circumstances to him, and they agree to flee.

Thus in 450 lines, in addition to all the necessary expository matter, Shakspere has contrived to bring in seven or eight distinct situations. By means of these situations Leontes' jealousy is given its origin and development, and the Polixenes-Florizel story is well introduced. To see how great is the change from the old methods of construction we have only to recur again to the treatment of Othello's jealousy.

In dramatizing Greene's old and popular romance, Shakspere, after the fashion of Beaumont and Fletcher, created a play distinguished by its effective situations and the constructive feat of its remarkable dénouement. How great the departure is from his earlier methods may be seen by comparing the *Winter's Tale* with *Pericles* (1607-8?) a play that seems to many to be connected with the romances.[5] There Shakspere was also dramatizing an old and popular story and one similar to the story of the *Winter's Tale*, but he gave it a form that is primitively undramatic and in most striking contrast with the constructive ingenuity of the later play.

Of the fourth act, one dislikes to say anything which may even appear to indicate a failure to appreciate its spontaneity: but even here Shakspere is only giving an original development

---

[1] I, 2, 1-108.
[2] I, 2, 108-146.
[3] I, 2, 185, seq.

[4] I, 2, 357.
[5] See Appendix.

to the inevitable idyl. We have already seen that the business of a girl gathering flowers in March had been seen on the stage before Shakspere was born.[1] The business of shepherds and shepherdesses was also an old and popular theatrical convention, and the dance of satyrs was an entertainment probably directly borrowed from a court masque. The reality given to these conventions and to the equally conventional love story is Shakspere's own, and is secured largely by the introduction of comic characters from real life.

Of the characters of the play; we have already considered many. It may be added that Perdita's vitality arises rather from that atmosphere of real life in the country scene than from anything individual in her own lines. The style, too, structurally considered, is the same as that of *Cymbeline;* and the various devices for stage effect have already been noticed.

The *Winter's Tale*, then, seems in its main traits a development from the same type as *Cymbeline.* Its most marked distinction from the imitative character of that play is found in the very vital connection established between the sentimental love story and the comic elements of real life. In the nature of the plot, in its mixture of tragic and idyllic, in ingeniously dramatic situations and dénouement, in weakened characterization, and in a more dramatic style, the play belongs to the romance type of Beaumont and Fletcher.

The *Tempest* at first sight seems to differ much more than the *Winter's Tale* from a romance like *Cymbeline.* This is perhaps mainly due to the fact that we always think of it as a poem and never as a play. More than any other of Shakspere's plays, it seems to embody a conscious effort at the expression of a definite artistic mood. The beauty of its idealized picture of life, the serenity of its philosophy, the charm of its verse make it a poem to be treasured and pondered over and loved. To understand, however, just what its effect must have been on the Elizabethan stage, we must minimize the effect of its poetry and recall some elements of the play which are no longer salient. We must analyze not the æsthetic mood which it creates in us but the structure of the play itself.

A few truisms may again be repeated. The play was not printed until Shakspere's plays were collected long after his death: it was written for and acted on the stage where it was evidently popular. While Shakspere's imagination has filled it with permanent beauty and truth, he could not have written it without having in mind its stage-effectiveness. If we look, then, at the qualities which distinguish it as a stage play, we find many indications of current dramatic fashions and many points of resemblance to the general type of romances.

---

[1] See p. 4, ante.

163

For the plot there is, as usual, a story of sentimental love and a correlated plot of intrigue and murder.[1] We have only to see the play on the stage to realize that the story of the bewildered courtiers (however uninteresting to modern taste) is the best acting part of the play. That story, probably from some Italian source, forms the basis of the plot. As Mr. Wendell has shown,[2] Shakspere has elaborated the dénouement into five acts. The play is simply the expanded fifth act of a tragicomedy—a surprising, romantic dénouement.

This is the distinguishing feature of the construction, but there are many other evidences that Shakspere was striving for stage effect. Perhaps for this reason he followed the unities of time and place, for whose observance Beaumont had praised Jonson. Moreover, he added to the tragic-idyllic story, incidents, characters, and scenes, almost surely suggested by tales of a voyage to the new world which were just then exciting general interest. The enchanted island, the magic of Prospero, the monster Caliban, and the fairy Ariel must certainly have been novel and interesting to Elizabethan audiences. As in the *Winter's Tale*, he also gained stage-effectiveness and lessened the artificiality of the idyllic element by introducing comic personages after the style of those in his early comedies. He also used some of the stage devices which he had earlier used in the *Midsummer Night's Dream*.

Most notable, however, of all the devices for stage effect, was the pageantry borrowed from the court masques. We have already seen that the *Tempest* was in part a stage pageant, definitely constructed on the style of those popular entertainments. In this respect it resembles Beaumont and Fletcher's *Four Plays in One*, which also combines romantic situations with masque-like pageants. In borrowing from the masques Shakspere was making use of a very popular fashion.

Most of the characters, as we have noted, are developments of the conventionalized types. Miranda says little or nothing which has a trace of direct individualized characterization. The speech which comes the nearest to this, her proposal to Ferdinand, sounds very much like one of Beaumont and Fletcher's heroines.

> "Wherefore weep you?
> At mine unworthiness, that dare not offer
> What I desire to give; and much less take
> What I shall die to want. But this is trifling;
> And all the more it seeks to hide itself,
> The bigger bulk it shows. Hence, bashful cunning!
> And prompt me, plain and holy innocence!
> I am your wife, if you will marry me;
> If not, I'll die your maid: to be your fellow

[1] Note also Caliban's attempted rape of Miranda.
[2] *William Shakspere*, pp. 317-318.

You may deny me; but I'll be your servant,
Whether you will or no."[1]

To-day the audience laughs as Miss Ada Rehan speaks the
lines. They have no individual vitality; and we are not used
to the Beaumont-Fletcher idyl.[2]

The style of the *Tempest* shows far more mastery than that
of the two other romances; but, for all its greater beauty, it is
structurally the same. From the nature of the play, something of a return to the old lyrical structure might be expected,
but there are no indications of this. One or two examples
will indicate that the disjointed, parenthetical structure of
Cymbeline is retained but used with greater skill. For an example of its use in passages involving intense action, take the
speeches of Antonio.[3] For its use in narrative take Prospero's
account of his misfortunes,[4] or his account of Caliban's plot.[5]
To see how far this structure had become a matter of habit
even in set declamations, take Prospero's speech at the beginning of the last act,[6] or Ariel's speech to the courtiers.[7]

In style, therefore, as well as in characters and plot, the
Tempest resembles the other romances. In style, however,
and in all other elements, the differences are not less notable
than the resemblances. The characteristics of the romances
of Beaumont and Fletcher which appear in *Cymbeline*, reappear
in the *Tempest*, but altered and transformed. While *Cymbeline*
seems an experiment suggested by *Philaster*, the *Tempest* is a
development of the 'romance' type, which is in the highest
degree masterly and original. Perhaps there is no better way
of appreciating its supreme art than by recalling some steps in
its creation. We can best estimate Shakspere's accomplish-
ment by remembering with what materials and conditions he
began.

Our analysis has shown that his transformation of the ro-

---

[1] III, 1, 76-85.
[2] The resemblance between Ariel and the Satyr in Fletcher's *Faithful
Shepherdess* has frequently been noticed. Not only is there a close
verbal resemblance between some of their lines; both have traits in
common, and each is the servant and nimble messenger of a superior
being. Fletcher's Satyr has also many points of similarity to the
faun-like satyrs and 'wild-men' of the early English pastoral entertainments; particularly to the satyr in Ben Jonson's *Complaint of
Satyrs against Nymphs* (1603). There the satyr is a singer, a piper,
a merry fellow, a companion of the fairies, and also serves as a messenger and sort of chorus. Possibly Shakspere's Ariel is a development of the same type, which may have received some suggestions
from the theatrical part of Fletcher's Satyr. See *Modern Language
Notes*, April, 1899; *the Pastoral Element in the English Drama.*
[3] II, 1, 226-290.
[4] I, 2, 106-188.
[5] V, 1, 268, seq.
[6] Note particularly V, 1, 61, seq.
[7] III, 3, 60-82.

mantic type involves much besides a more masterly expression of the artistic impulses which seem to have dominated his latest period. He was dealing as in the other romances with an idyllic love story and a counterplot of tragic possibilities, and he was trying to treat both with ingenuity and novelty. He found suggestions for much new and sensational matter in the reports of a recent voyage. He undertook a constructive feat in handling the dénouement such as he had experimented upon in *Cymbeline*, and for some reason he chose strictly to observe the unities. He borrowed many devices, conventions, and situations from earlier plays, and he constructed a stage pageant on the style of the court masques. In all these respects he was aiming to make his play effective on the stage, and in some particulars he was following methods and fashions used by Beaumont and Fletcher. Yet all his varied aims are perfectly harmonized in the final result. The Italian story finds its true home in the Bermudas, and marvellous adventures are told with strict adherence to Aristotle's laws. The love of a maiden, the old plot of villainous intrigue, the superb wisdom of Prospero, all find one haven through "calm seas, auspicious gales." The drunken clowns, the Italian courtiers, the strange monster, and the 'zephyr-like' Ariel play their parts with antick dancers such as Shakspere had seen in the court masques at Whitehall. Out of such varied driftwood rose Shakspere's enchanted island.

CHAPTER XI.

CONCLUSION.

A brief glance at our conclusions will serve for a recapitulation. The conjectural nature of some of these has often led us to avoid using one probable conclusion in support of another; taken together, however, their cumulative effect must be considered.

In the first place, an examination of the chronology of Shakspere's romances and Beaumont and Fletcher's plays showed that some of the latter certainly preceded the former, and that six of the Beaumont-Fletcher romances were probably written by the time Shakspere had produced three. *Philaster* seemed probably earlier than *Cymbeline*. An examination of the stage history of the period indicated that mutual influence between Shakspere and the younger dramatists was probable from the fact that they were all writing plays for the King's men at the same time. The evidence that Shakspere and Fletcher collaborated on two or three plays made this probability almost a certainty. Our study of the chronology and stage history of the plays discovered no evidence at any point contradictory to the hypothesis that Shakspere was influenced by Beaumont and Fletcher, made plain the likelihood of some mutual influence between them, and on the whole indicated that the first contributions of Beaumont and Fletcher to heroic romance preceded Shakspere's.

An examination of all the plays acted 1601–1611 revealed a surprising paucity of plays which could be classed with either set of romances and a still more significant absence of experimenting with romantic material. In the light of the work of other dramatists, it became clear that the romances were neither the development of current forms nor the results of manifest tendencies in the drama, but that they must have been an unexpected departure largely due to the innovation of either Beaumont and Fletcher or Shakspere. In showing the independence of Beaumont and Fletcher's revival of romance from current influence and in emphasizing the significance of Shakspere's abrupt change from tragedy to romance, our examination presented further indications that Beaumont and Fletcher were the innovators.

A study of the six romances by Beaumont and Fletcher produced before the end of 1611 demonstrated that they constituted a new and distinct type of drama. A similar study of the three plays by Shakspere showed that they constituted a type of drama decidedly different from the rest of his work. Both types of romances showed a revival of romantic material, a use of new dramatic methods, and an effort to secure varied and lively action on the stage with some added spectacular effects. They resembled each other so closely in all their distinctive traits that it seemed impossible that they could have been produced independently of each other. While some of these resemblances seemed due to current conditions and common purposes, we concluded that one set of romances was indebted to the other for the defining traits of the type. And there were not lacking further indications that Shakspere was the debtor.

An examination of *Philaster* and *Cymbeline*, each an early representative of either type and each written for the King's men before the fall of 1610, revealed further specific similarities which made it almost certain that one influenced the other. *Philaster* appeared to have been the earlier of the two; but apart from considerations of dates, the general character of the plays indicated that *Philaster* was the original. This was made still more probable by consideration of the habits and positions of the authors themselves. There seemed good ground for the supposition that Shakspere, desirous of producing a play which should have the same effect on the stage as *Philaster*, produced in *Cymbeline* a play of the same type and of many of the same specific characteristics.

It was admitted that this conclusion would be accepted only by those who believe that Shakspere wrote plays with a keen eye for theatrical success, and that he was as ready as any of his fellow-dramatists to follow current fashions and to receive suggestions from his contemporaries. This investigation was based on the premise that such a view is justified by a study of the recognized facts of his career, and on the *a priori* probability that further investigation might be expected to substantiate and enlarge the opinion that he was constantly indebted to his fellow-dramatists. Apart from the consideration of his relation to Beaumont and Fletcher, many specific results of our investigation increase our confidence that Shakspere was likely to have been the adapter.

In the romances which followed *Cymbeline*, Shakspere appeared to have so far mastered the romantic type that evidences of imitation became slight, and the plays seemed his by birth rather than by adoption. Instead of degenerating, as it did in Beaumont and Fletcher, into a pretty distinctly conventionalized form, the romance type developed under his genius into the *Winter's Tale* and the *Tempest*. Even in these plays he seemed still to be using the methods he had adopted in *Cym-*

beline and still to be answering the same theatrical demand which Beaumont and Fletcher had first supplied.

In analyzing Shakspere's obligations to their romances, we have noted many varieties from direct imitation in *Cymbeline* to original tranformation in the *Tempest*. Sometimes there is no indication of indebtedness; he is merely following the same fashion which they did or writing with the same purpose. Sometimes he seems to have adopted a method or a type of character which they had used successfully, sometimes to have tried to outdo them at their own game. In no case was he merely adopting or imitating, he always adapted and usually transformed what he borrowed; but in many details in *Cymbeline*, and generally in the material of his plots, his constructive feats, and his characterization, Shakspere appears to have been working either in conscious imitation or conscious rivalry of the younger dramatists.

On the whole the evidence seems sufficient to establish the probability of our two main hypotheses: first, that Shakspere's change from tragedies to romances is to be accounted for by the contemporaneous production of the Beaumont-Fletcher romances; and second, that these latter definitely influenced *Cymbeline*, a *Winter's Tale*, and the *Tempest*.

Shakspere's romances thus afford another illustration of the way in which his genius worked, transforming dramatic forms which other men had invented into vital creations of his own. They afford, too, another evidence of the great influence of Beaumont and Fletcher on the history of English drama, and they add greatly to the indebtedness we owe to the astonishing invention and poetic genius of those two dramatists.

APPENDIX. PERICLES.

Pericles is thought by many to resemble the three romances and to bear to them a relation similar to that borne by the early to the great comedies. This possible relation to the romances, rather than questions of date and authorship, is the problem before us. We must examine what evidence there is that in *Pericles* Shakspere was experimenting with the romance type and consider what bearing such evidence has on our conclusion that his romances were largely influenced by those of Beaumont and Fletcher.

Questions concerning date and authorship are important for our purpose, but they are complicated by so many difficulties that we can only arrive at solutions which are extremely conjectural. We must therefore be content with noting the conjectures that seem to afford the safest hypotheses and then pass on to the main problem.

Pericles was entered S. R. May 20, 1608, for Edward Blount, and was published by Henry Gosson in 1609. This first quarto states that the play was "by William Shakespeare" and had "been divers and sundry times acted by his Majesty's Servants at the Globe, on the Bankside." *Pericles* was not included in the first or second folio, but was added with six other plays to the third folio of 1663. It appeared in five different quartos before the end of 1630.

Whether the 1608 entry refers to the 1609 quarto or not, and how the publisher of the quarto got hold of the play, are debated questions. There is general agreement that *The Painfull Adventures of Pericles, Prince of Tyre*, by George Wilkins (1608), appeared after the play had been acted; but even this conclusion is open to doubt.[1] The latest limit for the date is fixed by the quarto, 1609; and, while there is no certainty that the play in some form may not have been acted earlier, verse tests indicate that Shakspere's part was written about 1608.

In thus accepting 1608 as the conjectural date we have been forced to rely on the hypothesis that the "Marina Story"[2] is wholly Shakspere's. At least that is in part surely his and

---

[1] There is probably no other case in Elizabethan drama where a novel was made out of a play as it is supposed was done by Wilkins. If he had a share in the play, such a proceeding seems the more surprising.

[2] The last three acts, with possible exception of scenes 2, 5 and 6 in Act IV.

171

is in a style distinct from the rest of the play. Some critics,[1] however, believe that he wrote the entire play; some believe that his share was very small;[2] and there are all shades of opinion as to his possible collaborators. The first two acts are assigned by some to Wilkins,[3] and the offensive scenes in Act IV to Rowley.[4] While there is little more than conjecture in such assignments, we are fairly safe in saying that three distinct styles are discernible, that the first two acts are not by Shakspere, and that only the Marina story can be with any certainty assigned to him.[5]

Working on these hypotheses, it seems likely that Shakspere did not work directly in collaboration with the other author or authors. Unlike his shares in *Henry VIII* and the *Two Noble Kinsmen* Shakspere's share appears quite distinct from the rest of the play.[6] Neither does it seem probable that he had much to do in planning the play or in retouching the first two acts. Nevertheless, *Pericles* was acted by Shakspere's company and published with his name, and he must to some extent be held responsible for its final form. In examining it, however, as a play of his, we are safest in keeping pretty closely to the Marina part.

Remembering that Shakspere's share in the play and its date are very uncertain, we may return to our main problem, its relation to the romances. If the play was as late as 1608, there is a possibility of Beaumont and Fletcher's influence just as in the romances. If *Pericles* is a play of the same type as the romances, and if Shakspere's part is a forecast of his later work, these facts are of importance on the general relationship between the Beaumont-Fletcher and the Shaksperean romances. We must consider to what extent *Pericles* was a forecast of the romances and to what extent it possesses traits of the two contemporary series of romances.

The plot is taken from Laurence Twine's *Patterne of Painfull Adventures* and Gower's *Confessio Amantis*. A sentimental love story appears, but is not given the prominent place that similar stories receive in each of the three romances and also in each of the Beaumont-Fletcher romances. The plot is, however, like those of the romances and particularly like that

---

[1] *Cf.* Introduction to *the Bankside Shakespeare*, Vol. XIV. New York, 1891, by Appleton Morgan.

[2] See H. P. *Outlines* I, p. 205.

[3][4] See the *Transactions of the New Shakspere Society* for 1874, pp. 130, 253, and also for 1880-86, p. 323, for articles by Mr. Fleay and Mr. Boyle.

[5] The offensive scenes (2, 5 and 6) in Act IV are more closely connected with the Shaksperean part than the first two acts; are in prose and less distinguishable in style; and on the whole of more doubtfully non-Shaksperean authorship.

[6] It is especially distinct from Wilkins' part, Acts I and 2.

of the *Winter's Tale* in dealing with a long series of tragic events leading to a happy ending. It presents, too, a similar variety of emotional effects and a contrast of tragic and idyllic elements; the idyllic elements, however, which we have found highly developed in all Shakspere's and Beaumont and Fletcher's romances, do not receive a similar development in *Pericles*.

Considered in detail, the plot contains incidents, common enough in Elizabethan literature, which Shakspere had previously used and which he used again in later plays. Thus the shipwreck, which had been used in the *Comedy of Errors* and *Twelfth Night*, appears later in the *Tempest;* [1] and the reunion of Pericles and Thaisa both recalls that of Ægeon and Æmelia in the *Comedy of Errors* and anticipates that of Leontes and Hermione in a *Winter's Tale*. The story of Marina is something like that of Perdita; but in the extraordinary emphasis placed on the trial of her chastity, it is more like the story of Isabella in *Measure for Measure*.

In *Pericles*, then, Shakspere chose to dramatize an old story which has some general and some detailed resemblances to the material he later used in the romances. There is, however, nothing of the invention and ingenuity of the romances and little of their emphasis of the love story and idyllic element. In general character the plot is not unlike those of the earlier comedies, and the leading motive of the Marina story is similar to that in *Measure for Measure*.

In construction, *Pericles* is hardly a play at all. It is astonishingly undramatic. The story is largely told by the rhymed narrative of the choruses or presented in the dumb shows. There is no effort made to secure effective dramatic situations, and no pains are taken with the dénouement. The final happy reconciliation has none of the dramatic importance that it has in the *Winter's Tale;* it is merely an explanation. In all the characteristics of dramatic construction, the most marked contrast exists between *Pericles* and the romances either of Shakspere or Beaumont and Fletcher.

Pericles, indeed, is not only altogether unlike the romances of varied dramatic situations and intense, heightened dénouements: it is so utterly lacking in dramatic construction that one wonders that it could have been written as late as 1608. Plays of this archaic style, however, were not uncommon even at so late a date. In 1607 the *Travels of the Three English Brothers* [2] was brought out by the Queen's men. The play dealt with the wonderful adventures of the three Shirleys in

---

[1] See *Pericles* III, 1; *C. of E.*, I, 1, 63, seq.; *T. N.*, I., 2; *Tempest*, I, 1.
[2] See *Chr.* II, p. 276. Wilkins, who is thought to have had a share in *Pericles*, had a share in the *Three Brothers*. For an account of similar plays, see p. 98, ante.

Russia, Turkey and Persia and the marriage of one of them to the Sophy's daughter. Its construction is decidedly like that of *Pericles*: dumb shows, narrative choruses, much parading, and no real dramatic action. It is repeatedly ridiculed in the *Knight of the Burning Pestle*, and evidently appealed to the same vulgar taste that contemporary references show *Pericles*[1] greatly delighted. We cannot be sure that the construction of *Pericles* was by Shakspere; but even in the Marina story the same archaic methods are adhered to and there is no attempt to secure dramatic effectiveness.

In construction, then, the plot of *Pericles* has no resemblance to those of the three romances. So far from using any of the innovations of Beaumont and Fletcher, Shakspere seems to have returned to the methods then recognized as primitive and ridiculous but which still aroused the delight of the vulgar.

The characters of the play have little importance except Marina. By some she is thought to anticipate the heroines of the romances. The similarity of her situation to Perdita's has been noticed, and she certainly resembles the later heroines more than she does the women of the preceding tragedies. Sentimental love, however, the dominant characteristic of Imogen, Perdita, and Miranda as well as of the Beaumont-Fletcher heroines, receives very slight exploitation in Marina. Of course she has a lover and marries him after the fashion of all heroines, but her utter devotion to him is not the theme of her story, nor is it her crowning glory. Shakspere used the sentimental love story and heroine as he had used them in the early comedies and in *All's Well* and *Measure for Measure*, but not as Beaumont and Fletcher used them nor as he used them in the later romances.

Marina appears mainly as a pure girl who in the most trying circumstances maintains her chastity. The same motive also appears in Imogen and Isabella. In Imogen it receives a treatment after the style of Beaumont and Fletcher and quite unlike that in *Pericles*. In Isabella, however, it receives a treatment very similar to that in *Pericles*. Her purity is brought into contrast with the same loathsome aspects of life; her chastity endures equally trying circumstances; and its defense involves considerable vigorous argument like Marina's. On the whole Marina resembles Isabella quite as much as the romance heroines. She resembles the latter in the nature of the story rather than in the treatment of her character.

The style of *Pericles*, according to verse tests, takes a place at about 1608 in the general development of Shakspere's versification. It shows nothing of the marked structural change of *Cymbeline* which also characterizes the other romances. In

---

[1] See *Centurie of Prayse*.

devices for stage effect, it is decidedly archaic with its dumb shows and choruses. There is a dance of the knights in armor, alone and with their ladies, after the fashion of the masque;[1] but the pageant of the knights and their devices[2] is after the fashion of such exhibitions in *Jeronymo*.

On analysis, *Pericles* thus proves to be a play dealing with a story similar to those of the romances, but giving this story an entirely different treatment. In construction, characterization, style, and general stage effect, it presents none of the leading traits of the romance type. It seems to have been one of those Elizabethan 'plays of adventures,' whose character and the character of the taste to which it appealed are indicated in the title page of the first quarto: "The late and much "admired play, called Pericles, Prince of Tyre, with the true "relation of the whole Historie, adventures and fortunes of "the said Prince: As also the no less strange and worthy "accidents, in the Birth and Life of his daughter Mariana."

A word remains to be said about the artistic mood of *Pericles*. There does not seem to me to be much in the Shaksperean part which indicates any definite mood. There is some very fine phrasing in the account of the tempest, a subject that constantly appealed to Elizabethan rhetoricians; and the choice of the Marina story may have some artistic significance. Its underlying mood seems to resemble that of *Measure for Measure* as much as that of the *Tempest*. Those who insist on the forgiving serenity of the romances can at best find only slight indications of such a mood in *Pericles*.

As a precursor of the romances, the most that can be said of *Pericles* is that Shakspere was using material distinct from that of his tragedies and resembling in some ways the material of the romances; and that his artistic mood may in a similar way be conceived to have altered from that of the tragedies and to anticipate slightly that of the *Tempest*.

Such opinions, however, have little significance in connection with our discussion of the romances. *Pericles* is doubtless earlier than Shakspere's romances, but there is no probability that it preceded all of Beaumont and Fletcher's. Even if it did, the mere fact that Shakspere used an old romantic story is the only evidence that he began to experiment with the romantic type earlier than did Beaumont and Fletcher.

About 1608, *Philaster* was acted as well as *Pericles;* and two more different plays can hardly be imagined. They not only differ entirely in their methods of construction and their general stage effect; they differ as well in their treatment of the sentimental love story, of the heroine's character, and of the happy ending. *Pericles* was a return to archaic methods, *Philaster*

---

[1] II, 3, 98 and 106.
[2] II, 2.

175

was a remarkable dramatic innovation. Probably shortly after these two plays, came *Cymbeline;* and there can be no doubt which play it followed. If Shakspere had already experimented with romantic material and in a romantic mood, he had certainly not determined the characteristics of a new romantic type. If we make all possible allowance for the influence of *Pericles* and of all other plays dealing with romantic stories upon the work of Beaumont and Fletcher, the evidence remains unimpaired that their type of romance was an innovation and that it distinctly influenced Shakspere's romances. *Pericles*, however, seems to me in no appreciable degree a precursor of the romances, but rather a return to the old chronological, narrative dramatization of stories of wonderful adventures, such as were popular on the stage even later than 1608. At any rate, for our discussion of the relations between the romances of Shakspere and of Beaumont and Fletcher, it has either little or no significance.